Building a Business Through Good Times and Bad

Building a Business Through Good Times and Bad

Lessons from 15 Companies, Each With a Century of Dividends

Louis Grossman
Marianne M. Jennings

QUORUM BOOKS
Westport, Connecticut • London

Library of Congress Cataloging-in-Publication Data

Grossman, Louis H.
    Building a business through good times and bad : lessons from 15 companies,
    each with a century of dividends / Louis Grossman, Marianne M. Jennings.
        p. cm.
    Includes bibliographical references and index.
    ISBN: 1-56720-519-4 (alk. paper)
        1. Success in business—United States—Case studies. 2. Corporations—
    United States—Case studies. 3. Stocks—United States—History—20th
    century. 4. Business cycles—United States—History—20th century.
    I. Jennings, Marianne. II. Title.

    HF5386.G784 2002
    658—dc21   2002017942

British Library Cataloguing in Publication Data is available.

Library of Congress Catalog Card Number: 2002017942
ISBN: 1-56720-519-4

First published in 2002

Quorum Books, 88 Post Road West, Westport, CT 06881
An imprint of Greenwood Publishing Group, Inc.
www.quorumbooks.com

Printed in the United States of America

The paper used in this book complies with the
Permanent Paper Standard issued by the National
Information Standards Organization (Z39.48-1984).

10 9 8 7 6 5 4 3 2 1

To our families for their love, support, and example
Oh, for 100 years with them!

Contents

Preface

With a project that began in 1986, it is difficult to list all those who helped see us through to the end. We are indebted to the late Professor Jeffrey Bracker for his help in the initial stages of exploration. He has left us too soon, but his commitment to quality management lives on through this work and its reminder of his scholarship. Professor Mark Pastin was a great support in the early days of the project as he insisted on its merits when self-doubts arose. Dean Larry Penley at the College of Business and the administrators of Arizona State University (ASU) have been supportive over the years in granting us the resources, including sabbaticals, for the completion of this work.

We are grateful to the officers and employees of the fifteen companies who accommodated us in everything from interviews to access to their archives. That high-ranking executives in these companies took the time to help us and offer their insights speaks volumes about the nature of those who run these firms. They were most gracious. Perhaps more importantly, they were honest and open about their successes, failures, and attitudes. Cognizant of what they might offer others who struggle, they permitted us the luxury of revealing searches for the truth.

We owe much to the exceptional students we have had the privilege of teaching over the years. As we inevitably shared our findings in classes with them, they offered their insights, thoughts, experiences, and criticisms. We have taught long enough to know that teaching, when done properly, is always a two-way process. From them we have learned, and we only hope they can say the same.

We are especially grateful to the students from Professor Noel Stowe's business history course. Professor Stowe, a colleague at Arizona State University, has taken a keen interest in our work on these companies. During one semester he assigned the students in his course on business history the task of looking into the backgrounds of some of these companies as a means of developing the skills necessary for creating the history of a company. The authors appreciate Professor Stowe and the work of those anonymous students who uncovered information for us about Scovill, Stanley, Corning, and Diamond as part of their studies and training at ASU.

There have been many graduate students over the years who have worked to bring information to us. We do mean "worked," as they struggled to find annual reports, financial statements, and news clippings. Clare Black and Vincent Curley were stuck with the lion's share of the work in serving two years under our project and us. They have sinced moved on to graudation and successful careers. Perhaps their relief and reward came with graduation and not having to find just one more piece of information for us. However, Ganesh Raghuraman's graduation date was not until May 2002, and he had the unenviable task of putting all the dividend and financial information into tabular and comparative form. His professionalism and diligence were a key to timely completion of this manuscript. His sense of humor made it all seem easy.

We are grateful to our editor, Eric Valentine, who worked weekends to make this final product clear, concise, and worthy of the companies and principles it describes.

We are both grateful to our families for their support and tolerance during this effort. For Louis' Gloria and Marianne's Terry, Sarah, Claire, Sam, and John, we remain devoted and in debt. Their love and support saw us through the times of challenge, the burdens of the work, and those inevitable periods of questioning our abilities and efforts.

Introduction

The hurrier I go, the behinder I get.

Pennsylvania Dutch Proverb

If you are looking for fast and easy solutions to running a successful business, you have opened the wrong book. If you are looking for management's new buzzword or gimmick, then read no further. We have none of that. If, on the other hand, you have looked around in this postconstruction era following the burst bubble and the fall of the new economy, wondering if something might have been missing from all those young and now gone companies, you have turned to the right place. While we labored mightily on this book and its simple advice for managers, the dot-com world was exploding. Earnings seemed irrelevant, dividends were passé, and our work and findings seemed terribly outmoded. Building and growing a business was a task that the dot-coms and companies of the new economy made seemingly effortless.

However, as we completed our work on fifteen companies that had paid dividends for at least 100 years, our centenarians, the market crashed. Because of that crash, the unique achievement of these fifteen remarkable companies took on new significance, and a certain mode of business repentance has positioned this book and our work for its insights. This is a book that offers timeless lessons somehow lost in time. This is a book that offers management principles, simple in description yet demanding in their execution. This is a book about companies that offer the principles of long-term success. In discovering those principles, we developed a profound respect for these companies and their ability to stand firm for those principles even during economic swings and social change that witnessed the demise of many other companies.

Amid the bells, whistles and fads of trendy business theories, basic principles of good management and the common sense of values have become uncommon. Many of the business books and management theories of today read like parody. In their zeal to become a Wall Street darling or meet incentive system targets, managers look to the next quarter and opt for the quick fix. Managing earnings is today's business strategy while managing to earn is nearly a lost art. The quick fix is the drug to which business managers are addicted. If reengineering is the new trick, they will try it. If downsizing will boost share price, it's done. If a culture change will bring earnings, then bring in the culture consultants.

Today we look for companies that dazzle us with the inexplicable. Their earnings and sales growth defy expectations and even gravity. But then reality brings the news. Sunbeam slashes its workforce and then its CEO. Then its CEO is charged with fraud by the SEC for his failure to disclose that a sale reflected on the books never really happened.[1] Long Term Capital jeopardizes the financial markets with its leveraged losses until its customers bail it out. A year later, its CEO admits that very few of its customers really understood how risky an investment they were.[2] Bausch & Lomb admits its managers were a bit creative in booking sales so that they could meet sales goals and earnings for the company restated for several years.[3] Enron entered bankruptcy and its auditor, Arthur Andersen was indicted. Xerox, Krispy Kreme, and others too numerous to list here have all been forced to restate their earnings. Enron announced restatement of its earnings to slice $600 million from its earnings for the period from 1996-2001.[4] The *Wall Street Journal* offered its analysis of the company in an article titled, "Fancy Finances Were Key to Enron's Success, and Now to Its Distress."[5]

Such earnings recalls have become far too commonplace. Warren Buffett has referred to these creative approaches to financial statements as "distortions du jour," as he has expressed his concerns about the disappearing transparency of financial statements for U.S. companies.[6] He has expressed dismay over what he has noted are all too often phony numbers that are later restated.

This zigzag style of chasing the gold works for a time. But the chase becomes confusing as the goal of long-term survival disappears in favor of the next quarter. Businesses neither grow nor survive this way. In sports, keeping one's eye on the ball is critical. In business, today's managers often ignore the ball while looking and hoping for a different court or game to relieve them of the work of chasing that ball with vigilance. Sometimes it seems as if the tricksters and the financial sleight of hand has won out over the plodding earner who plays by the rules.

During the dot-com mania of the late 1990s, there were few takers on any other way to do business than exponential growth, soaring stock prices, and burn rates that defied basic finance. E-commerce and B-to-B transactions were so dominant that history and market cycles seemed irrelevant. There was a sense of infallibility that permeated the market, the companies, the analysts, the auditors, and even the employees.

Then the market crashed. *Fortune* magazine ran its dot-com death watch, reporting each week on the demises of more and more "new economy" companies. As the stories of these failed companies emerged, we had to come to one conclusion: There were some fairly basic rules of doing business that these companies violated. As MicroStrategy watched its stock drop from a high of $333 per share in 1999 to $1.61 in October 2001, we were curious.[7] How did a company with so much potential fall so quickly and so hard? Its postmortem is revealing. Some outsiders were placed on its board. It began focusing on building a customer base.[8] It began using phrases such as "steady growth." MicroStrategy is but one example. There was Razorfish dropping from $56 per share in 1999 to $1.11 in 2001 and a resulting restructuring.[9] There are hundreds more who fell for the conventional wisdom of earnings at all costs. Our companies taught us that earnings always matter, but companies need values and long-term goals for weathering this downturn or any future market swings looking for answers.

Too many managers look for miracles and in all the wrong places. The common threads in these 100-year companies are what every investor interested in maximizing returns should be studying and applying. As will be noted, some of these centenarians have even lost their way on occasion with temporary and permanent consequences. When they ignored their own keys to long-term performance, they too lost their ways. Those details and missteps are also painfully documented as lessons for investors and managers.

Investors should look to these companies with their steady and certain growth and performance. Their investors have enjoyed stability and continuing success for over 100 years. These companies' perplexing quality of successful longevity makes them unique. Not sprinters, but marathon runners who endure, perform, and survive. There are not hundreds of them, only fifteen. Fifteen industrial companies have paid dividends without interruption for 100 years.

This book is a tale about these legends of the business world. Fifteen legendary companies that have defied the transient theories of business consultants and managed their firms in a unique fashion that allowed them to honor, for at least 100 consecutive years, the commitment to their shareholders of a return on their investment most easily seen in uninterrupted dividend payments. Through a worldwide depression, two world wars, and the industrial revolution, these firms never missed a dividend payment. Given their unique achievement, we couldn't help asking and researching: How and why did these fifteen firms alone generate such a consistent and unique record of achievement?

In exploring this question, we began this book as a simple exercise in curiosity; our exercise ended with lessons in values not only for us, but also for managers. The tales of these fifteen firms offer lessons of patience, leverage, diversification, employee involvement, customer relations, and insight into the basics of business itself, ignored far too often in favor of a more glitzy solution. The thicket of today's management gurus and gizmos blurs the clarity of perspective these fifteen companies have. They were worth examining simply for their unique dividend achievement. But, beyond their achievement, these companies bring to the forefront certain basic principles that can help managers find their bearings and return to matters at hand: growing and managing a business for increasing shareholder value.

There are definitive common threads among the fifteen businesses. While each firm is unique and no direct cause-effect relationships are claimed or proven, there are common elements found among these firms that offer some insight into business survival, growth, and success. Studying the experience and history of other companies is hardly a new approach to the case-laden business education experience of most managers. Studying the experience of fifteen firms with this historical achievement of dividend delivery is simply an extension of the case method. Survival for 100 years, along with consistent dividend performance, is indicative of something at the soul of these companies that gave them constancy during eras marked by everything from massive technological changes to turbulent business cycles to political upheavals to wars to dramatic social change.

There is between us, a professor of business strategy and a professor of business ethics, some guilt in simply stating for the world to read what was once called common sense. Within these pages, there are no miracles, quick fixes, whistles, or magic. What is within these pages is a reminder to find your values, put them first in business, and the rest will follow. There was a time when no one needed to write a book about that premise. Perhaps it was one hundred years ago.

NOTES

1. Norris, Floyd, "They Noticed the Fraud but Figured It Was Not Important," *New York Times*, May 18, 2001: C1.

2. Lewis, Michael, "How the Eggheads Cracked," *New York Times Magazine*, January 24, 1999: 24–32.

3. Jennings, Marianne, *Business Ethics: Case Studies and Selected Readings*. Cincinnati, OH: West, 1999: 152.

4. Oppel, Jr., Richard A., and Andrew Ross Sorkin, "Enron Admits to Overstating Profits by About $600 Million," *New York Times*, November 11, 2001: C1, C5.

5. Smith, Rebecca, and John R. Emshwiller, "Fancy Finances Were Key to Enron's Success, And Now to Its Distress," *Wall Street Journal*, November 8, 2001: A1, A8.

6. Henry, David, "Buffett Blasts Accounting Tricks," *USA Today*, March 15, 1999: 1B.

7. Elkind, Peter, "Firm Auditing MicroStrategy Settles Lawsuit," *New York Times*, May 10, 2001: C1, C2.

8. Ibid.

9. Elkind, Peter, "Dot-Com Ethics: The New Role of Directors," *Fortune*, March 20, 2000: 116-117.

Who They Are and What They Did

I

Who Are These Companies?

Diamond International has elected to pay dividends for 99 years in a row.

> Caption from an advertisement in the *New York Times Magazine*, February 10, 1980, p. 85

Over two decades ago, we saw a full-page ad in the *Wall Street Journal* that read: THE DIAMOND MATCH COMPANY. 100 YEARS OF CONSECUTIVE DIVIDENDS. How could you not be intrigued by such an ad? Through two world wars, a depression, and this country's most significant economic transformation period, this rather innocuous company had sufficient cash flow for the payment of uninterrupted dividends. When they paid their first dividend, James Garfield was president, and here they were still going strong under Ronald Reagan. There were three questions that we would spend the next twenty years researching: Are there other companies like Diamond Match? What do these companies have in common? What lessons can businesses learn from them?

THE COMPANIES

To answer the first question, there were indeed other companies with records as remarkable as Diamond Match. We excluded banks and utilities because of their peculiar financial circumstances, such as guaranteed rates of return and price controls. The oldest company in the larger group of all 100-year companies was the Bank of New York Co. Inc. (founded in 1784), and the longest unbroken quarterly record of consistent dividends was held by Chemical New York Corporation (founded in 1827).

We chose to focus on the market category of "industrial firms" because the nature of their products and operations was such that they were truly vulnerable to changes in demographics, markets, and economies. We found fourteen other companies with the same remarkable record as Diamond Match.

When we began this work, we identified only eight companies with 100-year records. But the nature of the work and the detail required twenty years for completion. While a first draft of a manuscript existed in 1982, new centenarians began appearing. We could not resist the opportunity to see if the principles for building and growing a business applied to newcomers.

With these fifteen, the unique set is complete. It will be some time, if ever, before another centenarian company exists. Our efforts not only fit the vision of plodding academics that surely comes to mind as a reader thinks, "Twenty years for one project?" but reflects that part of business longevity that we found to be critical—a carefully charted and steady course. Nearly all tasks in this research effort, from access to officers to companies' cooperation to data gathering, were painstakingly slow. But the passage of time enabled us to capture the full set of unique companies.

The fifteen industrial companies in descending longevity for payment of consecutive dividends during the period from 1865 through 1980 are: Scovill, Inc. (1856); Pennwalt Corp. (1863); Singer (1863); Pullman, Inc. (1867); Ludlow Corp. (1872); The Stanley Works (1877); Corning Glass Works (1881); Diamond Industrial Corp. (1882); General Electric (GE) (1892); General Mills (1898); Coca-Cola (1892); PPG Industries Inc. (1895); Colgate-Palmolive (1895); Procter & Gamble (1891); and Johnson Controls (1895). Pullman, Ludlow, and Stanley had unbroken chains of one century of quarterly dividend payments as well. Pullman's run consisted entirely of cash dividends. Table 1.1 provides a summary of the companies with brief descriptions of their initial business and current operations and products.

A CAVEAT ON THE FIRMS

Before embarking on the study of these companies and their common traits, it is important to understand that these companies were neither angels nor devils. All of the companies had their errors and actions that were deviations from their overarching values. As in human biography,

TABLE 1.1   Fifteen NYSE Companies Paying Dividends Consecutively for 100 Years or More

Year of Origin	Year of Initial Dividend in Current Study	Name of Company	Original Business for Firm	Examples of Current Businesses (1980)
1. 1802	1856	Scovill	Brass manufacturing; button-making; brass lamps.	Manufacturing wide variety of products; housing products—Nu Tone; housewares group—Hamilton Beach; garment industry accessories.
2. 1850	1863	Pennwalt	Mining of salt and production and sale of basic or commodity chemicals, initially caustic soda; in 1860s, petroleum refining and sale of kerosene.	Manufacturing several chemical, health, specialized equipment products—worldwide; commodity chemicals; pharmaceuticals, dental, and health equipment for medical field.
3. 1851	1863	Singer	Sewing machines, industrial, and later, consumer machines.	Manufacturing consumer and industrial sewing machines; aerospace and marina systems; motor products, furniture; air conditioning controls; electronics.
4. 1858	1868	Pullman	Manufactured railroad sleeping cars.	Engineering and construction, oil and gas processing, nitrogen fertilizers; petrochemicals; transportation equipment.
5. 1868	1872	Ludlow	Importer, manufacturer, and seller of jute products—yarn, fine twines, bagging, webbing.	Specialty supplier of high value-added papers, packaging, and other flexible materials with interests in selected home furnishing products; furniture, carpet cushion, mats, matting, and textiles.
6. 1843	1877	The Stanley Works	Manufactured bolts, tools, then machinery.	Production (domestically and abroad) of tools for the construction, industrial and consumer markets; also manufactures other household, builder, and industrial, products.
7. 1851	1881	Corning Glass Works	Glass manufacturing and fabrication.	Manufactures products made from specialty glasses including consumer products (tableware and housewares: Pyrex, Corning Ware, etc.); consumer durable components (glass bulbs); capital goods components (individual electronic components, optical waveguides, glass piping and fillings, specialty glass products).
8. 1881	1882	Diamond International Works	Manufactured matches.	Major manufacturer of packaging and of lumber (packaging includes production of folding cartons, labels and wrappers, molded pulp items, metal containers, plastic pumps, dispensers and corrugated

TABLE 1.1   (continued)

Year of Origin	Year of Initial Dividend in Current Study	Name of Company	Original Business for Firm	Examples of Current Businesses (1980)
				items, and pulp; lumber includes rough and finished products); operates a chain of 116 building materials outlets and wholesale outlets serving construction and "do-it-yourself" markets.
9. 1889	1892	Coca-Cola	A new concoction of a soft drink called Coca-Cola	160 brands of beverages including the Coca-Cola line of soft drinks plus Minute Maid orange juice, Cadbury Schweppes products; did diversify with acquisition of Columbia Pictures for a time.
10. 1837	1891	Procter & Gamble	Soap and candle manufacturing	Focus is on consumer products (Bounce, Joy, Comet), beauty care products (Cover Girl, Head & Shoulders, Vidal Sassoon, Secret), and food and beverage products (Crisco, Jif, Hawaiian Punch).
11. 1878	1892	General Electric	Established by Thomas Edison as the Edison Electric Light Company	Aircraft engines; appliances; GE Capital Services which includes 27 focused businesses in five core areas including equipment management, consumer finance, specialized financing, mid-market financing, and specialty insurance; information services; lighting; industrial systems; medical systems; plastics; power systems, transportation, and NBC.
12. 1866	1898	General Mills	Began as Cad Wallader Washburn Flour Mill; became General Mills in 1921 as a combination of several milling companies.	Following 30 years of acquisitions, General Mills divested to focus on consumer foods and restaurants including products such as cereal (Wheaties, Chex, Total, Cheerios), baking mixes (Bisquick, Betty Crocker), snacks (Pop Secret, Fruit Roll-ups), and Yogurt (Colombo and Yoplait).
13. 1883	1895	PPG Industries	Glass manufacturing	Paint, glass, chemicals, coatings, resins.
14. 1883	1895	Johnson Controls	Thermostats	Control devices for managing and monitoring buildings; batteries; automotive components; building temperature/climate control services.
15. 1806	1895	Colgate-Palmolive	Soap, candles, starch	International manufacturer of oral care (dentifrice), personal care, household surface care, fabric care, and pet nutrition (Hill's products).

mistakes and misjudgments are evident. These are not perfect businesses. Rather, they are companies with a singular achievement worth examining in an effort to determine commonality. No information about the companies is withheld. Even their current status and fates, as noted throughout the book, are presented in straightforward fashion. Nonetheless, their achievement of financial stability and continuing shareholder return cannot be discounted because of errors along the paths of their development.

THE RESEARCH

The levels of information available on the firms varied in many ways. While their financial histories are readily available, attitudes of managers and employees are not so easily gleaned. Initially, secondary sources (public records, newspapers, museums) provided background. Some of the companies (Coca-Cola, GE, Procter & Gamble) refused personal access while others (Scovill, Johnson Controls, Pullman, PPG, Inc., Colgate-Palmolive, Diamond, General Mills, and Stanley) provided full access including on-site visits and interviews with current company officers, board members, and retired officers.

In-house libraries of the companies were fruitful sources but not consistent in their depth and troubling in their, at times, self-serving nature. When using information from the archives, the authors found independent verification or were satisfied through interviews that the information in the company archives is accurate. Some firms provided direct access to current and historical files and records of the companies including board meeting minutes, internal memoranda, and company history.

Not all firms cooperated equally nor did all firms have equally rich archives. For example, Scovill references in the book are voluminous. Malcolm Baldridge, then Chairman and Chief Executive Officer, cooperated extensively with interviews, access to other officers and retired board members, and use of a very extensive collection of company documents. The Museum of Waterbury, an independent historical site, had an extensive collection of very early records of the company. GE would not grant interviews, but there is such extensive secondary literature on this company that its references rival those of Scovill. In all cases, regardless of archives or interviews, there was sufficient information on the companies and their histories to offer both a history and insight on their achievements.

THE CATEGORIES OF COMPANIES

There are three categories of companies we examined in the study. Pennwalt is a category-one company: a company that achieved 100 years of dividends but fell victim to the 1980s takeover fever, that is, was acquired and never again existed in the same form. Category two consists of those companies that achieved 100 years of dividends, fell victim to the 1980s takeover fever, and experienced an interruption in dividends but struggled through and emerged a viable entity. Category three consists of firms that survived the 1980s without an interruption in dividends, regardless of takeover attempts.

Category one consists of Scovill, Pennwalt, Pullman, Ludlow, and Diamond. These companies are part of larger firms having been absorbed by merger or acquisition during the 1980s. Category two is comprised of Singer, which filed for Chapter 11 bankruptcy on September 13, 1999.[1] Category three includes all remaining firms, that is, Stanley, Corning, PPG, Coca-Cola, GE, General Mills, Procter & Gamble, Johnson Controls, and Colgate-Palmolive. Corning broke its dividend record in 2001 because of losses from its heavy investments in fiber optics (see Chapter 6 for more details).

All of the fifteen were particularly vulnerable during the 1980s because they had cash, low debt, and potential. In most of the takeovers, the companies were targets because of their ability to pay greenmail and not for the takeover offeror's diversification or because there was shareholder dissatisfaction with management. In fact, in 1978, Johnson Controls diversified into batteries and plastics and purchased Hoover Bull and Bearing partially because of Victor Posner's threatened greenmail attempt. Because Johnson Controls was cash-rich and profitable, it moved quickly to use acquisition in order to avoid takeover. The lessons of the 1980s and the impact on all three categories of these firms are offered in subsequent chapters.

Part I explores the companies, who they were and what they did, along with the rationale for studying their performance, policies, strategies, and structure. Part II outlines the common threads. There are keys to building and growing a business that all fifteen had in common, and the chapters in this part provide a discussion of those five principles of keeping a business going in good and bad times. Finally, Part III offers some advice on how to do what these remarkable fifteen companies were able to do for so long and so consistently.

NOTE

1. "Singer Files for Chapter 11," *New York Times*, September 14, 1999: C8.

2

Why Study Fifteen Companies and 1,526 Years of Dividends?

"I ate bacon every morning. Maybe that was it."

"I still have all my teeth."

"I lived a good long life by doing nothing the doctor tells me."

> Quotes from interviews with centenarians,
> from the medical study of those
> who have lived at least 100 years.[1]

From childhood days, we learn to look at the success stories around us and gather data. When Julie, the next-door neighbor, got a new bicycle, we wanted to know where she got it. Then we wanted to know why she got it. If she bought it herself, we wanted to know how she got the money to buy it. We might even follow Julie's bicycle purchase plan. But, if our friend Sam also got a new bicycle, we investigated him and his acquisition just as thoroughly. Perhaps we would adopt the Sam plan for amassing childhood assets, preferring it to Julie's capital budget and funding. However, as the number of new bicycles in the neighborhood increased, our data gathering became more sophisticated, and we soon learned that Sam, Julie, and others of new bicycle fates had common traits. They were hard workers. They were savers. They were diligent shoppers and savvy purchasers. We took the lessons of Sam and Julie et al. and applied them, and soon we were the bicycle king or queen of the neighborhood for a time until the next great purchase.

We have lost our childhood ability to gather data and copy. Too sophisticated for those simple exercises of observation and application, we reinvent. This book is offered to bring you back to Sam and Julie and an understanding that they were indeed worthy of your research and their successful efforts deserving of study, if not duplication.

THE LESSONS OF HEALTH AND LONGEVITY

In 1999, several medical researchers released their findings on centenarians, those few souls in society who live to the ripe old age of 100. Their standing is unique, and their healthy survival piques both medical and individual curiosity.

Had the medical researchers approached their examination of these centenarians with preconceived theories, formulas, and conventional wisdom, the findings might have been no more insightful than a generic prescription of, "Take care of yourself if you want to live to be 100." Such a prescription is as deficient in its lack of specifics as it is in its motivation.

Instead, the researchers gave us a glimpse of the lives of these 100+ long-term survivors. They explored what they ate, what they did for work and play, where they lived, how long they slept, their beliefs, their attitudes, and their philosophies. What emerged was not a staid prescription, but several important keys to long-term survival. No one could point to a single food and conclude, based on the 100+ers, "Don't ever eat that." But, they could point to a trend among these happy subjects: they ate a variety of foods and a balanced diet. No one could say they all had 3.5 children, but did find they had strong and long-lasting interpersonal relationships.

If the medical researchers issued a report concluding that 4 of every 20 centenarians never ate eggs, the public would probably avoid eggs in their desire to reach the ripe old age of 100. Indeed, we lived through the no-egg era only to find that eggs are not bad for you. We went through the phase in which we believed that potatoes made you fat. Now we know that potatoes provide fiber, fill you up, and are generally good for you. We have gone back and forth between margarine and butter and are now living through a phase in which we are using artificial spreads that will see the frying pan decompose before they will melt in the heat of cooking. Convinced they are following a path to the fountain of youth, the latest trendy food avoidance converts eat all else, drink more, and are merry, all while ignoring the more important and challenging aspects of long-term survival such as exercise and moderation. Following all these trends, food avoidance techniques and the study of which foods make you fat and which burn fat, we have emerged a nation of heifers. We are heavier than we have ever been, with 61 percent of us overweight.

So it is when companies follow singular and trendy ideas on what makes for success in business. From our research of these companies with histories of 100+ years of dividends, we do not emerge with magical solutions. There is no "one thing," as Billy Crystal searched for in the movie *City Slickers*, that is the key to happiness.[2] But we emerge from our years of work with sound and simple advice for long-term growth and success in business. We found no magical fix, just as medical researchers found no magical food. We found no precise ratios or formula, just as the medical researchers found no exact weight or cholesterol count. But, also, just as the medical researchers found common factors among their 100+ers, we found sound and consistent factors among these firms that play a consistent role in long-term survival and success.

In that sense, the findings in our research and the pages in this book offer no singular key to whopping business performance. But that result is the profound recommendation of this book. We hope to break the addiction to trendy management theories and quick fixes. All we were able to find in our research of these companies was sound advice from sages who have been there and done it, the "it" being the achievement of long-term business success.

SUCCUMBING TO THE CARNIVAL MIDWAY

Immersing yourself in conventional business books and consulting with its newfangled terms is rather like touring the midway at a carnival. There are bells, balloons, and the lure of easy money. A businessperson could try one recommended game or formula and quickly gain or lose and then move just as rapidly to the next game to try a different approach. Like the carnival games, magical solutions hold their charm for business folk desperate for the big easy. Each new formula for business change is glitzy, new, and alluring. But also like the carney games, the odds are against a big win. The games may not be fixed, but the midway is shallow, with its solutions designed for a fast pace, getting attention, and long odds. Too many business advice books promise solutions without grounding in reality, let alone research.

The world of the midway is not one of values, constancy, and reasonable returns. The midway is bright, flashy, attractive, and awash in media coverage. Each new meaningless formula is pursued in search of success, and often managers finding a new fix become the sole purpose of the journey. Managers seem to compete on a level of whether they are nouveau thinkers, not whether they are old-guard earners. Succumb to enough midway distractions and managers can pass up the show in the big tent. While managers tinker with quick fixes, their businesses suffer.

But the alluring midway moves from town to town relying on new gullible faces who apparently fail to realize how many have been stung in the past when they focus on short-term results and Band-Aids as treatment for underlying infections.

So it is in current business wisdom with its singular recommendations. A focus on one key to business success is as risky as a focus only on margarine over butter or Alex Rodriguez over a solid team. Yet, managers buy into the latest trend as if the Holy Grail has been retrieved. If one expert says, "Reengineering is the secret to business success," managers reengineer and then reengineer what they just reengineered, all the while forgetting why they reengineered in the first place. "Earnings be damned, we're reengineering here!" seemed the mantra of the early 1990s. "Downsizing is what we need!" claimed other managers. During the dot-com era, we were falling hook, line, and sinker for the new theory of business, "Well, we would have been profitable if it hadn't been for all those expenses."

Too much of what is written, done, advised, and demanded in businesses today has a midway feel and results to it. In the quest for the ultimate business fix, the basic role and goals of business are lost: earnings. What is important is lost to what is new. Businesses move from being enamored of downsizing to madcap expansion. It's as if there is no formula for business success except the current formula. Tomorrow there will be another formula and another after that. An interesting study would be one that documents the costs businesses incur as they drift from one quick fix to another. Of even greater interest would be what they might have earned if they had ignored the quick fix and behaved as these fifteen firms with the focus on values that will unfold over the following chapters.

THOSE DAMN YANKEES AND THE BUSINESS OF SPORTS

The 1999 Yankees provide a sports analogy on the quick fix. The Yankees had no one on their team who could be called a home-run hitter. They had no players with records the world was watching. The 1999 Yankees had no megastars—just slow, steady, and quiet achievement that handed lukewarm Yankee fans the ultimate return. The 1999 Yankees brought home a World Series victory in a straight sweep. Who would have thought that a lot of singles, quality pitching, and defense could bring home baseball's prize? Slow but steady won the prize. It was calm Joe Torre, the man with a steady-as-they-go philosophy, who led those Yankees to the prize, demanding only performance, not superstardom. But, oh, did those Yankees perform. While other teams searched for that magical player and formula, the Yankees played steady, but good, baseball.

Interestingly, when *USA Today* asked five business experts to choose the ten companies that were the greatest business dynasties of the twentieth century, all ranked General Electric, one of the fifteen 100-year companies, as their first choice. Professor Rosabeth Moss Kanter, one of the panel members, said, "GE is the New York Yankees of the century."[3]

Baseball suffers financially today because business managers of the teams search for expensive and singular solutions. In fact, most have lost a focus along with a financial reality check in their starstruck quests. Anyone can sign a hopefully magical $20 million Alex Rodriguez. But Alex Rodriguez struck out in the Texas Rangers' first game following his megastar contract negotiated in 2001, and the Texas Rangers were not having a good season.

Too many businesses today use the Rodriguez formula. Managers think if I can just get that "one thing," I can surpass everyone. While it seems trite to say so, there is a bit of a tortoise-and-hare nature to business. These fifteen companies, with their long-term growth, taught us that fable once again.

THE REVELATIONS OF TONY BENNETT "UNPLUGGED"

In the latter stages of our research, we were struck by the presence of Tony Bennett on MTV, courtesy of children and grandchildren tuned to this new generation's television entertainment. His very presence there inspired a short piece for the *Wall Street Journal* that then became the foundation for this book.[4] We had spent our lifetimes listening to Tony Bennett on everything from hi-fi stereos to MP3 players, and now here was Tony Bennett in "Unplugged," on the same network that brings us Eminem and Alanis Morissette. How does a singer span three generations with the same formula? How do companies, regardless of externalities, perform well enough to pay their shareholders dividends for 100 years without interruption?

The answers to the questions about Tony Bennett's survival are the same as the answers to the two questions central to this work: why these companies and why 100 years? Like Tony Bennett, these companies knew what worked and stuck with it. For three generations, Tony Bennett remained true to his strength as a balladeer. Disco and rap have come and gone. "I Wanna Be Around" has the eerie feel of survival in the constant that it is to Mr. Bennett's performances.

A glimpse at the history and business of these companies provides not just an overview of who and what they are, but a bit of incredulity when it seemed that their product lines were almost certainly not the stuff of the long term. Mr. Bennett's body of work does not bring MTV immediately to mind. But, like these companies, he knew what mattered. Mr. Bennett had a formula that worked, and he stuck to his roots as a balladeer through the eras of Elvis, the Beatles, disco, and hip-hop.

Mr. Bennett delivered quality and focused on a long-term strategy. These are components to success that never have and never will change regardless of the passage of time, the presence of competition, the buffetings of the market, or even the latest management fad. We discovered these same Bennett components in our work. The stories of these fifteen companies, like that of Mr. Bennett's long-term success, have quality, consistency, and commitment as common elements. These companies are not the one-hit wonders such as Katrina and the Waves. There was one terrific song, "Walking on Sunshine," and then neither Katrina nor the Waves were heard from again. Nor are they Christopher Cross, who had one phenomenal album that swept the Grammy awards and a string of number-one tunes followed by two decades of nothing.

There are many one-hit wonders we could study from business today. The runs for the dot-coms were shorter than Katrina's. We could examine the demises of these short-lived companies and find that their collapses were the result of their failure to apply the lessons for spanning generations, eras, and cycles. We listen to Mr. Bennett because there is something about his quality and unique achievement that defies the odds of survival in a fickle music industry. We appreciate and study these fifteen companies for the same reasons. They offer quality and survival in a very fickle business environment.

THE ROLE OF THE BUSINESS BIOGRAPHY

While it may seem odd for two academics to find inspiration in a balladeer, such a source of light is consistent with the role of biography both in history and in learning. We read biographies about presidents, prime ministers, authors, and sports legends for inspiration, lessons, and applications. We learn from Babe Ruth's life story what can be accomplished despite enormous obstacles such as his childhood as an orphan. We learn from Margaret Thatcher's and Ronald Reagan's stories that personal convictions are critical in leading others. We learn from Ernest Hemingway about the demons of substance abuse. We learn of spunk from Harry Truman and motivation and leadership from Winston Churchill. We learn from Mr. Bennett about the importance of quality as a sustaining market tool. We learn, we are inspired, and we apply.

Not everyone who reads Margaret Thatcher's biography will become Margaret Thatcher in the sense of parroting behaviors or achievement. But studying the biographies of several successful leaders will provide common threads. Adopting those common threads increases the likelihood of achievement.

Despite the obvious importance of biography in history, the business biography is rare. So attuned are managers to the current that the past is, well, the past. Yet a company's story offers the same lessons as an individual's story. The case method, so popular in business, is but a snapshot of a moment in time. The biography is a moving picture of a company. These case studies span over 100 years. From these biographies, there are precautions to be gleaned, motivations to be drawn, and passions for success to be adopted.

There is a stunning lack of detail and resulting failure of appreciation for the rich veins of business history. While historians focus on political and social issues, little is done to document formally the evolution of companies and their products. Business historians are only now coming into their own as companies recognize the value of understanding their roots.

Institutional historians within companies are becoming increasingly rare because employee longevity has suffered (see Chapter 8 for more discussion of this issue). Companies, now beginning to understand their histories' play in future success and in the ability to avoid the mistakes of the past and/or reinvention of the wheel, have been hiring historians to document the longitudinal path of their companies. For example, Otis Elevator used its company history as developed by the work of the Winthrop Group to do some research for a contract it had been awarded for modernization of the circa 1930s elevators it had installed for New York Life in its company headquarters. Otis was able to get background details before performing the repair and updates, and the result was a savings of time and money for both New York Life and Otis.

Our 100-year companies have already been heavily involved in their company histories. Corning hired the Winthrop Group, a company of historians and archivists, to provide a scholarly look at Corning as part of its celebration of its 150th anniversary. The result of the Winthrop Group's work on Corning is two books: David Dyer and Daniel Gross, *The Life and Times of a Global Corporation* (Oxford University Press, 2001) and Margaret B. W. Graham and Alec T. Shuldiner, *Corning and the Craft of Innovation* (Oxford University Press, 2001).

Sadly, Corning may have delved into its own history too late to save it from its foray into fiber optics that forced it to halt its dividends in

2001. That expansion was in defiance of the company's historical approach to such expansions, which was good R and D followed by immersion into a new technology, but not a complete surrender of all assets and diversity in an effort to land all the eggs in one basket. Such a managerial decision ran contra to virtually every Corning management principle that had seen it through the years, all with a dividend.

Procter & Gamble hired the Winthrop Group to write its history due to be published in 2002. Procter & Gamble plans to use the book for training sessions for employees at all levels within the company. These company histories give employees the flavor of from whence they came and especially a sense of the values of the company's founders.

Professor George D. Smith, one of the principals of Winthrop, now busy working to recreate the history of Campbell's Soup advertisement campaigns, notes that one of the impacts of the multinational corporation, mergers, restructurings, layoffs, downsizings, and outsourcings is a lack of appreciation for history as what he calls a "strategic asset." He notes, "What's been lost in the modern era is the ability to track thought processes."[5] For example, one-half of Corning's 37,000 employees have been with the company less than three years.

Knowing company history is not only important for that company's employees and managers as they go forward with innovation using the same values and the lessons of the past, it is important for other businesspeople and companies so that they can learn those same lessons as they go forward. It is because of this notion of history and biography that these fifteen firms offer insight into the intangibles of success. It was not sophistication, mere sentimentality, or a lack of realism that drove our inquiry into these companies and their histories. While these qualitative motivations cannot be dismissed, they were not the sole reasons for our inquiry.

The corporate organization is no mere mechanical synthesis of appropriate elements. It is or should be the result of organic growth under dynamic leadership. Its success or failure in the future may depend, more than the economist, financier, or mathematician would admit, on the intangible factors of maturity, developed corporate intelligence, and working harmony among its component parts. A discriminating stockholder can use history to observe the sources of the company's strengths or weaknesses and to measure its present health. For example, Hewlett-Packard (HP) has been struggling to find its way back to the dominant market force it once was. Interestingly, its proposed merger with Compaq runs contra to its company history and tradition of the HP way of following R and D instead of the urge to merge. In addition, HP has traditionally groomed a significant depth in its ranks in terms of executive talent so that transitions from one CEO to another were seamless. The most current transition has not been a seamless step, and the approved merger only adds to the view that there is a management that is grasping, as opposed to managing. Ignoring the rich history of HP can be costly, and the objections to the merger came from those most familiar with HP—the descendants and family of the company's founders.

What follows are biographical tales of fifteen firms that hold an achievement unique in American business. Causation is not claimed, just as individual biographies cannot offer direct cause-and-effect analysis. But within biographies, when patterns emerge, readers are able to self-cobble a path for success. In the biographies of these companies, patterns emerged, and what follows is a cobbled plan both for business achievement and evaluation.

THE RISK OF CONVENTIONAL WISDOM

There has always been a certain dismissive attitude of this very basic look at what makes a business grow and how that growth is sustained. But, we learned that we were not alone in that feeling that these companies were sleepers, often ignored for their achievements. The companies we studied often felt undervalued and underrated, and sometimes their indignation at the failure of the financial community to recognize what they had accomplished became public. In 1976, when Pullman was dropped from the Fortune 500, it ran a two-page advertisement that included the following language:

> It isn't every year that a growing $2-billion global company gets dropped by the Fortune 500. We were. Thanks to a particular circumstance of our continuing growth, Pullman Incorporated no longer qualifies for membership in that elite group known as the Fortune 500 list of top industrial companies.
>
> Last year, our engineering and construction business generated more revenue than our manufacturing business: our 1976 results showed that more than half of our record corporate revenues of $2.1 billion came from technological activities such as the planning, design, and construction of plants for the fertilizer, chemical, steel, ceramic, and refining industries.
>
> Less than half came from our manufacture of railroad freight cars, passenger cars, mass transit cars, truck trailers, and the like.
>
> So according to the Fortune 500, which ranked us 184th in 1972, 166th in 1973, 144th in 1974, and 102nd in 1975, we weren't an industrial company in 1976.
>
> It seems a little sudden. But then, it isn't easy to classify an international company with a $3-billion order backlog, that's been paying consecutive quarterly cash dividends since 1867, longer than any industrial company. On any list.[6]

Like sleeper movies these companies offer quality and insight. It just takes word of mouth to gain appreciation for them. This book is that word-of-mouth endorsement of these sleepers.

NOTES

1. Yost, Barbara, "100 and Beyond," *Arizona Republic*, August 22, 1999: A14, A15.

2. *City Slickers* (Paramount, 1991).

3. Maney, Kevin, "The 20th Century's Greatest Business Dynasties," *USA Today*, November 15, 1999: 3B.

4. Jennings, Marianne and Louis Grossman, "The Tony Bennett Factor," *Wall Street Journal*, June 26, 1995: A12.

5. Browning, Lynnley, "Documenting Company Pasts," *New York Times*, August 19, 2001: BU4.

6. Pullman advertisement, 1976. From Company Archives.

The Stories of Past Survivors

You have to be an antique to appreciate them.

Fay Madigan Lange

This chapter provides the background information on the category one companies of the fifteen centenarians or those firms that emerged from the 1980s having been acquired by another company. We call them out in separate chapters not because of any perception of these firms as being less worthy of examination, but to distinguish them for purposes of their fates. In some cases, their acquisition was a strategic choice, something done for the benefit of the shareholders because of changing markets, particularly as a result of international business. In those circumstances in which the merger or acquisition proved not to be in the best interests of the shareholders, their vulnerability to such a change is instructive for companies and managers.

SCOVILL, INC.

The name Scovill is not one businesspeople immediately recognize or to which one would attribute achievement or even admiration, but one of Scovill's CEOs, Malcolm Baldridge, has become a name synonymous with quality. The Malcolm Baldridge National Quality Award (MBNQA) was named for Baldridge's obsession with quality, service, and innovation. Today companies tout the coveted Baldridge award for quality. That award has its genesis in the nature of its namesake's philosophy for doing business as he presided over Scovill.

Founded during the Jefferson Administration in 1802, Scovill began as a brass button manufacturer, answering the insatiable fashion demands of the time. In its original form, Scovill was a partnership known as Leavenworth, Hayden and Scovill. It was first chartered as a corporation in 1850, and it paid its first dividend in 1856. No New York Stock Exchange company has ever equaled the Scovill continuous dividend record and it seems unlikely that any company will in the future.

Its initial brass products were also used for clothing fasteners, snaps, and, eventually, slide zippers. However, realizing fashion's fickle nature, Scovill evolved and turned its expertise in brass with buttons into generic brass products. It was when Chauncey P. Goss assumed the role of president in 1900 that Scovill's diversification began in earnest. Goss was nothing short of a brilliant businessman. When he took over as president, Scovill had $1.6 million in total capitalization. When he retired in 1918, he left a company with $5 million in capitalization and "surplus and reserves" of $26 million.

Scovill's skill in manufacturing brass products was applied in other metals as the nature of home products changed. When the brass pot faded, Scovill was prepared. Because it had already moved into kitchen brass wares, it was able to capitalize on the skills and name recognition it had acquired in meeting kitchen demands. Recognizing that it needed a means of infiltrating the minds of consumers on modern kitchen products, Scovill acquired Hamilton Beach Company in 1923. The Racine, Wisconsin, appliance manufacturer was a ready-made entry into the world of kitchen appliances. Scovill then evolved into a kitchen appliance manufacturer, producing everything from juicers to irons, as well as its continuing success in small, simple metal products. By this time, Scovill was producing over 15,000 of these small items of metal, such as buttons, for other industries and retailers.

During World War II, Scovill played a key role in producing both armaments and brass buttons for the U.S. military. In fact, Scovill had supplied those same items to the U.S. military in every war in the nineteenth and twentieth centuries. When all available metal in the United States was being used for the war effort, Scovill sensed the demoralization of women on the home front. It developed the only wooden lipstick case that U.S. society has ever seen. The product was an immediate hit and a welcome substitute for women who were bearing up well handling both factory duty and the home front because so many husbands and fathers had gone overseas.

Along the way, Scovill became a manufacturer of brass locks, again taking the product into other metals. Its acquisition of Yale Locks combined its manufacturing expertise with Yale's consumer recognition. One Scovill CEO, William Goss, once remarked, "Scovill can make anything; the principle job is to sell it." Yale Locks continue to hold a dominant position in the market. With its expertise in locks, Scovill logically evolved into a manufacturer of electronic door locks and other forms of monitoring devices. It also entered the auto industry as a supplier of parts to manufacturers and as a seller of parts for auto repair. Within one year of his assuming the Scovill helm in 1955, Goss had turned Scovill around from its post–World War II depression in sales and income.

When Malcolm Baldridge assumed the position of CEO at Scovill, the company began a new era in both marketing and efficiency. Baldridge reduced small appliance inventories, flattened the lines of communication within the company, and made every employee financially accountable for the budget decisions and results in their area. Baldridge ran a smooth and profitable company until the mid-1970s when the supply market changed dramatically and Scovill would begin its most dramatic strategic changes.

In 1977, faced with a bottomed-out copper market, Scovill's plants were operating at a loss, something that had not happened before except during the Depression. Baldridge warned his board that Scovill needed to get out of the brass business, but the board felt a duty to the Connecticut community and the nearly 2,000 jobs that would be lost if Scovill sold its brass production plants. Finally, the board agreed to the need for the company to leave brass behind, if Baldridge would find a buyer for the plants so that the jobs could be preserved. With the help of then Connecticut governor Ella Grasso, Baldridge sold Scovill's plants to Century Brass Products, Inc., in a deal that included a promise to retain the employees in exchange for tax credits and other incentives.

Following the sale, Scovill was able to focus on its small appliance product area, and it continued its acquisition mode for these types of firms, such as its purchase of Dominion and Westinghouse Electric's small appliance division to supplement its Hamilton Beach line. Scovill also acquired NuTone, Inc., a manufacturer of housing products, and discovered that its expertise in door locks worked well with NuTone's expertise in door chimes, security systems, garage door openers, and other access-related products this home service firm sold.

Scovill had a rough go during the early 1980s because of the recession and the resulting impact on housing sales and consumer purchases. Furthermore, its sales in auto parts were curtailed because of the declining sales in the auto industry. Despite being on Standard & Poor's credit watch in 1982, Scovill emerged with the next building cycle when the 1980s boom took hold. By the time of the 1980s merger mania, Scovill, returning to its low debt position and possessed of well-developed divisions and product lines, was a prime takeover target, and as a result, it was acquired by a Canadian firm in 1985. Its dividend record ran for 130 years from 1856 until 1986.

PENNWALT CORPORATION

By the time the first shots were fired on Fort Sumter on April 12, 1861, the Pennsalt Chemicals Corporation was already eleven years old. Founded as the Pennsylvania Salt Manufacturing Company in 1850 by a group of five Quakers and twelve other Philadelphians with a total of $100,000 in capital among them, it was organized as a company "for the manufacture of salt and articles therefrom." The young company searched the state for a plant location and chose a site 21 miles north of Pittsburgh along the Allegheny River. Pennsalt named the site Natrona, from the Greek *natron*, which means soda. Its location on a salt deposit permitted it to sell and process salt, soda, ash, salt soda, and Glauber's salt. By the time Jefferson Davis was president of the Confederacy, Pennsalt held a patent for processing alkalies from salt.

The fledgling company struggled during those early years. Urban legend holds that CEO George T. Lewis, one of the founders of the company, was walking around Philadelphia on a gloomy day, concerned that he had lost the investment of his sixteen Quaker friends in his Natrona boondoggle. As he turned one corner, he saw a young woman standing at the back of a home, her sleeves rolled up, stirring a large kettle of soap. The labor-intensive process struck Lewis, even more so when he realized the young woman was on her final steps in the process, having already completed the painstaking task of leaching wood ashes for lye. Lewis realized that most consumers made their soap at home and could not be pleased either about the time it took to make the soap or its quality. He zeroed in on the time-consuming and messy step of extracting potash from wood chips. Interestingly, this process was not only crude, but also it released caustic chemicals in the home. Despite obvious consumer dissatisfaction with the home process, there was no product that gave them a convenient way of purchasing lye. It was no wonder there was a void in the market. Lye is a strong chemical and very difficult to package.

But, the urban legend holds, Lewis was inspired that day as the Philadelphia gloom was broken when the sun came from behind a cloud and so did the idea for selling lye. Lewis went back to work determined to develop a lye that could be sold in convenient form. The company finally created a form of flaked lye that could be sold in cans. The canned product was named Lewis Lye, after George Lewis. Still sold today, the product became a profit generator. By 1863, Pennsalt not only had the cash flow to finance the restructuring needed for buoying the salt processing, but it also had a nearly equal amount ($55,000) for the declaration of its first dividend. Its dividend run would last 118 years, until 1981.

Based on its success with the consumer market, Pennsalt looked for other processing opportunities that would yield end products suitable for consumer use. Pennsalt found that by refining petroleum, it could produce a by-product known as kerosene for home lighting. Sales of this convenient consumer item also began during the Civil War. Pennsalt would follow this formula of continuing research and product development, observation of consumer patterns and needs, and earnings reinvestment to expand both its product lines and production facilities. That drive and consumer savvy resulted in the development of over 400 products used in virtually every industry in the United States. Pennwalt's sales reached $90 million by 1960.

While not every processing foray yielded consumer products, Pennsalt continued expansion of its processing expertise along with the sale of chemicals, which were raw products for industrial products. Its production of soda alkalies was a profitable product line, but there was a continuing struggle to find and purchase the cryolite needed for processing. The largest cryolite deposit in the world was in Ivigut, Greenland. Pennsalt's CEO (then called a Superintendent), Henry Pemberton, learned of the large Greenland supply and the desire of the Danish government to sell more cryolite. Before the Civil War ended, Pemberton became a pioneer in international supply chain management and traveled to Copenhagen to negotiate a long-term supply contract with the Danish government. In what would become a turning point for Pennsalt, Pemberton locked up two-thirds of the cryolite production from Ivigut, a minimum of 6,000 tons per year.

The first shipment arrived in Natrona in 1865, and Pennsalt's contractual relationship with Denmark has been one of the longest continuous business relationships between a U.S. business and a foreign entity. The locked-in contracts on cryolite processing of soda alkalies gave Pennsalt an edge because cryolite proved a key component in the production of aluminum, insecticides, and abrasives. Pennsalt became the primary importer and seller of this raw material simply because Pennsalt was an astute observer that recognized not just the art, theory, and science of processing but its profit potential. Pennsalt expanded and adjusted its product line according to its own and others' discoveries about the use of minerals. Pennsalt's company history described the cryolite turning point as follows:

> [It] paved the way for the use of the "ice stone" in such modern materials as glass, porcelain enamels, ceramic ware, and agricultural insecticides. Pennsalt's strong position in cryolite prompted its later entry into the manufacture of alumina, a vital component for the production of aluminum.

Alumina was also used in making alum for paper, textiles, and water treating. Today some of the original alum buyers are still Pennsalt customers.[1]

Pennsalt's niche in processing and its resulting product diversification brought it significant government contracts during World War II for chemicals by-products. The name change from Pennsalt to Pennwalt in this era reflected its evolution from salt producer to chemical processor. At its peak, in the early 1980s, Pennwalt was selling one or more of its products to virtually every industry in America. It had 13,000 direct buyers and 75,000 distributors.

But it was also during the 1980s that Pennwalt ventured into a program of restructuring and diversification that resulted in revenue shortages and the tragic end to its streak in dividends. The lessons of that diversification and restructuring are found in Chapter 5, along with the story of resulting dissatisfaction among shareholders and finally, the 1989 acquisition of Pennwalt by Elf Aquitaine, France's largest oil company.

PULLMAN COMPANY

Pullman, founded in 1858, was and will be forever known as the sleeping car manufacturer. Its fame in constructing railroad train cars stayed with it even when it no longer made them. If you build it well, they will always remember you for it, even if you no longer build it!

The Pullman family had run a cabinet-making business with the father, Louis, as the cabinetmaker, and his son George as the salesman. When Louis died in 1853, George was the only child of the Pullmans' eight who was not yet married but who was old enough to support his mother. By default and fate, George became the head of the family business. George altered the direction of the company by developing moving equipment for building relocations and selling this equipment along with moving services for such relocations. Pullman played a critical role in all of the relocation required during the construction of the Erie Canal.

Rapid economic development during this era made the moving services indispensable, and Pullman's earnings soared with the company beginning a winning streak when it paid its first dividend in 1867. George's new equipment and construction expertise found him the typical consultant with regular travel and long train trips. Fascinated by what he called "the discomfort of existing sleeping cars," George designed a new sleeping car. While his brother Albert built them, George sold them, and the name "Pullman" became synonymous with comfort in rail travel.

Such a narrow focus with a product so tied to the transportation mode of an era would seem to imply a short-lived business. However, George and the expanded Pullman Company used their engineering and construction expertise gained in rail car construction to expand into other forms of construction such as commercial and industrial buildings and equipment. By 1950, when rail travel had declined substantially, Pullman had diversified sufficiently to maintain its growth and returns to shareholders. Its annual revenues went from $750 million in 1970 to $2.1 billion by 1976.

This rich cash position as well as Pullman's assets attracted the attention of the merger-driven financial markets of the time. The takeover offers began, and in 1980, Pullman, Inc. (changed from Pullman Company in 1927), with a dividend run of 113 consecutive years from that original payment in 1867, was acquired by Wheelabrator-Frye, Inc. Pullman became a subsidiary bounced from holder to holder, its exemplary management and record lost in the shuffle. Wheelabrator-Frye was later merged into the Signal companies in 1983, which was then merged into Allied-Signal, Inc., in 1985. Pullman was spun off from Signal in 1984, prior to its merger with Allied. It once again became the Pullman Company, but in 1988, Pullman was acquired by FLPC Acquisition Corporation.

Presently, Pullman is a little-known subsidiary of Forstmann Little Company—a leveraged buyout investment and management firm. Interestingly, Forstmann Little has been active in the school voucher movement, pledging and paying millions in scholarships for K–12 children in poor quality schools so that they can attend private schools. The response to this philanthropic program has been equaled only by the improvement in the children's scores and grades.

LUDLOW CORPORATION

Ludlow Corporation was formed in 1868 as an importer of jute from India. But Ludlow quickly evolved from importer to operator of an integrated supply and value chain when it began to use its imported jute for purposes of manufacturing twines, carpet yarns, furniture webbing, and cords at its plant in Ludlow, Massachusetts. Ludlow continually evolved, moving incrementally in logical extensions of its expertise. For example, Ludlow was manufacturing twine for packaging and expanded to the role of supplier of all forms of packaging materials. Ludlow was thereby able to offer consistent financial performance despite being in a business whose initial product was hostage to the volatility of the jute market.

In 1921, there was a price drop in jute of such significance that Ludlow's annual report included the following dismal news mitigated by favorable news that is also included from a company ever adjusting and always evolving. The strategic cushion enabled Ludlow to survive these dramatic swings in the jute market.

> With a shrinkage in the value of goods sold of over 56%, it has not been an easy task to bring about a favorable balance for the year's operations. To meet this condition it has been imperative to effect every possible economy consistent with maintaining the quality of our product and, in addition, to increase the efficiency of our operations wherever possible. We are pleased to be able to report that many substantial economies have been effected and that improvement made in methods will, we feel, show even more satisfactory results in the future than they have to date.[2]

Because of its subtle product line expansion, Ludlow had sufficient financial cushion to survive a 56 percent hit in reduced inventory value that year from the jute price drop and still pay dividends. Ironically, Ludlow's longstanding philosophy on carrying a sufficient cushion in its balance sheet poised it as a prime takeover target. Cash attracts takeovers, and Tyco Laboratories acquired Ludlow in 1981, the year in which Ludlow became an anonymous subsidiary, with its longstanding dividend record ending abruptly. Tyco today is a company in turmoil.

DIAMOND INTERNATIONAL WORKS

During the 1870s in the United States, there was ruinous competition in the match market. At that time, there were 79 match factories all vying for market dominance and profit in an era when a box of 300 matches sold for 5 cents. There were two dominant players in the market: The Barber Match Company of Akron, Ohio, which focused on midwestern and western U.S. sales, and the Swift & Courtney & Beecher Match Company, based in Wilmington, Pennsylvania, focusing its sales efforts on the eastern and southern United States. The two companies sold their matches in their respective territories and never the twain did meet. However, in 1878, Swift & Courtney & Beecher made the decision to take on the competition and built a factory in St. Louis, Missouri. Barber was offended by the competitive affront and so built a plant in Philadelphia. What William H. Swift would call "senseless destructive competition" soon followed.

On December 3, 1880, Barber, Swift, and eight other industry leaders met in New Haven, Connecticut, and agreed to merge. They incorporated themselves as the Diamond Match Company and opened that company's doors for business in 1881. The top ten companies had invested a total of $2.25 million in capital, and in exchange they were given all of Diamond's stock: 14,000 shares of common stock and 8,500 shares of preferred shares. This formidable combination of the top ten produced a company that would dominate the industry.

This newfound mega match firm was both a kindly and a profitable company. This seller of a simple household product began paying dividends in 1882 and continued through 1983 when it became a private company. However, it continued to do so even after 1911, when it deeded its patent for nonphosphorous matches to the public. Diamond dispatched its engineering staff to any competitor that asked for assistance on how to use the newly available process that was now part of the public domain.

Diamond Match was a company constantly on the watch for the winds of change and the potentially related fields it might explore. Its initial product was made of wood, and it explored opportunities in everything from the growing and harvesting of wood to its sale in prefabricated forms for houses. By the early 1900s, it was selling a complete house kit at its lumberyards for $1,950.

The one time Diamond was caught by surprise was when its supply of chlorate of potash, derived mainly from Germany, was cut off during World War I. Diamond quickly went to work to find potash in the United States. It discovered three primary sources and became the supplier for all manufacturers. It incorporated Uniform Chemical, Inc., as its subsidiary to handle potash retrieval and sales.

Perhaps the best word to describe the Diamond Match Company was "colorful." Creative and whimsical at times, Diamond was always trying new things. For example, by 1911 the company had equipped all of its retail yard managers with motorcycles so that they could travel about maintaining contact with customers, all the while collecting bills. Even the traveling auditor sent to the various yards was assigned a motorcycle. The rumble of the motorcycle engines easily signaled approaching Diamond employee auditors in advance. But the travel was cheap and the transportation was rapid.

Despite the colorful nature of even its audit operations, Diamond's top management over the years has traditionally been a quiet group. For example, Williams Armstrong Fairburn led the company beginning in 1909 and was described as a recluse. His biography in *Who's Who in America* read, "pres., Diamond Match Co. Office: 30 Church St., NY, NY," for that was as much information as the listing service was able to glean from the public records and neither Fairburn nor any other senior managers would voluntarily provide any personal information. What is documented is that Fairburn had been born in Bath, Maine, and worked in the Bath Iron Works, acquiring a keen sense of production, quality, and the supply chain. Educated in Scotland, he returned to the United States trained in architecture and engineering. Following work on both railroads and ships, he settled into Diamond Match bringing diverse experience, which some credit for the diversification of Diamond throughout its early years (see Chapter 7).

Diamond was a stellar performer from its beginning, and its increasing share price reflected its results in sales and expansion of its lines of business. Just prior to 1930, its stock was selling for $100 per share. Diamond offered a stock split in 1930. Shareholders received five shares of preferred stock and four shares of common in exchange for every old share of Diamond that they owned.

While Diamond began with one simple product, it diversified into timber production and manufactured other products made of wood such as toothpicks, ice cream sticks, corn dog sticks, tissues, paper towels, and egg cartons. The 1960s proved to be Diamond's most active decade in terms of acquisitions. It acquired the Heekin Can Company in 1965 and then purchased a series of paper companies including Penobscot Company, Groveton Papers Company, and the Vanity Fair and Blue Ribbon brands of paper. It even acquired the United States Playing Card Company in 1974 and was able to capitalize on the coming boom in gambling.

The 1970s were a difficult decade for most businesses because of the inflation that resulted from government spending during the Vietnam era. However, Diamond's enormous diversification efforts during the 1960s proved fortuitous, and it was insulated from the impact of the economic downturn owing to inflation. Its sales topped $1 billion in 1978. Having already gone back in the supply chain and acquired pulp and paper companies, Diamond then went the other way and acquired LMF Corporation in 1978, a chain of 52 building material and supply stores. By 1980, Diamond was a diverse company with 36 percent in packaging, 27 percent in retailing, 15 percent in pulp and paper, 11 percent in lumber, 5 percent in printing, and the remaining in other smaller lines of business.

In 1977, a struggle for control of Diamond, with its rich cash and asset position, began as Sir James Goldsmith, head of the French firm Generale Occidentale, acquired 23 percent of Diamond's stock through his U.S. subsidiary, Cavenham Holdings, Inc. The *Wall Street Journal* referred to this takeover battle as "noisy and hostile."[3] Generale Occidentale was a $7 billion enterprise, and Sir James was intrigued with Diamond's diversity and success. Diamond staged a fierce battle against Sir James in the takeover. Diamond had recruited a white knight to prevent the Sir James merger, and Wall Street's largest investment banks issued dueling opinions over whether the proposed alternative merger was fair to the Diamond shareholders. The battle drew daily business press coverage with the revelation that Sir James would personally earn a $3 million fee for the successful completion of the Diamond takeover.

With such diversity of opinion on which offer benefited shareholders most, Diamond Match sought a shareholder vote and knew it could obtain it through state corporation laws. Diamond filed suit in both Maine and Ohio in an attempt to invoke the protection of those state's takeover statutes, but a judge ruled that neither state's statutes applied because Diamond lacked a sufficient amount of assets in the states. This legal technicality resulted in the suit's dismissal, and Sir James was able to step in and assume control of Diamond. By 1982, Generale Occidentale had absorbed Diamond. Sir James sold off most of Diamond's assets, and Diamond Match was merged into Generale Occidentale S.A. It is now a private subsidiary of that company and has not released financial information since the time of the first quarter dividend payment in 1983.

SINGER COMPANY

Singer was a company blessed with the sewing machine: a new and much-needed product. Mahatma Gandhi called the Singer sewing machine "one of the few useful things ever invented." While Elias Howe was actually granted the patent for the machine in 1846, the machine was far from perfected. For example, Howe's original invention could sew only six inches at a time. The machine then had to be adjusted and could then sew for another six inches, followed by another adjustment. Furthermore, the quality control on the machines left something to be desired. Fewer than one out of every ten machines produced actually worked, and the rate of needle breakage meant that often the machines never made it to the point of sewing even six inches at one time.

Along came Isaac Singer, a man in his thirties who had never quite found his position in life. He had been everything from a traveling actor, with the various children of various women around the country to show for it, to a failed inventor of printing machines. He was fascinated when he saw Howe's sewing machine and noted that the curved and weak needle was the problem. Singer undertook improvements to the Howe machine and also applied for patents for his improvements, as did a host of others from 1846 forward. The Singer Company, founded in 1851 by Isaac, with his improved machine and peripheral patents, set as its goal achieving international appreciation for its product that equaled Gandhi's zeal.

Isaac Singer was not exemplary in business ethics or his personal life. Upon patenting his reliable Singer machine, Singer was sued by Elias Howe. Edward Clark, a young lawyer at the time, agree to defend Singer in the patent infringement suit in exchange for a one-third interest in Singer's business. Singer agreed, and Clark was able to end the patent litigation with a patent pool settlement agreement between Howe and Singer and among other manufacturers. Until 1877, the 24 sewing machine manufacturers in the United States would give $5 each to Howe and Singer for patent royalties. The settlement and resulting royalties were an amazing coup for both Howe and Singer in that each sewing machine cost only $15 to make.

As Singer began manufacturing and selling sewing machines, Howe was in England trying to sell his machines to a corset manufacturer. The corset manufacturer refused, and Howe was so destitute that he sold the patent for his machine in England for $100. When Howe returned to the United States, he saw what had happened with his patent, and he began filing patent suits against all the manufacturers, including Singer. Singer, anxious to get the product distributed, settled Howe's suit against him in return for a royalty of $25 per machine. However, this singular settlement was by no means the end, for there were now almost 24 patented improvements to the Howe machine, and the complexities of the intellectual property rights on these improvements and Howe's original rights resulted in patent litigation that had claims, cross-claims, and counterclaims. Singer, now a market leader, proposed that there be a pooling of the patents, called the Sewing Machine Combination, which allocated royalties from sales to the various patent holders. Each manufacturer paid $15 per machine, which was then allocated according to formulas the parties agreed on as part of the litigation settlement.

The introduction of the sewing machine was an issue of social responsibility and an uphill battle for Singer. The country had already been sensitized by extensive press coverage to the plight of the seamstress in the United States. Mostly immigrants, these women had to sew by hand for over 14 hours to make a man's dress shirt. With the sewing machine, the time for shirt construction could be reduced to under 2 hours. Commentary of the time voiced concerns about the economic implications of the introduction of the machine. The fear was that the women who were dependent upon long hours to be able to earn the wages they needed for survival would be displaced. Furthermore, Singer was faced with overcoming both the public perception and the reality that the initial sewing machines had functioned so poorly that there was little trust in either the machines themselves or those selling them.

In addition, Singer's private life became a bit of an issue for customers because he was no saint. By 1863, details about Singer's sordid private life became public. When it was revealed that Singer had 24 children by four women, public outcry affected company sales. Clark and Singer dissolved their partnership, and Clark took over as CEO, a position he held until his death. Singer had the good sense to sell his interest to save the company's reputation, and he fled to Europe to escape the negative publicity and disassociate his personal activities from the company's. He died in Europe in 1875.

To overcome the intense negative perceptions that surrounded the sewing machine, Singer sought contracts with the powerful, rich, and famous in order to gain attention for the company from the resulting marketing power and product identification. Ahead of its time, Singer understood the power of celebrity endorsements. Singer was one of the United States first multinational companies, with sales of its machines to Czar Alexander III for his country's use in making tents for the Czar's army. Admiral Bird purchased six Singers to take to Antarctica with him. Singer used the notoriety of these purchasers to advertise and position itself as the sewing machine of choice for royalty and explorers. Singer was perhaps the first company to recognize the power of international celebrity endorsements.

Singer conquered the market for sewing machines because it was a company that understood its customer. Singer was also the first mass producer of machinery to build its own sales force. Paid on a commission basis, these sales representatives pumped up the sales volume tremendously during the 1850s. However, Singer learned that these independent sales reps did not know the product well; they could not demonstrate, repair, or service the machines. As a result, Singer began a new distribution and sales system whereby it opened stores with four employees: a female demonstrator, a mechanic for repair and service, a salesman or canvasser for selling machines, and a manager who supervised the others and handled credit and collections.

By 1859, Singer had fourteen of these branch stores. During this period of its store implementation program, Singer did, however, continue to rely on independent commission sales because there was a considerable lag time in opening these branch stores and training the personnel needed. Eventually, the branch stores would be managed by regional sales representatives, and Edward Clark, Singer's partner and now mastermind for the business, continued to believe that having its own sales force was the key to Singer's success in sewing machine sales.

By 1876, with Singer's passing and Clark assuming the helm, the Singer Company had a strong international presence, despite having to compete overseas without the benefit of patent protection. Not only did Clark implement the branch structure in Great Britain, but he also began more careful supervision of credit, cash, collection, and accounting. The result was a steady and reliable cash flow from all operations based in London and Hamburg. With the patent protection expiring in the United States in 1877, that European efficiency was necessary for U.S. operations as the competition increased. Clark implemented the same types of administrative controls in U.S. operations with the same resulting impact of steady cash flow.

By 1878, Clark had perfected his sales and distribution systems throughout the world. In the United States, 25 regional sales offices reported to Singer's New York office, 26 regional offices in Great Britain reported to the London office, and 53 regional offices of northern and central Europe reported to Hamburg. Latin America, Canada, and the Far East reported to New York, and the rest of Europe, Africa, and the Near East reported to Hamburg. Singer was a company with a strong international presence prior to the turn of the century.

While Singer had achieved international market dominance by 1874, selling over half of the sewing machines it manufactured outside the United States, it still had not tapped into all of its potential. Indeed, by 1900, Singer was selling over 500,000 sewing machines per year and had achieved a position of market dominance both in the United States and around the world.

This aggressive and organized sales team put Singer at the top of the sales list worldwide, and its production facilities were expanded regularly. In 1874, Singer built the largest sewing machine factory in the world at Elizabethport, New Jersey. Despite building another factory nearly as large near Glasgow, with a capacity of 10,000 machines per week, Singer lost sales when it could not fill its orders on a timely basis. The head of London's Singer office said that the delays "utterly ruined" the company's reputation in Britain. Interestingly, these two large factories were financed entirely out of current earnings, with no debt incurred for their construction.

As the sewing machine market diminished, Singer diversified and eventually spun off its sewing machine division during the 1980s takeover activity. Singer would bounce back for a time in its original mode as a sewing machine/home appliance manufacturer and seller with respectable performance. However, Singer would never regain that market position because of sociological changes that it failed to recognize as being dramatic: that of fewer women at home and most women lacking the time needed for sewing. Even the structure of school courses changed as the once mandatory home economics, wherein young girls learned to sew, was eliminated. Singer declared Chapter 11 bankruptcy on September 13, 1999. Singer had purchased Pfaff, Inc., a German sewing machine manufacturer in 1998, and Pfaff had already declared bankruptcy earlier in 1999. Singer is the only company among the fifteen centenarians that no longer exists and the only one met with financial ruin. Its failure to use its entry into its customer's home for other appliances may have been its downfall. More follows on this issue of diversification in Chapter 7.

NOTES

1. Pennwalt Company History.
2. Ludlow Annual Report, 1932.
3. Metz, Tim, "Diamond International Says It Is Trying New Avenues of Defense From Takeover," *Wall Street Journal*, June 6, 1980: A7.

4

The Stories of Present Survivors

A good man (company) is always a beginner.

Martial

The present survivors are the companies that remain the same companies today as in their formation. These are the companies that emerged from the 1980s intact and, with the exception of Corning in 2001, are still going with unbroken dividend records. Again, they are called out in a separate chapter for purposes of distinguishing strategic goals and choices and whether their performances under the keys to longevity were any different from those of the fifteen companies covered in Chapter 3 that were acquired or merged during the 1980s. The interests of the shareholders remains a question, and discussion of the principles of long-term success in subsequent chapters will offer insight into this question and other strategic issues that the 1980s presented.

THE STANLEY WORKS

In 1843, in New Britain, Connecticut, Frederick T. Stanley, an entrepreneur, set up shop for the manufacture of wrought iron hardware. Stanley made door and shutter bolts and, under the name of Stanley's Bolt Manufactory, peddled his wares by horseback or wagon along the Eastern seaboard. Stanley's factory innovations brought the first steam engine to New Britain and earned his operation the labels of "daring" and "progressive." In 1852, the Stanley brothers applied for incorporation and used the name "The Stanley Works."

The Stanley Works grew in both size and reputation through expansion into tools of all kinds from hand to power. It has survived foreign competition in that market with its signature quality as well as its marketing designed to fuel the do-it-yourself market. Its dividend payment has been made every year since 1877 (124 years). The Stanley Works holds the longest uninterrupted record of annual dividends of any industrial firm traded on the New York Stock Exchange. Stanley was one of the fifteen firms to survive the 1980s merger fever, intact as a stand-alone entity despite its attraction to suitors because of its significant value, product lines, and low debt. Stanley remains yet today a survivor, a publicly held company in the same form as it began with its dividend uninterrupted.

CORNING, INCORPORATED

In 1851, Amory Houghton purchased an interest in a small glass company in Cambridge, Massachusetts. In 1864, Amory and his two sons expanded their glass operations with the purchase of the Brooklyn Flint Glass Company. Realizing they needed coal supplies, good transportation, and expansion, the Houghtons packed up their melting pots, loaded everything from their factory onto barges, and shipped it up the Hudson via the Erie Canal to the southeast region of New York. By 1868, they had moved all of their operations there because the Houghtons had found an ideal location for the three critical components of fuel, transportation, and growth potential. However, another company had found the ideal location prior to their arrival, and the Hougtons merged with a local New York firm called Corning Glass Works, located in Corning, New York. Initially, the name of the two merged firms was the Corning Flint Glass Company.

By the time of this move, Amory Hougton had already made a definitive strategic decision on his company's focus. Flat glass and glass containers were too competitive. Corning would make its name in specialty glass products. Corning's initial product line included thermometer tubing, pharmaceutical glassware, railroad signal glass, and tableware blanks. In 1875, when the company was incorporated, its name was changed to Corning Glass Works.

World War II brought significant changes to Corning. Realizing the potential for sales in the postwar construction boom in the United States, Corning sought to enter the foam glass insulation market. In 1943, Corning entered into a joint venture with Owens-Illinois Glass Company for the production and sale of fiberglass insulation under the name Owens-Corning Fiberglass Company. This joint venture would position Owens-Corning for market dominance because the dominant insulation product, asbestos, had evolved into little more than massive product liability and class-action litigation with the end of asbestos as a building material insulator. Corning was positioned for complete market infiltration with its infamous pink fiberglass insulation.

Corning not only developed new products, it also developed new manufacturing processes that provided it with market expansion potential. For example, Corning had developed a machine during the 1920s that produced 2,000 light bulb blanks per minute. During the war, there were only seven such machines in the world, and Corning's main source of revenue became the sales of bulbs from its self-developed, rapid-fire machines to a world in need of light bulbs. With other factories retooled for military production purposes, Corning occupied a unique position. It had used its talent to develop the tools for rapid production, and its plants stood ready to take advantage of an acute public need.

The war was a turning point for Corning in many ways. Although Corning's dividend run began in 1881, it did not go public until 1945 when the war was in its final days. It offered shares for sale on the New York Stock Exchange for the first time, all in anticipation of its capital needs for what would be a postwar competitive boom.

While the war proved to be a period of prosperity for Corning, the postwar period was one of unprecedented expansion. At the root of all the growth would be just one thing: the television. Corning had been producing the radar bulbs for use during World War II. Then CEO William C. Decker saw the radar glass picture tube, a mere seven inches wide in 1946, as something for the future of television and Corning. Decker realized Corning's experience with radar screens, and its production skills for the Defense Department might be put to good postwar consumer use. He assigned a team of scientists to the task of developing a manufacturing method that could mass-produce the glass screens. Corning scientists, as usual, rose to the occasion and discovered a process involving centrifugal force that spun television tubes at a rate of 800 units per day. It captured the television tube market in 1949 and continued its dominance from then to the present with a slight setback in 1982 and 1983, with the introduction of Japanese competition in television, when its dividend dropped significantly but was still maintained.

Corning produced a basic commodity—glass—but made this staple for everyone from scientists to defense contractors during both world wars while still diversifying its product lines with joint ventures such as insulation and construction materials with Owens-Corning. The Corning joint venture boldness continued after the world wars, and

Corning is a record holder among U.S. firms for the sheer number of joint ventures.

However, Corning's other joint venture entered into in 1943 would not prove as fortuitous. Corning and Dow Chemical formed the Dow Corning Corporation that year, designating the purpose of the company as one to develop, produce, and sell as its basic product silicones, which are semiorganic fluids, oils, greases, and resins. Corning had the development and production skills but needed Dow's help, as a chemical manufacturer, on marketing. The joint venture was enormously successful until Dow Corning developed silicone breast implants. That product resulted in a $3 billion settlement of class-action product liability suits against the company as well as its bankruptcy with liability issues regarding the parent corporations still pending.

Since the time of the settlement, the science on which the claims of ill effects from the implants in the women who had them has been established as "junk science." The ill effects from silicone impact about 5 percent of the population, the amount that most prescription drugs affect the general population. However, public perception controlled, and there was no reversing the tide once the fear factor became engrained in the minds of those with implants (see Chapter 7 for more information on this part of Corning's history).

Corning, like Stanley, also stands as a survivor of the 1980s, but it did experience management turnover and strategic realignment in 1983 when, for the first time in a decade, it changed its product designs. Corning had never performed market research prior to 1984 and did no advertising until 1985, when it launched a message for consumers designed to get the word out that its products worked in microwaves, the new kitchen tool of the century. Corning continues its evolution today, with its name remaining a household word synonymous with ease in cooking.

Corning's downfall came with its investment in the new economy with its foray into fiber optics. Corning ventured into an area in which it had not developed expertise and perhaps fell victim to the lure of what seemed to be easy money. Corning's 118-year dividend run ended in July 2001 as its cash picture from the disappointing fiber optics venture was bleak. Ironically, *Forbes* magazine did a story on Corning's venture into fiber optics in 1997. The author of the piece expressed concern about the wisdom of the decision on Corning's part to continue in such a risky area. Worse, Corning had sold off its reliable earnings producers in order to acquire and become heavily invested in the volatile telecom market. Chapter 7 offers some insight on the strategy Corning followed with fiber optics and it running contra to both Corning's pattern of success as well as the success patterns of the other centenarians.

PPG INDUSTRIES, INCORPORATED

A one-man company founded in 1883 by John Pitcairn, Pittsburgh Plate Glass began with the odds against it. Prior to its beginning, several attempts by others to start a plateglass industry in the United States had, in the words of a 1934 *Fortune* magazine article, "gone ruinously bankrupt, unable to cope with the difficult technique involved, the lack of skilled labor, and the competition from foreign glassmakers." Pitcairn was no exception, having failed twice in start-ups of plateglass factories at New Albany and Jeffersonville, Indiana. Finally, at a location 20 miles north of Pittsburgh, Pitcairn found a home with the Allegheny River's sand, nearby quarries, abundant Ohio limestone and salt beds, and cheap fuel in the form of Pennsylvania coal and natural gas.

The company, originally called the New York City Plate Glass Company, began with $200,000 from Pitcairn and the advice and work of John Ford. When the company was incorporated, it was named Pittsburgh Plate Glass Company and called PPG.

In was in 1895, with profits becoming respectable, that Pittsburgh Plate Glass declared its first dividend and moved company headquarters from Creighton to Pittsburgh. PPG has always taken steps to protect its earnings from the often severe swings that come with downturns in construction, the industry using its products. One of its most successful diversifications was into paint, which was a product in demand during construction cycles but also during construction downturns when people chose to fix up and paint rather than build. With this paint diversification, PPG moved into all areas of paint sales, including sales to auto manufacturers, a market in which it continues to hold a strong position today.

While PPG does have a record of diversification, it has still clung to its role of building and construction supplier where it seems to hold its greatest strength. In the 106 years since, the company has not missed a dividend even during the frenzy of the 1980s. PPG held its own during the 1980s, despite some misguided diversification, which is covered in Chapter 7. PPG continues today as a formidable force in the building supply and paint business.

JOHNSON CONTROLS, INCORPORATED

In 1883, Professor Warren S. Johnson, a scientist at the State Normal School in Whitewater, Wisconsin, was awarded a patent for the first electric room thermostat. This invention was the beginning of a new industry: building management and controls. With the financial backing of a group of Milwaukee investors, Johnson formed the Johnson Electric Service Company and paid them their first dividend in 1885.

Professor Johnson's natural curiosity found the company expanding into storage batteries, tower clocks, automobiles, and telegraph communication. When he died in 1912, management and the board refocused the company on temperature control in nonresidential buildings. That refocus, what some called curtailing, was foresight and a recognition of social change in the nature and size of buildings. Controls became critical as buildings became larger and more complex. The need for uniformity in climate in these buildings made the need for controls more critical. Johnson Controls was the first company to introduce a Pneumatic Control Center that enabled building owners to operate, monitor, and control all temperature devices from one central location. Johnson Controls diversification beyond temperature controls has been limited to batteries (1978) and auto components (1985), including auto interiors.

Johnson Controls became the first in the climate control industry to develop computer controls (1972), digital controls (1980s), and also intermanufacturer communication via computer for all of a building's operational systems (1990s). Today, Johnson Controls offers its customers building management services that allow them to control all their company facilities in one central location by experienced Johnson Controls employees. Johnson Controls is responsible for systems operations in 600 million square feet of buildings around the world including IBM's facilities in 20 countries and government facilities at Cape Canaveral.

Like Stanley, Johnson Controls was a strong survivor of the 1980s and took no precipitous steps during that time despite its cash-rich vulnerability. Its dividend record stands at 104 years.

COLGATE-PALMOLIVE, INCORPORATED

William Colgate, an English immigrant, founded his starch, soap, and candle company on Dutch Street in New York City in 1806 at the age of 24. An astute marketer, Colgate chose Dutch Street as the location for his first shop because the mayor and other prominent citizens lived there. All of these movers and shakers would have to pass by his shop and factory and become familiar with the name Colgate. Furthermore, visiting dignitaries of the mayor would also be forced to pass by the candle and soap factory with the name Colgate associated with it, a means of spreading the word about his product beyond the city. The original Dutch Street location would remain in use by the company until 1910, an occupancy of record-setting length in Manhattan.

It was an odd business that Colgate chose as his means of support in this new nation. At the time he opened his shop, over 75 percent of the households made their own soap and candles. Colgate was not only selling a product, he was also selling a justification for purchasing something that could be made at home. He ran his first advertisement in 1817, and the original of the advertisement hangs today in Colgate headquarters.

SOAP AND CANDLE MANUFACTORY
WILLIAM COLGATE & COMPANY
No. 6 Dutch Street, second door from the corner of John Street,
New York
Have for sale on the best terms a constant supply of Soap, Mould and
Dipt Candles
Of the first quality
Orders for exportation executed on the shortest notice
N.B. The highest price given for tallow
January 1817[1]

Francis Smith became a partner, and the firm was known as Smith and Colgate until 1813 when William's brother, Bowles, bought out Smith and together they renamed the business William Colgate and Company. When William Colgate died in 1857, his son Samuel and his nephews took over the operations, and the company has remained under family supervision and control since. Samuel Colgate died in 1897 and jointly William's five grandsons took over the management helm with family control continuing even today. Commentators have noted that there is a certain strength and duty that comes from the Colgate tradition in that whoever is managing the company has the burden placed upon them of passing along something better to the next generation to manage. In the Colgate family, it is not enough to merely pass along the reins to the company—they must pass along something better than what they inherited.

The company grew throughout Colgate's lifetime with both innovation in existing products and the development of new products. For example, in 1872, Colgate, through the perfection of the milling process, gave the country its first perfumed soap, trademarked as "Cashmere Bouquet." This scent theme, which proved popular among a population reared on lye and baking soda, was carried into other products and, in 1877, Colgate introduced the first aromatic toothpaste.

From 1898–1927, Johnson Soap Company was Colgate's primary rival with its Palmolive brand of soap. Johnson merged its Palmolive company subsidiary with Peet Brothers, becoming Palmolive-Peet in 1927. In 1928, Colgate merged with its competitor becoming Colgate Palmolive-Peet, which was shortened to Colgate-Palmolive in 1953. It is known in lay terms as simply Colgate.

Colgate's innovation was a sticking point for its competitors, for Colgate always seemed to be one step ahead of the consumer preference curve. For example, when Colgate developed its dental crème, as opposed to the existing firms' powder, it was an instant hit with the public.

Colgate not only made new and better products, but those products also smelled good and were placed in packaging innovations that played well with customers frustrated with the inconvenience of traditional packaging for items such as toothpaste. In 1891, Colgate replaced the awkward toothpaste jars with the novel idea of Colgate Dental Creme in a tube, one of many items to come from its research laboratories.

Unable to compete because of their lack of product development, Colgate's competitors chose a different tact and began a rumor that Colgate was a foreign-owned company, something that would be devastating to sales in the United States because of issues surrounding foreign investment and power. William Colgate ran full-page ads in newspapers around the country offering a $1 million reward to anyone who could prove that Colgate and Company was foreign-owned or foreign-controlled. There were no takers, and the effect of the ad was to quash the rumors instantly.

The 1980s proved a productive, expansive, and relatively calm time for Colgate as those around it reeled as targets. Instead, Colgate used the decade for acquisition and growth with Colgate-Palmolive's purchase of Softsoap Enterprises, Murphy's Oil Soap, Mennen Company, and S. C. Johnson's liquid soap lines. Finally, Colgate-Palmolive used the beleaguered 1980s to gain an advantage over competitors who were otherwise occupied with merger mania. It began an intensive buildup of its international presence and launched new products on the domestic front. For example, in 1980, Colgate introduced Fresh Start, the first detergent concentrate requiring only 1/4 cup for each washer load. Other innovations during this era returned Colgate to its original forte of repackaging its products. During the 1980s, Colgate put its toothpaste in pump bottles and introduced the first liquid automatic dishwasher soap. Its innovation was also a part of its expansive growth. For example, Colgate edged its market share higher with its addition of a tarter control toothpaste and baking soda toothpaste.

GENERAL ELECTRIC, INCORPORATED

Thomas Edison founded the Edison Electric Light Company in 1878, along with Grosvenor Lowry, with a total capitalization of $300,000. The purpose of the company was to develop and sell an incandescent lighting system to replace gas lights. Edison succeeded with his invention of the electric light bulb in 1879 and almost immediately saw the opportunities for derivative products, which resulted in a research-focused company looking into the generation, transmission, and control of electric power. The result of the research in these fields was the development of everything from the DC generator to streetcar systems run by electricity.

In 1889, Edison consolidated all of his many diverse efforts from streetcar companies to machine works into the Edison General Electric Company even as the Thomas-Houston Company introduced its AC system, which could transmit over longer distances than Edison's DC system. The incompatibility of these systems and the sheer competitive forces threatened to halt the advancement of electricity. Edison worked with Thomas-Houston to find a resolution so that electricity could be universally transmitted and used. As a result of Edison's efforts, he was able to oversee the merger of his company with Thomas-Houston into the General Electric Company (GE), thus ensuring the advancement of electricity prior to his departure from the company.

When Edison resigned as CEO, he chose to remain on the board, but he turned the helm over to Charles Coffin. Coffin was a visionary who concentrated on the company, not the product. Without him, GE would perhaps still be just a light bulb company. From Coffin's time forward, GE continued its creative expansion into all aspects of the use, generation, and transmission of electricity through acquisition as well as product development in its GE Research Laboratory, which was founded in 1900.

A company that had begun as one focusing on light bulbs, elevators, and trolleys was, by the 1920s, merging with AT&T and Westinghouse to take advantage of radio opportunities. It formed the Radio Corporation of America (RCA) to capitalize on America's love affair and growing dependence on the radio. GE has always been able to move one step ahead or in step with the baby boom generation. For example, following the war GE turned to the manufacture and sale of household appliances for which there seemed to be an insatiable demand as the GIs returned from the war, ready to marry and set up households. GE was poised for the infamous plastics movement of the 1960s even before Dustin Hoffman was given the infamous advice in *The Graduate* for future business success, "plastics." The result of this foresight was the timely development, quality, and perfection of GE's Lexan plastic, a product legendary for its performance in use and sales. GE was also ahead of the curve on nuclear power and has been involved since the 1940s in its development. Today, GE generators are a critical part of many nuclear plants as well as other forms of generation.

GE moved into all aspects of television with everything from manufacturing and selling to the ownership of what was being broadcast through its ownership of one of the three major networks, NBC. GE now moves into the markets that an aging population will expand, most particularly health care. The aging baby boomers, in need of health care as they age, find that GE does indeed bring good things to medical care, if not life. GE is the premier company for medical imaging equipment including magnetic resonance imaging, sonogram, and mammography equipment.

This facile movement into developing areas and new technology is the result of its early focus on the role of R and D and its willingness to spend the funds necessary for product development. GE holds more patents than any other company in the United States[2] and now produces everything from turbines for electrical generation to jet engines to consumer products such as hair dryers, skillets, electronic ovens, self-cleaning ovens, and electric knives.

While GE did some internal and external reshuffling during the turbulent 1980s, it survived that era with high levels of profitability, and in addition to its dividend record, remains the only company listed in the Dow Jones Industrial Index that was also included in the 1896 original index. As 2002 began, questions about GE's financial reporting emerged.[3] GE did take a first quarter adjustment, but continued to predict inceased revenues and earnings despite a resulting loss.

COCA-COLA COMPANY

John Pemberton was an Atlanta pharmacist who happened upon a concocted mixture in 1885. The mixture was tasty, unique, and eventually became known as the real thing, Coca-Cola, a name Pemberton's bookkeeper, Frank Robinson, coined. Asa Candler purchased the right to Pemberton's Coca-Cola in 1889 and incorporated the Coca-Cola Company in 1892. Pemberton transferred the rights to the drink's formula in exchange for 500 shares in the new company.

Just when Candler was beginning to see the company hit its stride, the regulatory environment brought dramatic change. Candler and Coca-Cola had labored mightily during the early years of the company to overcome the public perception that this newfangled product was not a medicine. Any progress they had made in this regard experienced a setback when the company was hit with charges and penalties by government regulators for sale of a product harmful to consumers.

Handed the ultimate penalty by regulators, Coca-Cola drink sales were banned by law except for medicinal purposes. However, prohibition is apparently prohibition, even when the legalities involve a soft drink, and Coca-Cola sales thrived, for it seemed "medicinal purposes only" knew very few limits. Eventually, the ban was lifted, and the company had its loyal following that then felt free to spread the word on the new soft drink. The result was continuing sales expansion.

Following the "Prohibition era," Coca-Cola began to face and has since faced the cyclical and continuing problem of sugar market volatility. Coca-Cola eventually evened out the impact of changes in sugar prices with better contract negotiations. The company learned to negotiate longer contract terms, price stabilization clauses, and even price guarantees.

Through its ties to celebrities and its recognition as a morale booster for troops stationed overseas in markets into which Coca-Cola had already expanded, Coca-Cola held a near monopoly in the soft drink market during World War II. However, Pepsi-Cola began grabbing market share in the 1950s and 1960s, and has been a relentless competitor. Coca-Cola has remained a solid performer, but its international presence has alternated in some countries with Pepsi-Cola. Coca-Cola has remained, however, the most recognizable soft drink in the world. Even the shape of its bottle is a trademark and a universal symbol for "the real thing."

Coca-Cola enjoys a unique position among these 100-year firms because its continuing sales and success are centered on its original product. While there has been expansion in types of beverages, the real thing remains at the heart of Coca-Cola's success. While Coca-Cola is not a one-product firm, its market share, brand recognition, and expansion appear to be tied to one product, Coca-Cola, with its distinctive taste.

Today, Coca-Cola's global sales are in a state of decline. It had negative sales growth in late 1999, with a slight upward tick in 2000 to 4 percent growth in sales. However, when you consider that it had a 14 percent growth rate in 1997, its current mode of introspection and the search for change is understandable. A new CEO, Douglas Daft, an Australian and the first foreigner to run a U.S. company, has taken over and promises to restore the growth rate for the company's mainstay beverage, as well as for innovation he plans around the world for the various markets that have emerged. In these markets, there is a desire and thirst for some alternative beverage to water and native drinks. Daft has made it his goal to quench those markets' thirsts with Coca-Cola products.

PROCTER & GAMBLE, INCORPORATED

Like Colgate, Procter & Gamble (P&G) was originally formed as a soap and candle manufacturer. With just $7,192 in capital, William Procter and James Gamble formed their company in 1837 in Cincinnati, Ohio, selling just candles. Its location on the Ohio River near major railways positioned it for excellent product distribution.

It was during the Civil War that P&G made its name by switching its emphasis from candles to soap. Because the Civil War brought a rosin shortage, P&G was forced to experiment with new ingredients and manufacturing methods. The result was Ivory soap, the product that would make P&G famous. Ivory soap was, quite simply, an accident, caused by mixing too much air with the soap compound. Not only did P&G benefit from its new product, it also gained an appreciation for R and D, something it has pursued ever since. The eureka effect of P&G was born. The Ivory soap accident not only instilled in the workers a serendipity, but also served as the launch for the ad campaign for Ivory soap. The workers' declaration upon witnessing the effect of their mistake was, "It floats!" Ivory soap's slogan that continues even today became, "So pure, it floats." The phrase even translated into French, German, and Spanish, and P & G became known internationally as being synonymous with cleanliness and sanitation because of its unforgettable slogan, all courtesy of its employees' fortuitous mistake.

P&G has repeatedly used this combination of discovery reflected in its ad campaigns. In fact, its products and the advertisements are so well known that many consumers refer to generic substances by their P&G names. For example, many consumers refer to shortening as "Crisco."[4] "Clorox" is the consumer name for bleach, and all disposable diapers are "Pampers."

During the early 1900s, P&G diversified from soap into the broader field of consumer products. Its first new product was Crisco, and from there it launched Tide, the detergent that would sponsor melodrama in the afternoon television soap operas. That stroke of marketing genius in television sponsorships of daytime dramas gave P&G a near laundry detergent monopoly.

The 1950s was the era of P&G acquisitions, done brilliantly. The small companies this giant took over included Duncan Hines, Charmin, and Clorox. But its expansion was not limited to acquisition. Its own R and D brought Pampers into the world, and raising babies would never be the same, for Pampers was the beginning of the end of the cloth diaper; convenience triumphed in every home in America with a baby or toddler.

Procter & Gamble, a company that weathered the Civil War, the Depression, and two world wars, was unfazed by the 1980s, and emerged stronger than dirt, just as its own soap advertisements promised. Even today, the company remains on the cutting edge of consumer products. Witnessing the required use of low-water use washing machines in Europe, P&G understood that the machine requirements would eventually make their way into the United States. The machines did indeed emerge in the United States, first as energy-efficient, environmentally-friendly washers that were high-end items such as the Maytag Neptune series. P&G developed its own Tide HE (for High Energy) for these new era washers. Procter & Gamble entered the market as a first mover. Other soap producers are just now releasing their own HE products as the requirements for the new washers take effect in 2001 and the new washers begin to dominate the market.

GENERAL MILLS, INCORPORATED

General Mills began in 1866 as the Cadwallader Washburn Flour Mill near St. Anthony's Falls near Minneapolis, Minnesota. There Cadwallader C. Washburn, in partnership with John Crosby, built a mill along the Mississippi that came to be called "Washburn's Folly" because the locals found it difficult to believe that the flour from Midwestern spring wheat would ever catch on.

The milling process for spring wheat, focused in the Midwest at that time, leaves darker bran fragments in the flour. The result was a flour with a gray look, not the bright white that winter wheat produces in its flour. However, Washburn was an innovator, and he used production to solve the product's consumer preference issues. He installed steel rollers to replace the grindstones and introduced the Middlings Purifier for sifting out the bran fragments. The result was a flour made from spring wheat that rivaled winter wheat. Customer demand grew, especially when the spring wheat proved to possess better baking qualities than the winter wheat. In 1880, the Washburn Crosby Company's spring wheat flour won the gold medal at the Millers International Exhibition. The "gold medal" was touted on the company's flour bags, and the flour has been known as "Gold Medal" ever since.

The result of the new product and its recognition was that both the Washburn name and Minneapolis became known as a center for milling grains. Having brought to the country the first innovations in grain processing, the country acknowledged Washburn and the Midwest processors as the mecca for flour.

It was during the 1880s that the company gained a position of market superiority that continues today. James Stroud Bell, often called the greatest merchant miller of his time, began the national expansion of Washburn Mills. His first move was to construct mills around the country, the first being one in Buffalo, New York, in 1904. Buffalo became a milling center because of General Mills presence there.

In the 1920s, the company moved slightly from milling products to actually selling products to consumers. In order to encourage consumer demand, the company offered a free pin cushion in the shape of a flour bag if customers could put together a jigsaw puzzle of a picture of the company's flour mill. When consumers sent in their puzzles in order to collect their pin cushion prize, they included questions about baking with the company's flour. In order to answer all of the mail, the Consumer Response Department, as it was called, created a pen name that appeared on all letters, "Betty Crocker."

In 1921, the efforts of the R and D folks, quality control, and the Consumer Response Department resulted in the joint creation of the Betty Crocker Kitchen in a small space at the factory so that a home economist could test each batch of Gold Medal flour. The home economist used different recipes in testing the flour and put those recipes on the flour bags, a tradition that continues today. Demand for the recipes was so great that the staff of the Betty Crocker Kitchen increased from one home economist to 21 staff members plus the head home economist. The success of the kitchen was used as a marketing tool. Washburn sponsored Betty Crocker cooking schools all around the country. A fictional Betty Crocker became a symbol on all baked goods products, where she remains today, albeit with an updated look that has been changed periodically over the years.

Attuned to its role in the Midwestern community and a sense of social responsibility that predated the era when such community involvement by corporations became popular, Washburn responded when one of the area's radio stations was experiencing financial difficulties by joining with civic organizations to help save the radio station, with its call letters changing to the acronym for the company name, WCCO.

The radio station venture happened to coincide with another marking point in Washburn's development with the introduction of its first cereal in 1924, Wheaties. Wheaties, still in existence and selling well more than 75 years later, was not an immediate smashing success. In fact, Wheaties sales dropped dramatically after its initial introduction, so Washburn used WCCO to air the first singing radio commercial for its waning product, Wheaties, to wit, "Have you T-R-I-E-D Wheaties?" Sales skyrocketed as audiences responded to the advertisement sung by what would become known as the Wheaties quartet. Wheaties sales also increased because of a marketing serendipity: the sports figure endorsement, using sports figures as marketing tools for Wheaties. General Mills was able to sell more Wheaties with sports figures coupled with what has become not only an international slogan but an idiom, "The Breakfast of Champions."

In 1928, under the direction of James Ford Bell, the son of James Stroud Bell, Washburn made a critical move in order to support the company's expanding retail demand. Bell began consolidating regional mills and acquiring mills around the country, including the Sperry Flour Company, the dominant presence on the West Coast. All of the mills became part of a new corporation, which consolidated their operations and became known as General Mills.

Substantially unaffected by the Depression because of its newly acquired national presence, General Mills actually grew during that era to become the largest flour miller in the world. It was during this time that a motto appeared on the walls of the company offices in Minneapolis, "Facts, Not Opinions." This credo became the basis for the company's decision-making process and also an integral part of its marketing philosophy.

During World War II, General Mills again emerged the good citizen as it adapted its Minneapolis facilities for the development and production of intricate torpedo directors for use by the Navy. Other General Mills factories around the country were also modified for military use. The Buffalo plant was used for the production of lens coatings, and California facilities made sandbags. When the war ended, General Mills was so pleased with the quality and efficiency of its war time production facilities that it entered the home appliance business using the retooled factories. Its first product was the "Tru-Heat" iron.

From the time of its 1920s consolidation, General Mills invested in R and D to find consumer products that were quick, easy, and convenient. Bisquick was the country's first big-seller baking mix after its introduction in 1930. General Mills would begin a trend with Bisquick of following the American homemakers as they transitioned from meals made from scratch to the effortless meals of today. General Mills also built on its Wheaties success with new forms of ready-to-eat cereal such as Cheerios, introduced in 1941. Since that time, no flavor, shape, or cartoon character has gone untapped in the search for new ready-to-eat cereals.

During the 1960s, General Mills underwent substantial change through a rapid-fire series of acquisitions and restructuring with purchases of snack food companies as well as diversification into toys. A few of its new consumer brands included Yoplait yogurt, Gorton's frozen seafood, and Chef Saluto frozen pizzas. Its acquisition of Kenner and Parker Brothers made it the world's largest toy manufacturer. General Mills diversification included ventures into clothing lines, including Eddie Bauer, Talbots, Ship 'N Shore, and Izod Lacoste. Even Monet jewelry was acquired as part of the Specialty Retailing Group. General Mills also expanded into the restaurant sales areas with the acquisition of Red Lobster, York Steak House, Good Earth, and the Olive Garden.

However, this rapid and widespread expansion proved too much to manage for a company with General Mills roots, and in 1985, it began a process of divestiture in order to return to its focus on consumer food products. Rather than merging and acquiring during the 1980s, General Mills went through a period of divestiture. Its only acquisition since its massive 1980s divestiture has been that of Chex cereals from Ralcorp, a logical fit.

The company remains headquartered in Golden Valley, Minnesota, just 10 miles from the site of Washburn's Folly and remains focused on what it does best: food for consumers, in all of its forms. General Mills remains committed to new products and R and D and continues to expand the James Ford Bell Technical Center (JFBTC) that continues to fuel the pipeline for new products of the company. Products that have sprung from employees at JFBTC include Nature Valley snacks, all new cereals, and any new Betty Crocker mixes.

General Mills was able to garner a strong international presence during the 1990s. It helped form the Cereal Partners Worldwide joint venture with Nestlé, and the result has been its dominant presence in the European cereal market. With Pepsico, General Mills formed Snack Ventures Europe, and these two companies have, through their combined marketing and distribution effort, dominated the European market since 1992.

HOW THEY DID: A LOOK AT THE FINANCIALS

While not all financial records were available for all of the fifteen companies for their full 100 years, we were able to piece together enough to place the dividends in the context of share price, resulting return on investment (ROI), and other baseline measures.

This project has had its share of naysayers, particularly during the now-but-a-memory "new economy" when we were told that dividends no longer matter. Dividend payments seem to be a proxy for cash and cash is king, or cash is at least indicative of a company teetering in solvency, as opposed to the phenomenal dot-coms who just needed an economic reality check from investors who finally realized the burn rate meant there was no cash in the company.

The naysayers found no nouveau charm in this project. But, a quick look at these firms' performances in market context is a picture worth 1,000 refutes for the naysayers. The financial stability of these companies was as certain as the market opening each day. These companies did not have the pot-of-gold rainbow stocks. Rather, they were more like the best-kept secret stocks. Just descriptions of their financial performance are enlightening. During George Pullman's tenure, the company's operating ratio averaged 45 percent. The ratio of all of Pullman's charges to gross revenue averaged 57 percent. Dividends paid in 1897 totaled $37 million while earned surplus still remained at $27 million. Pullman's price per share in 1892 was $200.

Table 4.1 depicts just the stock splits for General Mills, including phenomenal results during the past year of market struggles. The splits are reflective of a company doing so well that it could announce these splits with a certain amount of regularity.

The following tables offer some insight into the companies' financial performance. If exemplary dividends records are insufficient reason for

TABLE 4.1 General Mills Stock Split History

November 8, 1999	2-for-1 split
May 28, 1995	spin-off
	1 share Darden Restaurants, Inc., for 1 share of General Mills
November 7, 1990	2-for-1 split
November 7, 1986	2-for-1 split
November 7, 1985	spin-off
	0.3 share of Kenner Parker Toys, Inc., and 0.2 share of Crystal Brands, Inc., for 1 share of General Mills
October 10, 1975	2-for-1 split
August 31, 1967	2-for-1 split
August 28, 1959	3-for-1 split
August 21, 1945	3-for-1 split

further examination of the long-term culture, then a survey of that record as well as their general financial performances should offer motivation for a closer look.

Table 4.8 reflects the dividends actually paid by the companies. More details and graphic depictions can be found in the Appendixes, but this chart gives an indication of the steadiness of the companies' course and their, in many years, phenomenal payouts to shareholders.

THE BRIEF HISTORY WRAP-UP

All fifteen 100-year companies struggled at their inception and then evolved. Their patterns of development and present status vary, but they are identical in their unique achievement of providing consistent shareholder value for 100 years without faltering. Just their brief histories reveal stories of variations in their growth, decisions, and even marketing. But even in those variations are consistent themes that do explain their unique business statutes.

These were entrepreneurs, convinced of a contribution their products and businesses could make to society. These companies were made of people of humble beginnings who achieved success through determination and hard work. These companies met competitive, logistical, and regulatory challenges as their companies and product lines developed. These companies all grew and managed to do so while providing returns on shareholders' investments in them. These common factors, evident after just a brief review of their histories, are explored in greater depth in the following chapters.

TABLE 4.2. Book Value

COMPANY	1976	1977	1978	1979	1980	1981	1982	1983	1984	1985
COCA-COLA	$0.47	$0.53	$0.59	$0.65	$0.70	$0.77	$0.85	$0.89	$0.89	$0.97
CORNING	$4.25	$4.71	$5.23	$5.86	$6.23	$6.60	$5.99	$6.13	$6.30	$6.91
GEN. ELEC	$2.90	$3.26	$3.61	$4.04	$4.50	$5.01	$5.60	$6.76	$5.76	$3.81
GEN. MILLS	$3.65	$4.10	$4.56	$5.08	$5.69	$6.13	$6.42	$6.76	$3.38	$2.87
PPG INDUSTRIES	$4.09	$4.25	$4.54	$5.12	$5.62	$5.99	$6.14	$6.60	$7.20	$7.19
P & G	$3.57	$3.97	$4.41	NA	$5.44	$5.84	$6.29	$6.94	$7.61	$7.87
SINGER	NA	NA	NA	NA	NA	NA	NA	NA	NA	NA
STANLEY WORKS	$6.22	$6.88	$7.69	$8.71	$9.19	$9.66	$9.66	$10.35	$11.00	$12.03

COMPANY	1986	1987	1988	1989	1990	1991	1992	1993	1994	1995
COCA-COLA	$1.14	$1.08	$1.07	$1.18	$1.41	$1.67	$1.49	$1.77	$2.05	$2.15
CORNING	$7.60	$8.52	$8.78	$9.08	$10.0	$10.43	$9.30	$8.40	$9.92	$9.15
GEN. ELEC	$4.14	$3.88	$4.54	$4.96	$6.74	$8.28	$7.59	$7.26	$0.09	$2.96
GEN. MILLS	$1.90	$2.06	$1.93	$2.27	$2.48	$3.37	$4.14	$3.80	$3.63	$0.45
PPG INDUSTRIES	$8.28	$9.22	$10.24	$10.49	$12.01	$12.50	$12.72	$11.57	$12.34	$13.21
P & G	$8.48	$8.49	$9.35	$9.59	$10.80	$11.34	$13.21	$10.72	$12.68	$15.16
SINGER	NA	NA	NA	$2.26	$3.66	$6.48	$7.93	$9.20	$10.67	NA
STANLEY WORKS	$13.05	$14.59	$16.31	$15.67	$16.92	$15.59	$15.32	$15.23	$16.74	$16.55

COMPANY	1996	1997	1998	1999	2000	2001
COCA-COLA	$2.48	$2.96	$3.41	$3.85	$3.75	$2.68
CORNING	$4.20	$5.38	$2.19	$3.04	$11.47	$5.73
GEN. ELEC	$3.15	$3.51	$3.96	$4.31	$5.08	$5.52
GEN. MILLS	$0.97	$1.55	$0.61	$0.54	$0.00	$9.68
PPG INDUSTRIES	$13.35	$14.09	$16.45	$17.84	$18.41	$18.28
P & G	$8.55	$8.92	$9.15	$9.14	$9.41	$9.27
SINGER	NA	NA	NA	NA	NA	NA
STANLEY WORKS	$8.79	$6.85	$7.54	$8.27	$8.65	$9.78

TABLE 4.3   Earnings Per Share (US $)

COMPANY	1976	1977	1978	1979	1980	1981	1982	1983	1984	1985
COCA-COLA	0.10	0.11	0.13	0.14	0.14	0.15	0.17	0.17	0.20	0.22
CORNING	0.59	0.65	0.74	0.88	0.78	0.67	0.44	0.55	0.53	0.63
GEN. ELEC	0.52	0.60	0.67	0.78	0.83	0.91	1.00	0.18	0.21	0.21
GEN. MILLS	0.59	0.65	0.73	0.84	0.98	1.12	1.22	1.22	1.24	(0.41)
PPG INDUSTRIES	0.61	0.37	0.52	0.85	0.79	0.78	0.56	0.84	1.08	1.14
P & G	0.61	0.70	0.77	0.87	0.97	1.01	1.17	1.31	1.34	0.95
SINGER	NA	NA	NA	NA	NA	NA	NA	NA	NA	NA
STANLEY WORKS	0.76	0.92	1.17	1.42	1.29	1.40	0.93	1.28	1.73	1.90

COMPANY	1986	1987	1988	1989	1990	1991	1992	1993	1994	1995
COCA-COLA	0.30	0.30	0.30	0.36	0.42	0.51	0.61	0.72	0.84	0.99
CORNING	0.93	1.03	1.63	1.40	1.54	1.66	1.40	(0.09)	1.32	(0.23)
GEN. ELEC	0.22	0.26	0.31	0.36	0.40	0.26	0.46	0.41	0.46	0.64
GEN. MILLS	1.03	1.25	1.63	2.53	2.32	2.87	2.99	3.10	2.95	2.33
PPG INDUSTRIES	1.33	1.60	2.13	2.09	2.22	0.95	1.51	1.39	2.43	3.80
P & G	1.05	0.47	1.49	1.78	2.25	2.46	2.62	0.25	3.09	3.71
SINGER	NA	NA	NA	NA	1.02	1.36	1.57	1.81	1.92	1.64
STANLEY WORKS	1.84	2.22	2.40	2.71	2.53	2.31	2.15	2.06	2.80	1.33

COMPANY	1996	1997	1998	1999	2000	2001	AVG
COCA-COLA	1.19	1.64	0.42	0.98	0.88	1.07	**0.50**
CORNING	0.26	0.61	0.55	0.64	0.49	(5.89)	**0.53**
GEN. ELEC	0.72	0.82	0.93	1.07	1.27	1.47	**0.77**
GEN. MILLS	1.47	1.38	1.30	1.70	2.00	2.28	**1.59**
PPG INDUSTRIES	3.92	3.94	4.48	3.23	3.57	2.30	**1.86**
P & G	2.01	2.28	2.56	2.59	2.47	2.07	**1.65**
SINGER	0.56	0.59	NA	NA	NA	NA	**1.31**
STANLEY WORKS	1.08	(0.47)	1.53	1.67	2.22	1.85	**1.66**

TABLE 4.4 Price Earnings Ratio

COMPANY	1976	1977	1978	1979	1980	1981	1982	1983	1984	1985
COCA-COLA	16.6	13.9	14.5	10.2	10.1	9.6	13.4	13.1	13.1	13.4
CORNING	15.0	10.0	9.0	7.9	9.5	10.5	18.7	15.9	16.4	24.4
GEN. ELEC	13.5	10.4	8.7	8.2	9.2	7.9	11.9	13.1	11.2	14.1
GEN. MILLS	15.4	12.3	10.5	8.0	7.0	8.4	10.7	11.6	14.5	21.8
PPG INDUSTRIES	7.9	9.2	5.7	4.3	6.4	6.1	11.5	10.5	7.6	11.2
P & G	17.4	14.6	13.5	10.0	8.6	9.1	11.8	10.7	12.5	16.9
SINGER	NA	NA	NA	NA	NA	NA	NA	NA	NA	NA
STANLEY WORKS	9.5	7.8	6.6	11.0	9.0	8.3	17.5	14.2	10.0	11.2

COMPANY	1986	1987	1988	1989	1990	1991	1992	1993	1994	1995
COCA-COLA	15.6	15.7	15.7	22.8	22.8	33.0	29.3	26.6	26.0	31.3
CORNING	15.0	11.4	10.7	15.4	14.6	23.1	26.8	NA	22.6	NA
GEN. ELEC	15.7	18.9	11.9	14.7	11.8	15.0	16.0	18.0	20.0	19.0
GEN. MILLS	18.7	17.1	14.8	17.4	19.3	24.7	21.1	21.1	26.7	37.7
PPG INDUSTRIES	13.7	10.4	9.5	9.5	10.6	26.6	21.9	27.3	15.3	12.0
P & G	17.0	30.9	13.1	17.6	17.9	18.9	21.4	77.0	18.2	20.9
SINGER	NA	NA	NA	NA	NA	13.1	18.1	20.7	15.4	17.0
STANLEY WORKS	13.9	11.7	11.9	14.4	11.5	18.3	19.8	21.6	12.8	38.7

COMPANY	1996	1997	1998	1999	2000	2001
COCA-COLA	39.0	43.0	62.0	72.0	76.0	46.1
CORNING	62.0	34.0	27.0	65.0	23.0	NA
GEN. ELEC	24.0	31.0	36.0	49.0	47.0	21.4
GEN. MILLS	20.0	24.0	29.0	24.0	21.0	20.0
PPG INDUSTRIES	16.0	17.0	17.0	22.0	18.0	26.0
P & G	22.0	30.0	34.0	38.0	45.0	37.0
SINGER	NA	16.1	NA	NA	NA	NA
STANLEY WORKS	26.0	NA	15.0	13.0	8.0	26.0

TABLE 4.5   Closing Prices (US$)

COMPANY	1976	1977	1978	1979	1980	1981	1982	1983	1984	1985
COCA-COLA	$1.65	$1.55	$1.83	$1.44	$1.39	$1.45	$2.17	$2.23	$2.60	$3.52
CORNING	$8.91	$6.52	$6.56	$7.00	$7.45	$6.48	$8.23	$8.72	$8.63	$15.44
GEN. ELEC	$6.95	$6.23	$5.89	$6.33	$7.66	$7.17	$11.86	$2.44	$2.35	$3.03
GEN. MILLS	$8.59	$7.59	$7.41	$6.25	$6.75	$8.97	$12.19	$13.06	$12.72	$15.28
PPG INDUSTRIES	$4.79	$3.38	$3.00	$3.61	$5.09	$1.72	$6.47	$8.72	$8.22	$12.75
P & G	$11.70	$10.73	$11.11	$9.28	$8.61	$10.05	$14.78	$14.22	$14.25	$17.44
SINGER	NA	NA	NA	NA	NA	NA	NA	NA	NA	NA
STANLEY WORKS	$7.22	$7.17	$7.75	$13.96	$11.67	$11.67	$16.33	$18.17	$17.25	$21.33

COMPANY	1986	1987	1988	1989	1990	1991	1992	1993	1994	1995
COCA-COLA	$4.72	$4.77	$5.58	$9.66	$11.63	$20.06	$20.94	$22.31	$25.75	$37.13
CORNING	$13.72	$11.69	$17.34	$21.50	$22.44	$38.38	$37.50	$28.00	$29.88	$32.00
GEN. ELEC	$3.58	$3.67	$3.72	$5.37	$4.78	$6.37	$7.12	$8.73	$8.49	$11.95
GEN. MILLS	$21.56	$24.81	$25.94	$36.19	$49.00	$29.63	$68.50	$60.75	$57.13	$57.75
PPG INDUSTRIES	$18.22	$16.56	$2.02	$19.88	$23.50	$37.38	$32.94	$37.94	$37.13	$45.75
P & G	$19.09	$21.34	$21.75	$35.13	$43.31	$28.38	$53.63	$57.00	$62.00	$83.00
SINGER	NA	NA	NA	NA	NA	$17.75	$28.38	$37.38	$29.63	$27.88
STANLEY WORKS	$25.50	$25.88	$28.50	$39.00	$29.00	$40.88	$42.50	$44.50	$35.75	$51.50

COMPANY	1996	1997	1998	1999	2000	2001
COCA-COLA	$52.63	$66.69	$67.00	$58.25	$60.94	$46.10
CORNING	$15.40	$12.36	$14.99	$42.94	$52.81	$8.92
GEN. ELEC	$16.46	$24.43	$33.97	$51.53	$47.94	$21.40
GEN. MILLS	$28.69	$31.63	$34.13	$40.19	$39.69	$42.36
PPG INDUSTRIES	$56.13	$57.13	$58.19	$62.56	$46.31	$51.72
P & G	$45.31	$70.63	$91.06	$89.25	$57.19	$63.80
SINGER	NA	NA	NA	NA	NA	NA
STANLEY WORKS	$27.00	$47.19	$27.75	$30.13	$31.19	$41.00

TABLE 4.6 Return on Assets

COMPANY	1976	1977	1978	1979	1980	1981	1982	1983	1984	1985
COCA-COLA	15.0%	14.7%	14.5%	14.3%	12.4%	12.5%	10.4%	10.6%	10.5%	9.8%
CORNING	8.1%	8.5%	8.5%	9.0%	7.7%	6.0%	4.1%	5.1%	4.7%	5.2%
GEN. ELEC	7.7%	7.9%	8.2%	8.5%	8.2%	7.9%	8.4%	8.6%	8.6%	9.2%
GEN. MILLS	8.1%	8.0%	8.0%	8.4%	8.5%	8.3%	8.3%	8.1%	8.2%	4.3%
PPG INDUSTRIES	7.5%	4.3%	5.7%	8.3%	7.4%	7.1%	4.7%	6.4%	7.9%	7.4%
P & G	9.8%	10.3%	10.3%	10.2%	9.8%	9.6%	10.3%	10.6%	10.0%	6.6%
SINGER	NA	NA	NA	NA	NA	NA	NA	NA	NA	NA
STANLEY WORKS	6.8%	7.7%	8.4%	9.0%	8.0%	8.3%	5.9%	7.5%	10.0%	10.0%

COMPANY	1986	1987	1988	1989	1990	1991	1992	1993	1994	1995
COCA-COLA	11.1%	10.9%	14%	14.0%	14.8%	15.8%	17.0%	18.2%	18.4%	19.8%
CORNING	6.8%	7.1%	10%	7.7%	8.2%	8.0%	6.2%	-0.2%	4.6%	-0.8%
GEN. ELEC	7.2%	5.4%	3.0%	3.0%	2.7%	2.6%	2.2%	1.7%	3.0%	2.8%
GEN. MILLS	8.8%	9.7%	9.9%	10.9%	11.4%	11.9%	11.7%	10.9%	9.0%	7.7%
PPG INDUSTRIES	6.8%	7.5%	9.0%	8.2%	7.7%	3.3%	5.6%	5.2%	8.7%	12.3%
P & G	5.4%	2.4%	6.9%	7.4%	8.7%	8.7%	7.8%	1.1%	8.7%	9.4%
SINGER	NA	NA	NA	NA	NA	NA	NA	NA	NA	NA
STANLEY WORKS	6.4%	6.9%	7.3%	7.8%	7.1%	6.1%	6.1%	5.8%	7.3%	3.5%

COMPANY	1996	1997	1998	1999	2000	2001
COCA-COLA	21.6%	24.3%	18.4%	11.2%	10.4%	17.7%
CORNING	7.9%	8.7%	6.5%	7.8%	2.3%	-42.9%
GEN. ELEC	2.6%	2.6%	2.7%	2.6%	2.6%	2.9%
GEN. MILLS	14.4%	11.4%	10.9%	12.9%	13.4%	13.0%
PPG INDUSTRIES	11.5%	10.3%	10.8%	6.3%	6.8%	4.5%
P & G	10.9%	12.3%	12.2%	11.7%	10.3%	8.4%
SINGER	NA	NA	NA	NA	NA	NA
STANLEY WORKS	5.8%	-2.3%	7.1%	7.9%	10.3%	7.7%

TABLE 4.7 Return on Equity

COMPANY	1976	1977	1978	1979	1980	1981	1982	1983	1984	1985
COCA-COLA	21.0%	20.9%	21.5%	21.9%	20.3%	19.7%	18.4%	19.1%	22.6%	22.7%
CORNING	13.9%	13.8%	14.1%	15.1%	12.6%	10.1%	7.3%	8.9%	8.3%	9.0%
GEN. ELEC	17.7%	18.3%	18.7%	19.1%	18.5%	18.1%	17.8%	17.9%	17.9%	18.1%
GEN. MILLS	16.1%	15.8%	16.0%	16.7%	17.2%	18.3%	20.0%	19.0%	11.3%	-6.5%
PPG INDUSTRIES	14.8%	8.6%	11.4%	16.4%	13.9%	13.0%	9.1%	12.5%	15.0%	17.7%
P & G	17.0%	17.6%	17.6%	17.9%	17.8%	17.3%	18.7%	18.8%	17.5%	12.1%
SINGER	NA	NA	NA	NA	NA	NA	NA	NA	NA	NA
STANLEY WORKS	12.2%	13.5%	15.1%	16.3%	14.0%	14.4%	9.6%	12.1%	16.3%	15.5%

COMPANY	1986	1987	1988	1989	1990	1991	1992	1993	1994	1995
COCA-COLA	26.5%	28.4%	31.2%	34.2%	35.9%	36.5%	48.4%	47.7%	48.7%	55.5%
CORNING	11.9%	12.3%	18.7%	14.8%	15.3%	15.2%	14.5%	-0.88%	12.3%	-2.38%
GEN. ELEC	16.8%	16.4%	12.8%	18.3%	18.8%	19.8%	20.4%	18.3%	17.1%	22.4%
GEN. MILLS	21.5%	31.4%	41.1%	60.0%	49.5%	49.2%	39.9%	39.1%	37.7%	52.0%
PPG INDUSTRIES	15.9%	18.4%	20.8%	20.3%	18.6%	7.5%	11.8%	11.9%	20.1%	29.8%
P & G	12.4%	5.7%	16.1%	19.4%	21.4%	23.1%	20.9%	3.7%	25.5%	25.4%
SINGER	NA	NA	NA	NA	NA	NA	NA	NA	NA	NA
STANLEY WORKS	14.0%	15.4%	14.8%	17.4%	15.3%	13.4%	14.0%	13.6%	16.8%	8.0%

COMPANY	1996	1997	1998	1999	2000	2001
COCA-COLA	56.7%	56.4%	42.0%	25.5%	23.6%	34.9%
CORNING	34.8%	32.3%	21.4%	20.6%	3.8%	-101%
GEN. ELEC	22.1%	23.3%	23.8%	23.9%	25.1%	25.2%
GEN. MILLS	90.0%	221.7%	221.7%	325.5%	-212.7	1274%
PPG INDUSTRIES	29.9%	28.4%	27.8%	18.28%	20.0%	12.5%
P & G	25.9%	28.3%	30.8%	31.2%	28.8%	24.3%
SINGER	NA	NA	NA	NA	NA	NA
STANLEY WORKS	12.4%	-6.8%	20.5%	20.3%	26.3%	19.0%

TABLE 4.8 Dividend Record
Dividend paid per share of common stock

Year	Scovill	Pennwalt	Singer	Pullman	Ludlow	Stanley	Corning	Diamond	GE	Gen. Mills	Coke	PPG	CP	P&G	JC
1957	$2.00	$1.85	$2.20	$4.00	$2.45	$2.70	$1.50	$1.80	$2.00	$3.00	$5.00	$2.75	$3.25	$1.95	$2.00
1958	$0.75	$1.85	$2.20	$4.00	$1.60	$2.00	$1.50	$1.65	$2.00	$3.00	$5.00	$2.20	$3.50	$2.00	$2.00
1959	$0.50	$1.20	$2.20	$4.00	$1.60	$2.60	$1.63	$1.20	$2.00	$2.55	$6.50	$2.22	$2.45	$2.20	$2.50
1961	$1.00	$0.75	$2.60	$2.00	$2.20	$0.85	$2.00	$1.50	$2.00	$1.20	$2.40	$2.20	$1.40	$1.70	$1.60
1962	$1.10	$0.80	$3.10	$1.70	$2.40	$1.00	$2.00	$0.75	$2.00	$1.20	$2.40	$2.22	$1.40	$1.50	$1.45
1963	$1.20	$0.90	$2.13	$1.90	$2.50	$1.00	$2.50	$1.95	$2.00	$1.20	$2.70	$2.25	$1.30	$1.60	$1.45
1964	$1.62	$1.00	$2.00	$1.90	$2.45	$1.00	$2.50	$2.25	$2.00	$1.20	$3.00	$2.40	$1.20	$1.75	$1.45
1967	$1.40	$1.25	$2.20	$2.80	$1.76	$1.20	$3.25	$1.75	$2.60	$1.33	$2.10	$2.60	$1.00	$2.20	$1.60
1968	$1.40	$1.30	$2.40	$2.80	$1.48	$1.30	$3.25	$1.80	$2.60	$0.80	$1.43	$2.70	$1.11	$2.40	$1.60
1969	$1.40	$1.30	$2.40	$2.80	$1.08	$1.40	$3.25	$1.80	$2.60	$0.84	$1.32	$1.40	$1.20	$2.60	$1.00
1970	$1.40	$1.20	$2.40	$2.80	$1.08	$1.45	$3.25	$1.80	$2.60	$0.88	$1.44	$1.40	$1.30	$2.05	$0.80
1971	$1.40	$1.20	$2.40	$2.00	$1.08	$1.20	$3.25	$1.80	$2.00	$0.94	$1.58	$1.40	$1.40	$1.45	$0.80
1972	$0.73	$1.20	$2.40	$2.00	$1.08	$0.82	$3.38	$1.80	$1.40	$0.98	$1.64	$1.46	$1.46	$1.53	$0.80
1973	$0.78	$1.20	$2.45	$2.07	$1.08	$0.90	$1.40	$1.90	$1.45	$1.02	$1.80	$1.60	$1.03	$1.68	$0.80
1974	$1.00	$1.24	$2.45	$1.55	$1.08	$0.96	$1.40	$2.00	$1.60	$1.11	$2.08	$1.70	$0.60	$1.80	$0.80
1975	$1.00	$1.36	$0.30	$1.60	$0.73	$0.98	$1.40	$2.00	$1.60	$1.24	$2.30	$1.73	$0.70	$2.00	$0.80
1976	$1.05	$1.54	$0.10	$1.23	$0.40	$1.13	$1.50	$2.00	$1.65	$0.72	$2.65	$2.00	$0.82	$2.15	$0.95
1977	$1.25	$1.75	$0.25	$1.34	$0.40	$1.21	$1.56	$2.05	$2.00	$1.88	$1.93	$1.95	$0.94	$2.60	$1.30
1978	$1.40	$2.00	$0.75	$1.45	$0.48	$1.26	$1.73	$2.20	$2.40	$1.04	$1.74	$1.69	$1.00	$1.90	$1.03
1979	$1.43	$2.20	$0.50	$1.65	$0.65	$1.16	$1.94	$2.20	$2.70	$1.20	$1.96	$1.88	$1.08	$3.00	$1.13
1980	$1.52	$2.20	$0.10	$0.95	$0.80	$0.82	$2.17	$2.20	$2.90	$1.36	$2.16	$2.12	$1.09	$3.60	$1.23
1981	$1.52	$2.20	$0.10		$0.60	$0.72	$1.74	$2.20	$3.30	$1.56	$2.32	$2.31	$1.14	$3.90	$1.33
1982	$1.52	$2.20	$0.10		$0.20	$0.76	$2.32	$1.80	$3.30	$1.74	$2.48	$2.36	$1.20	$4.20	$1.43
1983	$1.52	$2.20	$0.10			$0.78	$2.32	$0.35	$2.65	$1.94	$2.68	$2.14	$1.26	$2.40	$1.54
1984	$0.38	$2.20	$0.10			$0.90	$1.60		$2.00	$2.40	$2.76	$1.40	$1.26	$2.50	$1.25
1985		$2.20	$0.30			$1.00	$1.56		$2.20	$2.24	$2.96	$1.64	$1.30	$2.60	$1.86
1986		$2.20	$0.40			$1.00	$1.40		$2.32	$2.36	$2.08	$0.13	$1.36	$2.68	$2.00
1987		$2.25	$0.40			$0.82	$1.40		$1.92	$1.44	$1.12	$1.38	$1.39	$2.70	$1.06

56

TABLE 4.8   (continued)
Dividend Record

Year	Scovill	Pennwalt	Singer	Pullman	Ludlow	Stanley	Corning	Diamond	GE	Gen. Mills	Coca-Cola	PPG	CP	P&G	JC
1988		$2.40	$0.10			$0.92	$1.48		$1.40	$1.74	$1.50	$1.33	$1.58	$2.80	$1.10
1989			$0.88			$1.02	$1.40		$1.64	$2.04	$1.36	$1.48	$1.56	$3.30	$1.16
1990			$6.13			$1.14	$1.38		$1.86	$2.38	$1.00	$1.64	$1.80	$1.85	$1.20
1991			$9.63			$1.22	$1.35		$2.04	$1.38	$0.96	$1.72	$1.51	$2.00	$1.24
1992			$0.20			$1.28	$0.62		$2.24	$1.58	$0.70	$1.88	$1.15	$1.60	$1.28
1993			$0.20			$1.34	$0.68		$2.52	$1.78	$0.68	$2.08	$1.35	$1.17	$1.36
1994			$0.20			$1.38	$0.69		$2.16	$1.88	$0.78	$1.67	$1.54	$1.32	$1.44
1995			$0.20			$1.42	$0.72		$1.64	$1.85	$0.88	$1.18	$1.76	$1.50	$1.56
1996			$0.20			$0.91	$0.72		$1.84	$1.97	$0.63	$1.26	$1.88	$1.70	$1.64
1997			$0.20			$0.77	$0.72		$1.56	$2.09	$0.56	$1.33	$1.57	$1.66	$1.08
1998			$0.20			$0.83	$0.24		$0.42	$1.06	$0.60	$1.42	$0.55	$1.01	$0.92
1999						$0.87	$0.24		$0.49	$1.08	$0.64	$1.52	$0.59	$1.14	$1.00
2000						$0.90	$0.24		$0.53	$1.10	$0.68	$1.60	$0.63	$1.28	$1.12
2001						$0.94	$0.12		$0.64	$1.10	$1.00	$1.68	$1.00	$1.40	$1.24

Dividend Pay Outs
(Dividends per share/EPS)

Company	2001	2000	1999	1998	1997	1996	1995	1994	1993	1992	1991	1990
Coca-Cola	93.0	77.3	65.3	42.3	34.2	36.2	37.3	39.4	46.4	49.9	39.1	39.2
General Electric	45.0	44.9	44.9	45.2	43.9	44.4	43.2	53.8	51.6	42.1	68.6	39.6
General Mills	63.0	55.0	63.5	81.5	73.9	63.7	80.7	63.8	54.4	49.5	44.6	47.4
Procter & Gamble	69.0	51.8	44.0	39.5	39.5	39.8	40.2	42.6	(114.6)	41.6	42.2	41.1
Colgate-Palmolive	28.0	37.1	37.6	42.3	46.9	48.0	176.0	43.8	131.0	42.7	137.0	42.5
Stanley Works	52.0	40.5	52.1	54.3	(164.0)	67.6	107.0	50.0	65.0	59.5	54.5	45.4
Johnson Controls	23.0	23.0	23.6	27.1	27.6	32.2	36.5	40.0	45.6	46.9	58.8	58.5
Corning Inc.	NA	50.0	36.4	42.9	39.3	80.0	(313.0)	52.2	(755.0)	(725.0)	40.2	29.7
PPG Industries Inc.	78.0	44.8	47.1	31.7	33.8	32.1	31.2	46.3	1040.0	62.6	66.7	37.1

TABLE 4.8 (continued)
Dividends as a Percentage of EPS

Year	Coca-Cola	General Electric	General Mills	Procter & Gamble	Colgate-Palmolive
1990	39%	40%	47%	41%	42%
1991	39%	69%	45%	42%	137%
1992	50%	42%	50%	42%	43%
1993	46%	52%	54%	-115%	131%
1994	39%	54%	64%	43%	44%
1995	37%	43%	81%	40%	176%
1996	36%	44%	64%	40%	48%
1997	34%	44%	74%	39%	47%
1998	42%	45%	82%	39%	42%
1999	65%	45%	64%	44%	38%
2000	77%	45%	55%	52%	37%
2001	93%	45%	63%	69%	28%

Year	Stanley Works	Johnson Controls	Corning Inc.	PPG Industries Inc.
1990	45%	59%	30%	37%
1991	54%	59%	40%	67%
1992	60%	47%	-725%	63%
1993	65%	46%	-755%	1040%
1994	50%	40%	52%	46%
1995	107%	37%	-313%	31%
1996	68%	32%	80%	32%
1997	-164%	28%	39%	34%
1998	54%	27%	43%	32%
1999	52%	24%	36%	47%
2000	41%	23%	50%	45%
2001	52%	23%	NA	78%

58

TABLE 4.8 (continued)
Year-End Share Price

	Coca Cola	GE	Gen. Mills	P&G	CP	Stanley	Johnson	Corning	PPG
1990	11.63	4.78	24.50	21.66	9.22	14.50	12.50	7.48	23.50
1991	20.06	6.38	36.81	23.47	12.22	20.44	18.00	12.79	25.25
1992	20.94	7.13	34.25	26.81	13.94	21.25	22.44	12.50	32.94
1993	22.31	8.74	30.38	28.50	15.59	22.25	26.56	9.33	37.94
1994	25.75	8.50	28.56	31.00	15.84	17.88	24.50	9.96	37.13
1995	37.13	12.00	28.88	41.50	17.56	25.75	34.38	10.67	45.75
1996	52.63	16.48	31.81	53.81	23.06	27.00	41.44	15.42	56.13
1997	66.69	24.46	35.81	79.81	36.75	47.19	47.75	12.38	57.13
1998	67.00	34.00	38.88	91.31	46.44	27.75	59.00	15.00	58.19
1999	58.25	51.58	35.75	109.56	65.00	30.13	56.88	42.98	62.56
2000	60.94	47.94	44.56	78.44	64.55	31.19	52.00	52.81	46.31

Dividend Yield

	Coca Cola	GE	Gen. Mills	P&G	CP	Stanley	Johnson	Corning	PPG
1990	8.60%	38.90%	9.71%	8.54%	19.52%	7.86%	9.60%	18.38%	6.98%
1991	4.78%	32.00%	3.75%	8.52%	12.36%	5.97%	6.89%	10.55%	6.81%
1992	3.34%	31.44%	4.61%	5.97%	8.25%	6.02%	5.70%	4.96%	5.71%
1993	3.05%	28.83%	5.86%	4.11%	8.66%	6.02%	5.12%	7.29%	5.48%
1994	3.03%	25.41%	6.58%	4.26%	9.72%	7.72%	5.88%	6.93%	4.50%
1995	2.37%	13.67%	6.41%	3.61%	10.02%	5.51%	4.54%	6.75%	2.58%
1996	1.19%	11.17%	6.19%	3.16%	8.15%	3.37%	3.96%	4.67%	2.24%
1997	0.84%	6.38%	5.84%	2.08%	4.27%	1.63%	2.25%	5.82%	2.33%
1998	0.90%	1.23%	2.73%	1.11%	1.18%	2.99%	1.56%	1.60%	2.44%
1999	1.10%	0.94%	3.02%	1.04%	0.91%	2.89%	1.76%	0.56%	2.43%
2000	1.12%	1.10%	2.47%	1.63%	0.98%	2.89%	2.15%	0.45%	3.45%

The remaining pages offer more details on these firms' beginnings and strategies for growth. The biographical inspiration for change has just begun.

NOTES

1. Colgate company archives.
2. Jenkins, Jr., Holman W. "There Are No Markets without Trust," *Wall Street Journal*, March 27, 2002: A19.
3. Timmons, Heather and Diane Brady, "How Does GE Grow?," *Business Week Online*, April 8, 2002.
4. In October 2001, Proctor & Gamble completed negotiations to sell off Crisco and Jif peanut butter products.

II

How They Did What They Did

Five Keys to the Long Term: Purpose, Performance, Perfection, Priorities, and People

"I don't know. I haven't caught any yet."

> Yogi Berra's response when asked what was wrong with the pitches during a bad game for Yankee pitcher Whitey Ford in which every batter got a hit.[1]

After reviewing these brief histories of fifteen 100-year companies, the question that comes to mind is: What could these firms, from soapmakers to glass producers to grain processors, possibly have in common? What is it about Singer and its sewing machines that gave it a 100-year record, and how does Ludlow and its jute accomplish the same thing? The histories seem to reveal nothing but diversity. But, while these companies were diverse in products, history, and style, they did have some elements in common. We begin with a discussion of the physical commonalities and then proceed to a discussion of values, the drivers behind their longstanding success.

THE OBVIOUS COMMON TRAITS

Apart from the obvious common thread of being old and regular dividend-paying companies, there are other common traits that deserve mention. While some of these factors might be labeled as the true reason for the 100-year success, there is sufficient diversity of industry, risk, economic, and social change among these companies to provide support for the notion that their achievement is something more than just good fortune or being in the right place at the right time and then capitalizing on that position. Causality between the values (covered later in this chapter) and long-term success of these companies is a critical component in their unique achievement. But an analysis of them is unfair and incomplete without a look at other common factors.

Nonluxury Products

These were not firms in the business of producing luxury items. Salt, brass, sewing machines, yarns, hammers, matches, soap, electricity, toothpaste, cereal, and glass are day-to-day products. Coca-Cola is the only company with a quasi-luxury product. What these companies made has continued to be in demand over time. Nonetheless, there have been many publicly traded casualties that also specialized in basic commodities yet were not able to maintain a dividend record. Coal, oil, gas, and food are also examples of day-to-day commodities, yet not all companies involved in these forms of production have reached the 100-year level. As the remainder of the book reveals, even production of a basic commodity is no guaranty of long-term success. These companies' achievements did not result from simply choosing a product line in which demand was preexistent and ongoing and then meeting that demand. Even staid items' demand shifts, and technology or consumer taste can easily displace what was once thought to be a permanent and absolutely necessary product.

Manufacturers All

Not surprisingly, the companies all produced products for resale as their initial lines of business. Such a phenomenon is natural, with the exception of the banks excluded from the study, as there were not many service firms around 100 years ago. These companies reflected the era in which they began. They were, as were most U.S. businesses of that time, in the business, at least initially, of commodities manufacturing. This focus on commodities will enjoy some introspection as the U.S. migrates its way through the shifting international economy. These firms were performers in every Wall Street sense. During their 100 years, as could be expected, their trends were not always linear. They progressed and regressed, were fluid and occasionally frozen in strategy. But then tactics changed, and they adjusted as the market responded. Coca-Cola remains the only company wedded mainly to its original product. However, Coca-Cola has diversified from one beverage to over 160 brand names.

Merger Fates

Precisely because of their financial and strategic positions, the fifteen companies were enormously attractive takeover targets during the 1980s. Low debt, rich cash positions, valuable assets, and stable earnings brought the barbarians to their doors. Table 5.1 provides a summary of the companies, their dividend records and fates. Nine of the companies remained unaffected by the 1980s merger/acquisition activity (Stanley, Corning, PPG, Coca-Cola, Johnson Controls, General Mills, Procter & Gamble, General Electric, and Colgate-Palmolive). Singer, still struggling for its niche and normal operations, emerged again following a raucous series of transfers and takeovers as well as a period during which it was a privately-held company. However, eventually, as noted earlier, Singer filed for bankruptcy. The remaining four firms—Pullman, Ludlow, Diamond International, and Pennwalt—were all acquired by large conglomerates with the performance of those firms that acquired them generally consistent and on an upward trend. For example, Tyco, Inc., Forstman Little, Allied-Signal, and Elf Aquitaine are all companies that acquired centenarians, and their stock performances have been steady, with the usual economic fluctuations according to the nature of their industries. Tyco's 2002 difficulties related to its financial reports and its CEO have just begun emerging, and it is presently impossible to know whether its reflected performance to date has been a reality.

The Risk of Obsolescence and the Blessings of Innovation

The fifteen companies all had a high risk of obsolescence. While they may have begun their businesses with basic demand commodities, their product lines could have been limiting, easily replaced by new products through research and development, technological changes, competition from competitors' products or replacements, or even the generic and often fickle consumer whim.

Singer had to cope with the competition of cheap, ready-to-wear clothing and the sociological phenomenon of women entering the workforce and abandoning the time-consuming skills that once fueled Singer's market. PPG could not rely on glass as its sole product because of the cyclical nature of construction activity with its devastating swings tied to the economy, as well as new architectural trends that favored a modernistic windowless design and look. GE experienced the issue of fast-developing products and technology in the fields of electrical products and generation and has even diversified into a focus on financing the high-dollar items it sells, as well as other general financing. Colgate-Palmolive began as a retail outlet for soap and has emerged as an international producer and seller of all types of hygiene products.

TABLE 5.1 Fifteen Companies: Their Records and Fates

Company Name	Dividend Period	Time	Fate
Scovill	1856–1985	129 years	Acquired by Canadian corporate raider Samuel Belzbergon August 15, 1985, for $540. One share of common stock ($6.25 par) exchanged for $42.50 in cash.
Pennwalt	1863–1989	126 years	Merged into Elf Aquitaine, Inc., on October 11, 1989. Each share of $1 common par stock exchanged for $132 cash.
Singer	1863–1988	125 years	Sewing machine company spun off in 1986, called SSMC. Semi-Tech (Hong Kong) acquired SSMC in 1987, reinstated Singer name, and took it public. In 1988, Singer was taken over in a leveraged buyout by corporate raider Paul Bilzerian.* Each $10 par common share was exchanged for $50 cash. Between July and October 1988, Bilzerian sold 8 of Singer's 12 divisions. In 1989, Singer company's name changed to Bio Coastal, Inc., and James H. Ting purchased the Singer name and divisions for the sewing machine and consumer products. Singer filed for Chapter 11 bankruptcy in 1999.
Pullman	1868–1980	112 years	Acquired by Wheelabrator-Frye, Inc., in November 1980 in a common stock sweep. Merged into Signal Companies in 1983; merged into Allied-Signal Companies in 1985; Signal spun off Pullman in 1984; Pullman merged into FLPC Acquisition Corporation in 1988; each 10-cent par share exchanged for $9.25 cash. FLPC is now part of Forstman Little Co.
Ludlow	1872–1980	108 years	Acquired by Tyco Laboratories in 1981.
The Stanley Works	1877–1999	122 years	Remains as The Stanley Works; no merger or acquisition activity in the 1980s with Stanley as the target.
Corning Glass	1881–1999	118 years	Remains as Corning; no merger or acquisition activity in the 1980s with Corning as the target.
Diamond Int'l	1882–1983	101 years	Merged into Generale Occidentale S.A. in 1982.
PPG Industries	1895–1999	104 years	Remains as PPG (Pittsburgh Plate Glass); no merger or acquisition activity in the 1980s.
Johnson Controls	1885–1999	104 years	Made acquisitions during 1980s to make itself less attractive; survived the 1980s

TABLE 5.1 (continued)

Company Name	Dividend Period	Time	Fate
			unscathed except for cash it used to purchase companies as well as debt incurred for such.
Colgate-Palmolive	1895–present	104 years	Remains a soap, toothpaste, and cream manufacturer with large international market; high profitability. Acquired companies during the 1980s.
General Electric	1899–present	100 years	International conglomerate continues with no impact from the 1980s save some GE acquisitions and considerable diversification into financing.
Coca-Cola	1892–present	107 years	Only effect of the 1980s was strong competitive surge from Pepsi; remains a beverage seller with 160 products; strong performance is waning and suffering effects of competitors' diversifications.
General Mills	1898–present	101	Used the period of the 1980s for more acquisition of companies, which it eventually divested; General Mills was an acquirer, not an acquiree.
Procter & Gamble	1891 to present (1887–there were profit distributions to employees as part of the pshp.—referred to as "dividend day.")	109 years	Remained intact during the 1980s; used this era to expand its product base.

*Note: Bilzerian was convicted of nine counts of security fraud on charges related to the Singer takeover. Interestingly, Bilzerian was the focus of the 2001 hearings on Congress in bankruptcy reform because he declared bankruptcy following the government charges on the takeover, but escaped with his multimillion dollar Florida home because of exemptions under Florida law. His financial excesses were also a subject of considerable financial punditry.

General Mills went from grain processor to producer of ready-to-eat cereal because consumers' lives, demands, and preferences changed.

For a time, Stanley was forced to respond to competition from cheap foreign tools that U.S. customers initially found attractive for their price. Stanley also coped with a three-decade decline in home tool use, a trend only recently reversed with the popularity of do-it-yourself shows and stores. Some have opined that Stanley paved the way for Home Depot and its success as it fueled the do-it-yourself drive. Procter

& Gamble evolved with new products, expanding its line of soaps from personal hygiene to soaps for the new age of dishwashers and washers. Corning competed in everything from plastics to problematic joint ventures such as the ill-fated Dow Corning implant venture. Coca-Cola has had to cope with forty years of intense competition from Pepsi and even a health craze during which it found its way to juice-based beverages.

The fifteen companies have all stood at the precipice and would have faced complete demise had they not the requisite strategic nimbleness necessary to move with evolving markets, consumers, and technologies. When it comes to retaining the competitive edge, these firms had a stealth quality—always poised to move based on accurate intelligence, which was a relentless process. They were all innovators, generally assuming the lead as their industries changed. It is nearly maddening to observe the chaos that exists in these large organizations because of the desire for creativity and innovation. Colgate-Palmolive executive Stephen Patrick explained this role and how his company accomplishes the innovation leadership position.

> When people come to us from other companies, often the new young executive will ask: What is your list of 25 things to do to launch a new product? And then we say, well, we don't have such a list. We don't believe in bureaucracy. Look, if it's a good idea, throw it on the table and we'll work with everybody to make it go and it will go. If it's not a good idea, it won't go and a list of 25 things is unnecessary. We're fighting against severe competitors, some of whom are larger than we. Therefore, we must be nimble and fast.[2]

In short, these firms faced the same unknowns and uncertainties as those that did not reach the 100-year mark. What made the difference? Our review of what they had in common also led us to five key values: purpose, performance, perfection, people, and priorities. These key values are not just an explanation for their long-term success, but they are also a blueprint for any company seeking to attain longstanding financial success.

THE FIVE KEY VALUES OF LONGEVITY

These centenarian companies had five common keys that were responsible for their long-term survival and success. Despite their diversity in product, geography, and means of growth, these companies all had business climates that focused on the long term. A long-term culture seems antiquated to a financial community addicted to quarterly returns and acting on a quarterly returns time frame. Over any twenty-year period, investment in the stock market has always proven to provide better returns than any other investment, yet many have drifted from that long-term picture to one of making decisions to buy and sell based on three-month intervals. Businesses have labored for so long in complete deference to the next ninety days that the long-term focus is not easily recognizable and even more challenging to create and follow.

Nonetheless, there is a difference between the climates in these companies and the companies of today that announce with great regularity and little remorse that they will be cutting workers, restating earnings, or shocking with the sheer amount of reported losses, as Lucent Technologies did with its July 2001 revelation of a $3.25 billion loss coupled with the permanent slashing of half its workforce. A long-term focus is different from a failing Sunbeam that was once riding high on workforce reductions alone.

As U.S. airlines faced the implications of the 2001 World Trade Center and Pentagon attacks, most cut their flights, workforces, and service, including the suspension of meal service. Only one airline, Southwest, did not, and its executives cautioned about the need to stay focused on long-term success. Following the five principles, including low debt, Southwest is in an expansion mode in challenging times, as the other airlines respond only to a temporary condition, not the long term.

A long-term focus is one affixed on the future, not on conventional wisdom and certainly not on the next quarter. For example, when Singer introduced the sewing machine, it was competing with at least one dozen other companies with the same wondrous machine. How did Singer survive as the others fell by the wayside? How was General Mills able to sell a product such as spring wheat flour, which no one dreamed was even a possible consumer product? How was Colgate-Palmolive able to convince women that buying soap and candles was a good idea when everyone else had failed to make that case for the homemaker? Why did PPG make a go of a glass factory in the United States when everyone else who came before it had failed?

Likewise, the converse questions apply to the business icons of today. How was Amazon.com not able to turn a profit in a market in which it was a first mover and the dominant player with technological innovations no one else had? How did IBM lose its dominance of the computer in the workplace? Why does Hewlett-Packard continually struggle with its future course?

Both the common factors of the 100-year firms and the answers to these questions can be found in five key components we discovered to be at the heart of these fifteen companies: purpose, performance, perfection, priorities, and people. These five key Ps represent the components of the long term or a business climate that is fiercely determined to be successful over the long term.

Key #1: Purpose—Why Are We in Business?

Long-term performers have a firm and definitive answer to the question, Why does a business exist? Why are we in business? is a critical question for businesses committed to long-term success. The answer to the question is we are in business to earn money. How odd that such a statement should have to be made. While there is no question that these fifteen firms made substantial contributions to their communities and the social fabric (these contributions are discussed in detail in Chapter 9), they had a clear goal that all employees understood: We need to make a profit for the shareholders. While they would not make that profit by sacrificing their values, and the five values were their parameters, they did understand the goal of making a profit. These fifteen companies had a clear commitment to their shareholders for continuing profits.

These companies stated aloud this reason for being in business so that employees and shareholders alike were clear on the role of the company. Because of the longstanding debates on the role of business in society, employees can become confused about their role and the role of their companies. Just recently, Prime Minister Tony Blair, in a speech on corporate social responsibility, touted the virtues of the triple bottom lines: income, earnings, and social responsibility. Blair touts accountability to stakeholders and laments that businesses seem to be in it only for the money. Blair has come to believe that government intervention is needed to make businesses socially responsible and would grant tax breaks to businesses that fulfill their social responsibilities, whatever those are and however they are defined. Many scholars have proposed requiring proof of social responsibility as a prerequisite for the renewal of a business license or the continuance of a corporate charter. Such public policy proposals may be well intentioned but can serve to confuse employees on the company's motivations and goals.

These fifteen companies had a way of helping their employees understand the social contributions of a well-run business. The employees appeared to understand the difference a company with a long-term focus could make in society. While they knew profits were the goal, they also knew long-lasting profits were possible only with a respect for the social fabric of their communities as well as the environment. These businesses performed so well so consistently that their employees had the stability of continuing jobs, their communities had the revenues and taxes from increasing sales to do with as they please in terms of social goals, their suppliers had the steady flow of incomes from continuing and long-term contracts, and their customers were able to use the firm's products in ways that generate even more benefits for those beyond the companies themselves.

The danger of not striking a balance for employees between the goal of paying dividends and social goals is that the quest for both will be defeated. Ben & Jerry's was and always has been committed to doing social good, but this company has had difficulty with its long-term success. It has gone through a series of chief executives in search of something to make it a regular earner. While there is much companies can accomplish as social agents, a goal of social change without the parameters of accountability to investors is not a path to long-term success but rather a source of confusion for employees because of mixed signals about why the business exists, what its goals are, and what their role is in achieving those goals.

There was a sense of social responsibility within these fifteen companies, but, perhaps remarkably, these firms, their managers, and employees unabashedly stated pervasively and with great regularity their commitment to Key #1: They were there to make money, to increase shareholder wealth. For many, the social responsibility movement has given rise to guilt in employees of businesses and the demonization of the profit motive. However, these companies had a clear position: Profits enable us to achieve much social good so long as we do not violate our principles in earning those profits.

Doing good is indeed what businesses do, but they can not do good without turning a profit. Anita Roddick, founder of The Body Shop, has received countless awards from academic societies and schools of business. She once remarked that she did not "give a bloody damn about the money," for she was in business to do good.[3] In 1998, Roddick resigned as head of her own company as it faced earnings difficulties, suits from franchisees, and questions about sources for its product lines. Ben Cohen of Ben & Jerry's has long boasted of his company's desire to help Vermont, save the rainforests, and eliminate human rights violations.

Both Ben and Jerry had to resign as officers of their company in order to bring in other managers who could turn the company around and turn a profit. Eventually, Ben & Jerry's was sold to Unilever with great lamentation until Unilever proved able to take the products and turn them into something profitable, even as it continues to honor the social goals of Ben & Jerry and its commitment to the people of Vermont.

Adam Smith's observation, "It is not from the benevolence of the butcher, the brewer, or the baker that we expect our dinner, but from their regard to their own interest," though often dismissed in today's discussions about the role of business, was recognized by these firms as not just a sound business philosophy, but the best means for achieving social good.

These fifteen firms were in it for the money and all the good that sprang from that philosophy, but it was their clear philosophy that they were there to make money. In 1887, Procter, one of the founders of P&G, offered this insight into what he called his "common sense principles of economics" as he spoke to the employees of his company.

> The first job we have is to turn out quality merchandise that consumers will buy and keep on buying. If we produce it efficiently and economically we will earn a profit, in which you will share. But profits can't be distributed unless they are earned. And if the company is to take care of its equipment, expand normally, and remain in a sound financial position, part of earnings must be plowed back into the business. That will safeguard your future, as well as the company's.[4]

That William Procter could discuss economics with his workers in such an easy and straightforward fashion is indicative of a CEO with an attitude very different from some CEOs today. Procter, unlike many business leaders today, is not apologetic for his company nor does he subscribe to the notion that all business is evil because of the profit motive.

These fifteen companies seemed to understand that a business and its shareholders benefiting from profitable operations is not the issue. For them, it was how they got those profits that constituted the ethical issue and defined the nature of good company versus evil company. For example, General Mills has long included the following goal in its materials and background history and description:

> General Mills was a pioneer in the ready-to-eat breakfast cereal market. The company continues to provide cereals that are both nutritious and appetizing. Nutritionists point out that breakfast is the most important meal of the day. By providing a wide variety of convenient and wholesome cereal, General Mills aims to make the most important meal of the day a meal that everyone can enjoy.[5]

General Mills declares that it does far more than make a profit—it improves the demeanor and nutrition of America. Others in the fifteen companies also achieved social good through their quality products. Procter & Gamble and Colgate-Palmolive made personal hygiene a goal for their products. The result was limitations on the spread of disease; healthy skin, hair, and teeth; and a nice return for the shareholders. Coca-Cola's presence in a country has often reduced the rate of alcoholism there. GE's role in the fight against breast cancer is a critical one as its scanning equipment continues to improve, and the resulting early detection rate provides almost a guarantee of recovery for the patients diagnosed with cancer. The social goals these companies and their products achieved are too numerous to list. However, these companies also made no bones about the fact that they met those social goals without giving short shrift to their financial goals.

Key #2: Performance—What Business Are We In?

The key purpose of making money was Key #1, which focused on their performance in executing that goal or the hows and whats of making money. Key #2 is tackled in the form of the following question: What business are we in? This second key requires constant attention to an evolving strategic position. These firms explored, revisited, refined, and redirected their product lines and chains of distribution. For long-term survivors, there is an ever-present entrepreneurial spirit poised to capture evolving trends and markets. GE refused to define itself as a light bulb company. Diamond would not limit itself to matches. PPG was more than a glass company. These fifteen companies engage in a continuing struggle to be certain they know what business they are in and that their business is moving in the direction of existing and potential customers.

There is nothing complacent about these companies, even when they were at undeniable peaks of success. These companies were unwilling to believe that they had reached the summit and that there were no new products to be found. Staying focused on the question of what business they were in helped them to remain focused on what they were good at.

Using this performance key of staying focused on what business they were in, these companies grappled with the issues of diversification, expansion, and acquisition with a continuing mode of rethinking their strategic position. In a never-ending process of examining their products and customers as well as social changes, these firms were able to grow with trends, jettison the obsolete, recognize mistakes, rectify errors, and acquire assets and resources necessary to do both.

However, these companies' perspectives on their roles and where they stood were not so limited that they could not see opportunities that, while seemingly different, still capitalized on their strengths. For example, Singer's strength was not cabinetmaking, but Singer was in the business of selling sewing machines to consumers for use in their homes. As it turned out, the coveted consumer had an obstacle to the purchase of a sewing machine: no place to put it in their homes. Singer stepped in with a slight variation in its product, that is, a cabinet is not a sewing machine, but it seems to sell sewing machines. The effort was all still geared toward that overriding business that Singer was in: selling sewing machines.

Key #3: Perfection—Will We Ever Be Satisfied?

In a way it was maddening to study the histories of these companies because it was as if we were following bouncing balls or small children. Like Yogi Berra, we are not sure we have caught one yet. They never stayed in one position for very long. They were always moving along to another project, and they never seemed satisfied with what they were doing and were always ready to move on to something else.

All fifteen companies began as the new economy firms did—as small businesses, often as a one-person or two-person enterprise, then grew into conglomerates. What was so different about them that allowed them to ride from seizing the moment in a consumer trend or industrial revolution to a century of continuing success? These firms are clearly different from the flashes in the pan. Along the way from start-up to century-long performers, these firms encountered crises and developed coping mechanisms. But it is their adaptation and growth, despite times of crisis, that offer management revelations.

Paul Lawrence and Davis Dyer described the importance of a firm's internal capacity in its ability to "cope creatively with significant changes in their environment."[6] Their work documents the problem that most firms, as they mature, lose their capacity to adapt and focuses on "adaptation . . . [as] a powerful metaphor."[7] Like evolutionary biologists, Lawrence and Dyer spoke in theory about organizations adjusting to their environments in order to increase the likelihood of survival. Long-term cultures mean that the organizations change with the times, technology, and growth.

A recent *Harvard Business Review* article offered the following five phases for business organizational development and growth: make it, sell it, create efficiency of operations, expand markets, consolidate the organization, and, finally, solve problems and innovate.[8] This theory of management proposes that as firms grow, managers have different roles and functions that evolve in a sequential fashion. Both Lawrence and Dyer and these more recent theorists treat the phases as distinct, compartmentalized developmental stages. Firms move from one phase into another, with the latter phases being those of a higher level of business operations.

These theorists are wrong. Moving from one phase into another, defined in theory as the next progressive or higher step, is precisely what produces stagnation, something that runs contra to the culture of long-term success found in this research. These fifteen firms did not see consolidation as a phase or a goal or even as a desirable activity. In fact, these firms would ask the question, How did you get to a point in your operations and strategy where consolidation became necessary? Who was not paying attention when you became disjointed and dissipated?

These fifteen companies had all five phases working at the same time from their inception. Their focus never shifted from adaptation. There was no movement from the phase of focus on efficiency of operations because with needed adaptations in markets and competitive and sociological change, such was not possible without continually increasing efficiency.

These fifteen companies practiced a form of business evolution that defies existing theory because their only evolution was that of continual reinvention. Adaptation and survival resulted because they paid attention to their world and had the flexibility to behave as entrepreneurs despite their size. Yet, their journeys from start-ups to conglomerates were not at the expense of their values or at a loss of the spirit and flexibility of their start-up days. They had flexibility coupled with a keen awareness of their environment, which produced rapid-fire responses. Lawrence and Dyer documented a developing stagnation among businesses associated with growth and time, but these firms defied that model.

In these fifteen companies, employees reacted and interacted in order to ensure a competitive vitality despite company size and growth. In defiance of management theory, these fifteen companies operated in all phases concurrently. There was a continuing self-perception of start-up status that was chaotic yet dynamic. There was never rest nor comfort with operations as usual or the existing product line. A simple example on financial issues illustrates this dynamism. As the U.S. economy expanded, the nature of business capital changed from private funding to publicly owned. Ownership by those who did not work in a company was a new experience for U.S. businesses when the expansive notion of publicly-traded companies took hold. Those owners who did not work at the plants and offices of the companies in which they held stock had a desire for detailed information on how their investment was performing.

Initially, corporations with this new breed of outside financing failed to recognize this new breed of investors' need for accurate and complete information. Yet one of these centenarian companies, Pennwalt, was sensitive to Wall Street perceptions and used information about its performance to gain access to this new capital market. Pennwalt may have been the originator of the concept of investor relations. While other companies fretted about the shifting sources of capital, Pennwalt seized the new opportunity.

These companies' perpetual motion was perhaps best exemplified by their dedication to perfection of the manufacturing process as they constantly revisited the question, Is there a better, faster, and cheaper way to do it? Not satisfied with holding the "gold medal" flour of the world, General Mills moved to have a national presence through the acquisition of mills and the installation of new equipment in its Minnesota facilities. Furthermore, the executives asked, why must there be only one type of flour? Would refined flour serve a purpose in baking pastries? Voila! Softasilk cake flour was born. Could flour have baking ingredients added to make it easier to bake? Bisquick, a baking mix and home staple, was born.

Ludlow used microscopes to study types of jute and determine how to maximize the growth and production of the strongest yet lightest jute fibers. Its company archives include the slides from the microscopes wherein Ludlow R and D scientists uncovered the vast differences in jute quality. Here was a company not completely convinced it could not top Mother Nature with some changes in jute. William Colgate experimented with batch and vat sizes to see what he could do for the production rate of candles and soaps. His experiments began from the moment he opened the Dutch Street store and have never stopped; even today Colgate unveiled a new product that combines toothpaste and mouthwash into one—apparently they crossed the vats at Colgate and a new product was born.

There is a certain impetuousness to these companies. In a phrase, they were never satisfied. But coupled with this drive was a certain serendipity and creativity that served to drive their discoveries and adaptation. There was certainly no fear of experimentation. It is just difficult to know which came first: the experimentation that resulted in new products and processes or the drive for new products that resulted in experimentation? The question is moot for however they arrived there, the companies never left. There was constant motion in the quest for the new and improved. Their famous "new and improved" ad campaigns, to borrow a phrase from P&G's legendary marketing, was not only effective for selling products, it was true. "New and improved" was descriptive of these companies' constant refinement of products and product lines. These companies were on a continual quest for the new and improved.

Key #4: Priorities—What Will We Do and What Won't We Do for Results?

While there is clearly a feeling of chaos in these companies from their constant pursuit of new ventures, it is a different form of chaos from the type prevalent in some companies today. This is not the chaos of accounting irregularities or earnings restatements. The chaos of today is not from work, change, and relentless pursuit of profit, but from failure to communicate what the company will do and will not do.

When a company states unequivocally to employees that it is in business to make money, it sends a strong signal to employees to meet earnings goals. In some companies, such a clear goal produced the kinds of results we have witnessed: earnings goals met with later reversals of earnings when the eventual truth emerged. For example, Bausch & Lomb had earnings goals for its various divisions and performance rewards were tied to achievement of those goals. Furthermore, the sales teams and managers understood what would happen if they fell short of these goals. As a result, the various divisions cooked their books. The managers included as sold goods, for example, contact lenses shipped to ophthalmologists even though the lenses had not been ordered. "We'll worry about making up for it next quarter when the docs ship them back," was the thinking.

More recently, FINOVA Capital Corporation watched its stock dive from over $60 to $0.88 per share as it headed into Chapter 11 bankruptcy. This fine firm, once ranked as one of the top ten corporations in America to work for, has hit the skids because its managers postponed the inevitable write-down of a $70 million loan to a California computer manufacturer that had gone bad. Its refusal to write it down raised questions from the outside auditors, and FINOVA then fired the auditors and delayed the release of its annual report. The newly hired auditors offered the same advice, and the write-down was taken along with some other corrections to accounting practices and financial reports. Unfortunately, the actions were too little, done too late, and the market lost confidence in FINOVA. FINOVA managers were laboring under the demands of the executive team's goals of continuing double-digit growth, a goal of an ever-increasing price for its stock, and the temptation of bonuses tied to such performance. The values Bausch & Lomb and FINOVA might have had were lost in the isolated statement and goal of making money and meeting quarterly expectations.

There is nothing wrong with the clear objective of making money; we stated so unequivocally as a value of the long-term culture. But, employees must understand that there are parameters of predefined values in making that money. Throughout the history of these fifteen companies, we were unable to find examples of accounting improprieties or earnings restatements. The companies sent clear messages to everyone who worked for them that there were certain things that were *malum in se* and could not be used to reach their goals.

These fifteen companies' goals were always subservient to their values. Their goals, ventures, and even their chaos were always encased in a set of values held inviolate. They knew where they were headed, and they constantly examined what they needed to do to get there. But, more importantly and the heart of Key #4 to long-term survival is that they understood what they would *not* do to get there. They kept their eyes on the ball, particularly when tempted with the lure of diversification and other fads and fashions of business, including earnings management and financial statement distortions. These firms encased their first three keys in an overriding set of values. Their fourth key to success forced them to ask, answer, and think about: What will we do and what won't we do to get there?

Pepsi-Cola has been an intense competitor of one of the 100-year companies, Coca-Cola. Its culture is notorious for the achievement of competitive advantage. Coke is a formidable competitor, but its culture is different from Pepsi's. In a 1980 interview in *Business Week* about the culture of Pepsi, one vice president said, "Careers ride on tenths of a market share point."[9] Certainly such signals are motivational, but if taken in isolation of values or devoid of values, it means that Pepsi had created an environment in which manager and employees do whatever it takes to achieve the numerical goals.

Specifics on long-term values are covered in detail in the remaining chapters, but a cursory glance again illustrates a unique aspect of these companies. Their values developed a focus on achievement and a steadiness of course that contributed to their long-term success. So encased were their values (listed in Figure 5.1), that production line employees understood them and felt comfortable raising concerns when they felt those values were in jeopardy. These values were expressed in unequivocal terms. These values were their list of what we will do and what we won't do, expressed in simplest terms.

Key #5: People—Who Matters?

These companies gave their employees positions of honor, a common characteristic that is the fifth key to long-term success: a focus on people. These companies understood their employees to be a great asset. GE, Corning, Coca-Cola, Stanley, PPG, Colgate-Palmolive, General Mills, and Procter & Gamble consistently appear on business publication lists such as The 100 Best Companies to Work For and America's Most Admired Companies. These companies are loved by their employees and beloved by their constituents for that mutual respect. These companies see their employees as assets and are willing to heed employees' input and advice. From within their own ranks, they groomed and retained solid management teams.

It is not coincidental that many of the companies had family roots in their founding and in their succession practices with their children and grandchildren learning the business by working their way up through the ranks. As discussed in Chapter 10, it was rare for these companies to even step outside their own management ranks to recruit for their CEOs. All of the fifteen firms were dependent upon well-trained and groomed executive material from within their own ranks. Their succession planning consisted of years of work with managers with potential in order to create a pool with depth from which the next generation of executive management could be chosen.

These companies valued employee input and feedback. Each company has its stories of the CEOs interacting with employees in every

1. Purpose: Why are we in business?
2. Performance: What business are we in?
3. Perfection: Will we ever be satisfied?
4. Priorities: What will we do and what won't we do to get there?
   a. Low debt: risk and risk aversion
   b. Low costs
   c. No quality compromises
   d. Long-term, not short-term gains
   e. It ain't our money: Stewardship
5. People: Employees as assets: Let them know criticism is good and keep 'em home-grown

Figure 5.1 The five keys of long-term success.

situation from having them in the boardroom to visiting them where they do their jobs to see what insights they might offer for that perfection process. It also appears that employees of these fifteen centenarians understood that they had a role in the company in terms of contributions. These were not climates of subservience and silence. These were interactive climates in search of ideas, improvements, and change, no matter what the source.

The result of this type of interaction was a peculiar confidence among the employees about their role in the company and a dedication to its success. Employees appeared to understand that they played an integral role. Their treatment as team players generated not just ideas but a sense of loyalty and dedication that served these companies well in everything from quality to cost controls.

The five keys of long-term success are summarized in Figure 5.1.

THE LONG-TERM CLIMATE'S CONTRAST WITH CONVENTIONAL WISDOM

The long-term climate appears to run contra to the market's current desires. In a market fixated on even just the predictions of quarterly earnings statements and not the actual earnings themselves, how does someone sell the long term as a virtue?

The fixation on quarterly earnings and short-term progress actually defies both the cycles and realities of the stock market. In this era of $400 per share IPOs, we have lost sight of that principle, choosing instead to opt for the quick fix and those immediate returns, shunning the old-fashioned dividend. Warren Buffett is a proponent of share appreciation as the key to delivering value to shareholders, a view he shares with Bill Gates. But, even Buffett's share appreciation in

Berkshire-Hathaway is the result of a 50-year run. Dividends still do drive share appreciation and an examination of companies with consistent dividends is perhaps the same as an examination of a company with longstanding share price increases.

The study of the dot-com economy in juxtaposition with the 100-year companies provides a fascinating study in contrasts. While there is always risk in business and the resulting risk for investors, the fall of the dot-com economy is attributable to something more than the risk inherent in such investments. There was a yearning on the part of investors and managers alike for quick returns, those gravity-defying, double-digit growth figures were what they wanted and what they invested in. Both investors and managers ignored the age-old adage: If it sounds too good to be true, it is too good to be true.

While we have not penned a book about plodders, there is a bit of a tortoise and hare story here. The crash of the dot-com economy is evidence once again that if we periodically check out from the principles of sound investment and somehow immunize ourselves from the realities of growth, markets, and economic cycles, we do suffer tremendous consequences. There is not much new under the sun. However, that does not end the quest for the novel product. These fifteen companies teach us that the novel product is the key, not earnings adjusted for the creative impact of advertising dollars. Furthermore, these fifteen companies were focused on earnings from their products, not earnings made from dealing inputs and calls in the company stock.

There is no such thing as a sure thing in business, but what we have uncovered are the secrets to long-term success. Even among these companies there are occasions and eventual fates that resulted from their failure to follow the principles of the 100-year survivors. Much of what was discovered in the course of this research runs contra to current fads in financial wisdom and management consultancies. Indeed, that is the focus of this book—that we offer some profound discoveries that should make us all wonder how we lost sight of things so basic in successful companies. Perhaps we had become so used to the sleight of hand in everything from earnings management to the nonpayment of dividends that we forgot what it was like when businesses had values and planned for longevity. Perhaps our demands for immediate returns introduced a self-fulfilling defeat of expediency.

This study of the keys to long-term success is as much for managers as it is for investors. Investors have learned their lessons from the short-lived bubble. The questions now become: Have managers learned their lessons? More importantly, do today's managers have the courage to manage for the long term? Can today's managers take the lessons from these long-term survivors and apply them to maximize shareholder returns?

Today's managers can glance about and understand that of the companies still standing in this new economy, the vast majority of them are closer to compliance with long-term survival principles than the once darlings of the new economy. For example, how did we forget about something as simple as earnings in valuing stock? How did we invest so much in companies with no assets? We were not much better than the investors of the great Holland Tulip bubble when investors, realizing they could not obtain the flowers or the bulbs, began pouring $10,000 into the tulip market for bulb futures. When that market collapsed, as all investments in air must, the destruction of companies, individual investors, and the Dutch economy was inevitable. What was so different about bidding up MicroStrategy to $333 per share only to have it collapse under the weight of creative accounting? We were as foolish about dot-coms as the Dutch were about flowers and bulbs. The tulip is a lovely flower, but it takes more than looks to sustain a company.

Webvan is gone, but The Stanley Works is still selling tools. Dell's earnings are down, and General Mills is still selling Cheerios. Microsoft does not know where it goes next, and Colgate-Palmolive has a new toothpaste. Sometimes there are answers in what has always worked.

There is something different about these fifteen companies that has seen them through a Depression, two world wars, and now a burst bubble. They emerge not just as survivors, but also as old reliables. No matter what the world brings, they remain solid performers with something new just around the corner as they innovate. These centenarian companies demonstrate that there are keys to long-term success that apply no matter what the economic cycle or social or political culture. Even after 100 years, these companies still had the charm, potential, chaos, and behaviors of an entrepreneur or a fast-growing small business. They had earnings by sticking to what they knew they were in business to do. It surely could not have been easy for them as they were assured that the new economy was passing them by. But, the new economy did not pass them by—it was but another temporary fad for them to endure as they take their shareholders on to steady returns and appreciation.

These companies dealt in cause, not treatment of effects. The lack of focus, values, and input in the flip-flop and fickle reorganizations touted in today's management theory would surely amuse even the 1890 frontline employees of these fifteen companies who understood constant adaptation, refinement, and redefinition to be routine parts of their jobs.

DELIVERING WHAT INVESTORS WANT

During the time we examined and researched these companies, businesspeople have expressed skepticism about the value of this work.

The question skeptics raised most frequently to us is, "Why would we care about companies that have paid dividends? That's not a good indicator of delivering shareholder value!" or "Dividends are dead! It's share buybacks that count."

But, there was the very soft sort of assurance that dividends give that continued to intrigue us. These companies and their continuing payments provided shareholders with monetary returns and quiet reassurance that their investment was secure. With earnings reversals so common these days and the Securities and Exchange Commission (SEC) threatening regulatory action if companies do not adhere to fair notions of financial reporting, a company that offers continuous cash sounds like a gem.

Despite these kinds of nonquantitative points, the skeptics remained. Dividends, they assured us, were no measure of value for an investment. Then we looked more closely at the market and the reality of share appreciation and the role of dividends.

WHO CARES ABOUT DIVIDENDS? EVERYONE, NOW!

While the dot-com bubble was growing, the dividend was a kiss of death. In 2000, 39 of the 52 companies that were removed from the S&P 500 had paid dividends. Twenty-one of the companies that replaced the fallen 39 paid dividends, and the remainder did not. For us, in the midst of a decade-long research project focused on the value of dividend-paying companies, things could not have looked worse.

But, one day in April 2000, the cracks in the bubble began to appear. When the bubble burst, there was a chorus of calls to return to the old standby: dividends. This cry for dividends will only increase as the once-aggressive and high-flying baby boomer investors become dependent on income from investments to finance their retirements. This post–new-economy economy is one that demands more steadiness and certainty. Baby boomers and their analysts may talk a sophisticated game of share appreciation and buybacks, but when it comes to retirement, they want the same steady income that offered their parents a good life with regular income in Florida and Arizona. The dividend is back.

USA Today proclaimed in a recent headline, "Old-line firms thumb their noses at naysayers."[10] The so-called new economy was not what it promised. Indeed, that may have been part of the problem. By jumping off the "we're different" cliff, investors, managers, and boards abandoned the basic principles of business these fifteen 100-year companies have left engrained in us. Because we have studied their wisdom, insights, and experience for so long, we have emerged tainted. We know no other way to do business than the way these fifteen companies did for 100 investment-returns-packed years. However, even the survivors of the new economy appear to share many of the same traits of these centenarians. Petsmart has emerged as a winner, and Pets.com is liquidated. H & R Block flourishes while Intuit software stock is down 9%. Barnes & Noble is performing well with its brick-and-mortar stores, and Amazon.com continues to struggle to meet that ever-elusive goal of earnings. EToys languishes in bankruptcy while Toys "R" Us sallies forth into higher sales, earnings, and stock prices.

The new economy's captivation, devoid of basic business principles, is perhaps best summarized by an analyst who bet against the high tech stocks and is doing well, along with his clients. His feelings about the new economy are obvious in his pithy observation, "These new-economy companies say things such as, 'Well, if we hadn't had expenses, we would have had earnings.'" Earnings are back and with them, dividends, a glorious determinant of success and achievable over the long term. As Dick McCabe, the chief analyst at Merrill Lynch, has observed, "It's back to reality."[11] Because we were focused on these companies during the full run of the new economy, we never left. In perhaps quite timely fashion, we offer the new economy antidote in the form of the lessons of these marvelous companies.

THE ANTIDIVIDEND SCHOOL DEBUNKED

The antidividend theory in the new economy was that cash reinvested by the company or in the company benefited shareholders more. There was the continuing focus on growth of the company and in share value. But there was also the tax argument that shareholders could sell their shares to realize the gain in value and pay taxes on the gain as capital gains, as opposed to paying income tax rates on dividends, something that theoretically ate away at the shareholder's net gain.

However, the post-bubble burst has brought us the realization that the argument against dividends was a bit hyped and certainly dismissive of stock market history, as well as the returns and performance of these companies. First, there was a flaw in the logic of reinvestment by the company because no one was really quite sure what those reinvested dividends were doing. The theory was strong, but often the management was weak and too willing to invest in anything that came their way. Many of the companies with cash to spare because they paid no dividends simply made acquisitions (and not the measured kinds of acquisitions these centenarians made; see Chapter 6), which usually resulted in a lower return on assets (ROA). Professor Jarrad Harford of the University of Oregon noted in a 1999 piece in *The Journal of Finance*, "Investors should be concerned when they see their companies doing well but they're not increasing payouts. The cash tends to burn a hole in the pockets of management and they end up doing value-decreasing things with it."[12] In short, mischief happens when managers have too much cash in hand or, hopefully and better in terms of honesty, in the till.

This addiction to reinvestment, growth, and acquisition was evident by just a cursory review of the business headlines prior to the market drop. But as investors fretted over the next acquisition and quarter, there were those within the centenarians' management who were cautioning about the zeal for acquisition for the sake of acquisition and spending cash.

Roberto C. Goizueta, former CEO of Coca-Cola, generated stories in praise of his management style when he passed away just a few years ago: Selling more Coca-Cola at a price that makes it more readily available to a wider economic spectrum. Goizueta, whose management style was typical in all fifteen companies, ignored acquisition fever and made his reasons clear in an unequivocal statement on the act of acquisition for the sake of acquisition.

> There's a perception in this country that you're better off if you're in two lousy businesses than if you're in one good one . . . that you're spreading your risk. It's crazy.[13]

Coca-Cola is now at 108 years in its annual consecutive dividend payments, and Goizueta's philosophy of business was like the leaders in all the firms in that he possessed unique self-assurance through his clarity. Goizueta's self-described management style was earnings encased in values, respect in an atmosphere of innovation, and entrepreneurship in a conglomerate. He included in his three-part summation the five values of the 100-year companies.

During 23 of the last 74 years, stock prices for the S&P 500 have declined. One-third of the time, investors have not seen any gain in share price. There may or may not be gains on the share price, but, if a company has paid dividends to shareholders, those shareholders at least had those funds and that return on their investment. The high-tech bubble is an example of the ROI phenomenon. Dividends dropped 2.5 percent in 2000, the largest drop in dividends since 1951 and the first drop since 1991. No one complained about such a change in focus for rewarding investors, for dividends seemed irrelevant in an era of double-digit gains in stock prices. But, this in-depth study of long-term success stories shows that double-digit growth is simply not sustainable for long periods of time. The irony of the new economy is that even as the share prices were increasing, corporate profits grew at a slower rate, thus precluding dividend payments in some cases and reduction of dividend payouts in other companies. But, it seems, in the new economy, not only was no one paying attention to dividends, but they were also largely ignoring earnings.

A look at the dividend yield for S&P's 500-stock index shows that, overall, the yield has fallen since 1990, beginning in that year at 3.41% and declining to 1.1% in 2000. In 1990, when Unisys announced that it was eliminating its common stock dividend in 1990, its stock price fell 23% in one day. Annual growth in dividends fell from 12.5% in 1990 to –4.6% in 2000. But, as the high-tech boom ended, companies with consistent and increasing dividends have earned newfound respect. Dana Parts, Inc., having achieved its 255th consecutive quarterly dividend, is touting it and watching its share price climb while attributing its success to investors' realization that "Does anything grow forever?"[14] One investor, in describing what has happened to investors since the high-tech bust, notes, "As those companies prove there was no profit, I think people will shift emphasis to companies that do pay dividends. I think people are coming back." Professor Jeremy Siegal, a finance professor at Wharton, notes, "A little more than a year ago, people laughed at dividends. In the future I believe that more attention will be paid to dividends and current earnings and less to growth."[15]

The lowly dividend is regaining its stature, and companies that pay dividends have regained Wall Street respect. High-yield blue chip stocks are holding their own during a bear market. In 1973, blue-chip stocks gained 3.88 percent while the S&P dropped nearly 15 percent. So far this year, dividend-paying companies are up 15.7 percent while the companies not paying dividends yielded 2.2 percent. When the going gets tough, market-wise and economically, dividend-paying stocks emerge as the preferred option for investors. There are keys to finding companies most likely to deliver on long-term dividend success.

GIVE THE FIVE VALUES A GOOD LOOK AND A LONG STUDY

At times, the values of these long-standing companies fly in the face of popular trends. At times, their values seem impractical. But, in the study of business, introspection following a look at these companies will bring managers to a reckoning. If these values are not part of your company's operations, should they be? Are you short-changing your shareholders? Are you or your employees falling prey to theoretical distractions? In the complexities of theory, management mazes, and confusing models, the simplicity of these companies' approaches and successes are refreshingly profound.

NOTES

1. Interview with Tim Russert, MSNBC, November 22, 2001.

2. Interview with Louis Grossman, January 17, 1999.

3. Entine, Jon, "Shattered Image: Is the Body Shop Too Good to Be True?," *Business Ethics*, September-October 1996: 23.

4. *A History of Procter & Gamble*, p. 12.

5. Pamphlet materials, Public Relations Folder, General Mills.

6. Lawrence, Paul R. and Davis Dyer, *Renewing American Industry*. New York: Free Press, 1983.

7. Ibid.

8. Greiner, Larry E., "Evolution and Revolution As Organizations Grow," *Harvard Business Review,* May-June 1998: 55.

9. "Corporate Culture: The Hard to Change Value That Spells Success or Failure," *Business Week*, October 27, 1980: 151.

10. Krantz, Matt, "Old-line firms thumb their noses at naysayers," *USA Today,* August 23, 2001: 1B.

11. Ibid.

12. Harford is quoted in Clements, Jonathan, "Don't Forget to Remember the Dividends," *Wall Street Journal*, July 11, 2000: C1.

13. "Roberto Goizueta in His Own Words," *Wall Street Journal*, October 20, 1997: B1.

14. Vinzant, Carol, "The Return of the Dividend?," *Washington Post*, August 5, 2001: H1, H5.

15. Clements, Jonathan. "Dividends, Not Growth, Is Wave of Future," *Wall Street Journal*, August 21, 2001: C1.

6

Key #1: Purpose—
Why Are We in Business?

I am not aware of any bankrupt corporations which are making
important social contributions.

Ed Harness, Procter & Gamble

Over the long history of these fifteen companies, the owners, operators,
and managers never lost their strategic focus largely because of a ready
answer to the perennial question, Why are we in business (WAWIB)? In
these companies, everyone from the CEO to the production workers
understood: The goal was to make money. Spelled out most explicitly
in their literature was that they were in business to make money. The
first key to long-term survival is to make sure everyone understands
that without making money, a corporation is not worth the paper its
charter is written on.

THE STATED "MAKING MONEY" PROPOSITION

It is clear from all sources, both primary and secondary, that these
fifteen companies saw the function of making money as the ball, and
their eyes were affixed with steadiness. In 1995, J. E. Dempsey, CEO of
PPG, described the role of business as follows:

Probably a good place to start in forging a new social contract is with a
definition of the role of management, which is one of the first things every
business school student learns. That role is simply to perpetuate the

enterprise and reward the shareholders, which is only common sense, since everything else flows from it. If management cannot do that, nothing else happens.[1]

PPG executives often explored the relationship between "good deeds and performance" or "results and ethics." Their conclusion was that good deeds often bring about good performance, but their definition of good deeds was different from the traditional social responsibility issues raised today. For example, PPG explored the possibility of derivatives investments but declined. Their decision was based on simple financial analysis: The returns did not justify the risk.

In interviews, PPG executives could make no distinction between good business decisions and socially responsible decisions. They saw them as one and the same for their decision-making processes. Still, their decisions were always geared toward return on shareholders' investment. One PPG executive likened the importance of ethics and the social contract of business to the story of the goose and the golden eggs. For businesses, profits are the golden eggs. Geese can be forced to generate more in a short amount of time, but there are consequences for such demands on them. Long-term production requires attention to the geese and a regard for their health and well-being. While one could push the goose to the limit to maximize short-term gains in golden eggs, the risk is that the goose may not be around so long. Long-term profits are dependent upon the well-being of the entire production process. The goose must be treated well and with respect in order for the eggs to keep coming.

During the 1970s, Pullman ran a series of public service advertisements in *Business Week, Sports Illustrated, Forbes, Newsweek, Scientific American, Financial World, Fortune, Harvard Business Review,* and *Institutional Investor* with the goal of acquainting "members of the business and financial community with Pullman's point of view on major issues affecting the national and international economy." One of those memorable ads was titled, "What kids should be getting out of business," and it addressed Pullman's participation in Junior Achievement programs around the country. The only words in the ad, apart from a full-page color photograph of a young boy receiving 75 cents for shoveling snow, were these:

Children quickly catch on to the idea that if you do something really well, and care about how it turns out, then you're probably going to get something more out of the experience than just a flat, dull sense of duty accomplished.

This satisfying process is one of the reasons why Pullman Incorporated and our operating divisions support Junior Achievement programs all across the country. As a responsible international business, deeply involved in key global battles against the energy shortage, the food shortage, pollution, mass transit problems and distribution costs, we are convinced that JA is an excellent way for young people to learn—through direct personal experience—how the profit motive and the free market system actually work.

We know it's an important lesson because we are reminded every day that other interests in other parts of the world have lessons to teach.

While it may be true that enough oversimplification of complex problems will not solve them, regulatory overcomplication hasn't worked either.[2]

When Scovill president C. P. Goss (1900–1918) was asked on the factory floor what his company made, he responded, "Money."[3] When Isaac Singer was asked about the sewing machine invention and its contribution to society, he responded, "I don't care a damn for the invention. The dimes are what I'm after."[4] Rosemary Mazon of Pullman, in response to a question about the focus of business management, responded simply, "The earnings."[5] Stephen Patrick, the CFO of Colgate-Palmolive, described the goal as follows:

> What is the primary reason for being in business? To make money for our shareholders. That's our primary reason we are here and if we can't do that, you should replace us. We believe it is very important to think of the communities in which we work and sell our products, and be responsible citizens. So is our primary objective to make money? The answer is yes, while being a responsible member of the community in which we work because we're not going to be here for one year; we're going to be here for 1,000 years.[6]

When William Procter presented the company's first profit-sharing proposal in 1887 to the workers at the Procter & Gamble plant, he took a few minutes to remind the workers about what he referred to as "economic principles."

> The first job we have is to turn out quality merchandise that consumers will buy, and keep on buying. If we produce it efficiently and economically we will earn a profit, in which you will share. But profits can't be distributed unless they are earned.[7]

In 1953, H. B. Nicholson, a senior officer of Coca-Cola, said, "We have been soft spoken about our soft drink from the beginnings—though not overlooking, of course, the hard money."[8] Woodruff, the 60-year president of Coca-Cola, said Coca-Cola was "not selling the world short, but playing the world long," to which Nicholson added, "if it is profitable for me, it must also be profitable for my neighbor."[9]

In response to critics who chided the corporation for not putting social responsibility above profit-making, Ed Harness of Procter & Gamble noted, "I am not aware of any bankrupt corporations which are making important social contributions."[10] Harness went on to elaborate:

Procter & Gamble has succeeded throughout the 140 years since its founding for many reasons. Key among these is the fact that company management has consistently kept profit and growth objectives as first priorities while recognizing that enlightened self-interest requires the company to fill any reasonable expectations placed upon it.

Somehow we have managed to keep our priorities straight and yet have the sense of civic responsibility to achieve many important secondary objectives. Somehow our predecessors were wise enough to know that profitability and growth go hand in hand with fair treatment of employees, of customers, of consumers, and of the communities in which we operate.[11]

He was describing the corporate conscience of America, but he also described the attitude of these companies: make money with your priorities straight. Johnson Controls officers put it very simply: "The goal is profits and that benefits the shareholders."[12] However, Johnson Controls also encouraged all employees to own stock so that they could adopt an attitude of "us" together in lieu of the traditional management/employee attitude of those times: employees versus management. Furthermore, Johnson Controls executives never discussed the profit motive without a discussion of their values and a credo that was distributed to every employee in trifold pamphlet form (see Chapter 10 for more information).

Throughout the archives of Diamond International, you find evidence of the company's and individual employees' involvement in community activities. For example, their employees in lumberyards in Chico competed each year to build the best float for the annual Humane Society Parade, an activity documented as early as 1911, long before even first-generation animal rights activists were born. Diamond's lumberyards around the country entered similar types of competitions, and when the managers of the yards had their annual meeting, they would begin by bragging of their community achievements and donations. They ended the meetings, however, by comparing notes on everything from their operations to their profit margins to ways of maximizing sales and minimizing shrinkage. These were managers with earnings goals who were a welcome presence in their communities.

There is a certain natural comfort these companies have with their social contract. Their social responsibility was a matter-of-fact commitment. We found no one who viewed the multitasking as an either/or assignment. Making money was inextricably intertwined with social responsibility, a part of the decision-making and production processes.

There was also a faith and optimism in business. While the phrase "walk the talk" is generally associated with living the code of ethics of a company, these managers walked the talk of business and capitalism. Their enthusiasm for their companies, their companies' contributions, and the potential for sharing the gains with everyone were infectious. Reflected in annual reports and our interviews, these companies were possessed of a sincere belief in doing as much good for as many as possible. They saw a certain synergism when business and community worked together. In its annual report on its 20th anniversary as a company in 1900, Diamond's CEO wrote the following on the progress of the company and his faith in it:

> Those who have followed the fortunes of the Company the closest have no cause to regret their action. Had we, who had so prominent a part in the organization of the Company, invested all of our money in its stock, we would all have been much better off. An original investor who simply retained to date the amount of stock that he first acquired in the Company, selling its increases at market price, would have received a 28½ per cent per annum on his holdings up to the beginning of last year, and if he had retained such increases the result would have been even more to his advantage. I give this hint to the younger members of our Company, to inspire them to invest all of their surplus earnings in the business, and to prompt them to build it up and extend it. The Company has the best equipment in the world, without any doubt, for the manufacture of Matches, and there is no reason why, in time, it should not become the standard for the production of Matches in the entire world, and the Home Company draw tribute accordingly.[13]

There are several striking things, as it were, in this excerpt from the annual report of a match company. First, the CEO, O. C. Barber, a lawyer by training, reflected tremendous faith in the Diamond Match Company and wanted his executive team and other employees to invest in their company not just to realize the gains he explains as forthcoming, but to serve as a testament to their confidence. Second, the paramount goal appears to be not just the earnings, but setting the standard for the production of matches in the world. In other words, Barber was touting the quality and safety of the Diamond process and how it would lead the way to a better product and safer production. Interestingly, as noted earlier, Diamond did place its formula for production of matches into the public domain and even permitted its employees to travel to other companies to show them how to use "the standard for the production of Matches."

Finally, this quote evidences a company with a commitment to quality and returns. It is not accidental that the two topics appear in the same paragraph or that this paragraph was the final one in the annual report. It was simply a reflection of the attitudes of the executive team on performance and the ultimate contributions its company made to society.

Diamond's 1962 annual report reflects that understanding of the synergism between business and the social contract; this is a company that sees the role of its voluntary actions in protecting its stakeholders (in this case its employees) and the impact of both such voluntary actions and the resulting protected stakeholders on the bottom line.

> Outstanding safety records achieved at our installations during the year included more than two million man-hours worked without a disabling lost-time accident at our Lockland fabricating plant and paperboard mill; and the National Safety Council's Award of Merit presentation to our Oakland, Maine, plant for 1,661,223 accident-free hours. Comparable safety attainments applied to other facilities. These accomplishments were beneficial to the company in terms of a reduction in lost production time, decreased compensation payments and better employee morale.[14]

A company manufacturing combustible products earned a National Safety Council Award! This is also a company that recognized the potential for returns from its safety record: It saved money, produced more, and had happier employees.

In expounding on the role of caring and responding to stakeholders in relation to the purpose of his company and business, Colgate-Palmolive CFO Stephen Patrick noted,

> Caring may sound like an altruistic concept, but I don't think a company can be in business for long term unless they care. How many of the companies that didn't care are still here? If you don't care about your employees, your employees don't care about you. If you don't care about your environment, sooner or later the environmental police are going to come after you. And, if you don't care about your consumers, you don't care to be in business.[15]

WHAT OF SOCIAL RESPONSIBILITY?

While these fifteen companies were all in some way responsible for the growth and development of all the communities in which they located, their motivation remained profit, and they stated so unabashedly.

However, one cannot conclude, as some do today, that because they were focused on returns for their shareholders that they were not socially responsible. Again, they saw social responsibility as part of the return on investment. At the time that these companies understood and undertook social responsibility, they faced the demands of the investment community even as they worked voluntarily on improving their communities and the quality of life for everyone from employees to neighbors.

Their attitudes deserve recognition for their foresight and continuing devotion. All of their "doing good" was not without its risk. For example, voluntary activities on company time mean additional costs that their competitors might not incur. This "volunteerism" was undertaken despite an investment community that was in a continual demand mode for returns, returns, and more returns. Donald Davis of the Stanley Works explained the pressures to make money as follows:

> In the fast track, inflationary environment we live in, if you don't have 20% or close to it return on equity, you're not really a good investment: you don't have a good multiple, and you are not up there in the top quartile; you are risking the survival of the business because your stock is going to be priced down, you could be a good takeover target candidate to say nothing of the fact that your stockholder is not getting a maximum return on his investment which is really the name of the game in the final analysis.[16]

Davis' definition of being "socially conscious" was making certain that Stanley was not only good for its investors, but also good for the people who work for Stanley as well as for the people who use Stanley products. Davis worked to make a bigger and better Stanley for one simple reason: "I am interested in making a bigger pie so everybody can have more."[17]

Examples of the inherent fiber of social responsibility of these companies are found in the following subsections.

PULLMAN AND THE COMPANY TOWN

George Pullman built the town of Pullman, which many considered an enormously philanthropic act on the part of the Pullman Company. However, Pullman himself explained the generosity from a business perspective. The Pullman Company employees lived in Pullman, a town with no bars. The company's construction of a dry town increased factory productivity levels by eliminating the problems of employees going to work drunk or hungover. This noncash form of philanthropy was tied directly to the bottom line. Pullman may have been helping a community, but it was doing so by reducing costs through more efficient and productive workers.[18] These companies recognized that the pursuit of dollars was not only good, but it produced more good. It was as if these executives we spoke with were saying, "Look, we do better when we exercise social responsibility, and we have understood that for a century."

LUDLOW AND LABOR UNREST

When Ludlow executives noticed the labor unrest in other textile mills in New England, it raised its workers wages 15 percent and opened a co-op so that its employees could enjoy the reduced prices of their formidable purchasing power. Furthermore, they undertook these two additional costs at a time when they were facing great political uncertainty and resulting pricing uncertainty with the importation of jute from India. The management buzzword "proactive" applies to these types of choices and actions, all undertaken voluntarily with benefits to both the employees and the bottom line. That Ludlow made the changes so quickly and so easily is indicative of the blending these companies saw in voluntary actions and the returns to shareholders.

P&G AND THE LOADED DIAPERS

During the 1980s, Proctor & Gamble faced a crisis with regard to social responsibility. It was in the midst of environmental protests over the disposable diaper, and it was the largest manufacturer in the world, with its Pampers. In fact, P&G was the number-one seller in the market, holding over 50 percent of the market. By the late 1980s, photographs of landfills became an environmental call to action, and the statistics on diaper use made the sense of urgency even greater: The average child uses 7,800 diapers in the first 130 weeks of life, which is 18 billion disposable diapers per year going into landfills. The 200–500 years required for breakdown of the disposable diapers was also tossed about in stories on Pampers and other diapers. Here was a company faced with backlash against its top-selling product.

Regulation appeared to be growing, and more was imminent. Twenty states considered taxes or complete bans on disposables. Nebraska banned nonbiodegradable disposables, with a law that took effect in October 1993. Maine required day care centers to accept children who wear cloth diapers. New York considered requiring that new mothers be given information explaining the environmental threat of disposables. In 1990, the Wisconsin legislature barely defeated a measure to tax disposables.

Faced with mounting activism, P&G commissioned an Arthur D. Little study comparing the environmental impact of cloth and disposable diapers over the products' lifetimes. The Little study concluded that cloth diapers consume more energy and water than disposables. Cloth diapers also cost more (not counting diaper service fees) and create more air and water pollution through washing. The study was a sophisticated "life cycle analysis" that used elaborate computer models, and Arthur D. Little is considered an eminent research firm.

Armed with this study and its own marketing surveys that showed P&G would have been free to simply sell disposable diapers, P&G seemed to have a free pass in terms of what it could do to keep selling and promoting disposable diapers. Four of five American parents preferred disposables—P&G had a free pass in terms of public acceptance of its product. However, Procter & Gamble still provided R and D dollars to finding a means for reducing the time for biodegradation. Procter & Gamble also created advanced techniques for industrial composting of solid waste and spent $20 million to develop diapers that break down into humus.

After the Little study appeared, parents' guilt about rain forests and landfills was relieved, and by 1997, 80 percent of all babies were wearing disposables. Many attribute the change in attitude as well as the halt in legislative and regulatory action to Procter & Gamble's effective public relations using the Little study results. Also, Allen Hershkowitz, a senior scientist at the Natural Resources Defense Council, said, "The pediatric dermatology clearly seemed to favor disposables, while the environmental issues were murky."[19]

The entire disposable diaper debate is a study in the role of business in social issues. P & G undertook to find out how it could deal with the issue in a responsible fashion. It paid for research studies and appears to have preserved what has become an environmentally friendly product. Disposable diapers now decompose at a faster rate, and research has permitted the introduction of much thinner, but equally absorbent diapers so that landfill space used is minimized.

P&G, SOCIAL RESPONSIBILITY, AND ADS

Procter & Gamble continually struggles with its ad placements and its role in sponsoring programs with content that it finds offensive or that is too sensitive for general television audiences. For example, it recently withdrew its ads from planned CBS reruns during the summer of 2001 of an episode of *Family Law* because the episode dealt with a situation in which a son is shot by a gun owned by his mother and kept in their house. P&G also canceled its sponsorship of CBS's *Big Brother* series because of "offensive content." P&G has released explanations for its withdrawal of ads by stating that it monitors the programs on which its ads appear so that the content does not offend consumers and cost customers.

This interesting stance is a critical distinction between social responsibility and social responsibility with an eye on one's stewardship to shareholders. P&G does nothing that would cost it customers and has realized that social responsibility in ad sponsorship and not losing customers are one and the same.

COKE AND ATLANTA

Roberto C. Goizueta, a long-time CEO of Coca-Cola, summarized his modification of Coke's marketing plan and focus from one that he referred to as a peacenik theme to simply selling more Coca-Cola. Referencing its ads on world peace from the 1970s, Goizueta said, "We used to teach the world to sing. Now we teach them to drink Coca-Cola."[20] It was through Goizueta's bullish growth of the company that the world did indeed benefit and sing. The streets of Atlanta are lined with trees that are there because of Coke revenues. One Atlanta pediatrician notes that because of his investment in Coca-Cola stock, he was able to give up his suburban practice and build and work full-time at an inner-city free clinic providing health care for children. His clinic is a short distance from Coca-Cola headquarters, which he says reminds him that it is because of his holdings in Coca-Cola and the dividends that he is able to provide this service to the community without pay.

Emory University and four Atlanta-based foundations are funded in large part by Coca-Cola holdings. One foundation employee said, "Just think of the good from that stock."[21] It is hard to find a building on the Emory University campus that does not have a Coca-Cola-related name. Emory had an endowment of $250 million in 1981, just before Goizueta took over and changed the focus to selling Coke, and by 1997, that endowment amount, because of Coca-Cola holdings, was $3.8 billion. When Goizueta's son appeared on his father's behalf at an Emory University ceremony to open a high-tech building for business students, he said, "Dad believes very strongly that business is the best way to contribute to society—because it is how opportunity is created."[22]

SCOVILL AND SAFETY

These companies had a trigger finger when it came to the discovery of safety issues. For example, in 1892, Scovill discovered that its "Old Factory," its main production facility that had been erected in 1846, had structural integrity problems. When the structural problem was discovered, the plant manager was notified, and he contacted a vice president who then contacted the CEO. The CEO called an emergency meeting of the board of directors regarding shutting down Old Factory because of safety issues. Such a shutdown meant that Scovill's primary production source would be halted. By 6:00 PM that same night, the board of directors had shut down Old Factory. Scovill rented rooms at the American Mill Company on the Mad River near the Scovill facilities and proceeded with production until new production facilities were available for use. Their reaction was swift, and they protected workers above costs, production, and sales. Moreover, they did so without any government supervision or requirement. The decision was made within one day because while Scovill was in business to make money, it did not sacrifice others in that quest.

HOW EMPLOYEES BENEFIT FROM JUST MAKING MONEY

In a 1906 Colgate-Palmolive pamphlet celebrating its 100-year mark in business (1906), the following words appeared on the front page:

> There has been an unbroken century of good will and harmony—the executives and the co-workers in all departments having by honorable and faithful industry mutually contributed to the upbuilding of the business, and maintenance of the high ethical standard of the revered founder, William Colgate.

Among the employees in these fifteen companies, we saw team players on teams with goals that were stated and achieved without apology. The employees of these fifteen companies felt pride not just in their work, but also their work for a proudly successful company. Work and profits were not evil forces for these companies. While the fifteen firms did not subscribe to the isolationist philosophy of "what's good for GM is good for the country," they were plainly Friedmanesque in their desire to benefit others by making money as their primary business focus.

THE DANGERS OF CORPORATE VOLUNTEERISM

Their commitment to community was based on an understanding that their success was inextricably intertwined with the success of others, including community, employees, and neighbors. Their work within communities was volunteerism because of a sincere dedication to the greater good.

While these fifteen companies had long histories of employees with significant contributions to their communities, they were not the same as the corporate volunteerism of today, often used as a substitute for underlying values and a hoped-for means of earnings returns. Volunteerism is not a substitute for earnings. Nor is it a substitute for responsible conduct by the company. For example, Sam Eichenfield, the former CEO and Chairman of the Board of FINOVA, Inc., was an unparalleled philanthropist in the Phoenix area. His generosity was documented continuously on the society pages of the local newspaper. However, FINOVA's quick descent into bankruptcy following the, at a minimum, ill-timed disclosure of a loan write-down could not have been prevented by any more volunteer work. Furthermore, the generosity of management is not a substitute for good values in business operations. A bad loan is not justifiably concealed because the officers and employers are good citizens.[23]

THE SOCIAL ACHIEVEMENTS OF PRODUCTS

The Model T was not produced with the idea of helping mankind. In fact, Henry Ford acknowledged that its long-term success depended upon the creation of a mass market. A mass market was dependent upon an affordable product. Ford stepped up production with wage incentives of two times the going rate and mass-produced a car that resulted in enormous profit. Unquestionably, society moved forward as a result of Ford's prescient efforts. But Ford's goal was the profits. Public benefits came from the knowledge of mass production as well as the availability of the automobile to the common man.

Stephen Patrick of Colgate-Palmolive described the interrelationship of earnings and quality: "While we are in business to create value for our shareholders, the way to choose to do that is through excellence and the development and marketing of consumer package goods."[24] While Colgate-Palmolive prospered, consumers benefited with perfumed soap, toothpaste tubes, concentrated detergent, and a constant stream of innovative products and convenient packaging as well as reduced costs for those products, not to mention the hygienic and health results that stemmed from the products.

These companies had a nobility in the way they generated earnings: by a quality product, good customer service, and continuing innovation. Procter & Gamble states in its purpose: "We will provide products of superior quality and value that improve the lives of the world's consumers. As a result consumers will reward us with leadership sales and profit growth, allowing our people, our shareholders, and the communities in which we live and work to prosper."[25]

Perhaps these companies were able to sustain this comfort level with their stated goals of making money because of their parallel zeal for business ethics. Their view of business ethics stemmed not just from the notion of social responsibility, but also from their mandates on basics such as honesty and full disclosure at all levels of operation.

HONESTY IN DISCLOSURES

These fifteen companies had a quality of forthrightness stunning in contrast to the public relations spins of annual reports and press releases of some businesses today. Perhaps a concern about today's standards for measuring ethics is whether a self-declared dedication to social responsibility has given companies a free pass in terms of the forthrightness of their disclosures and activities. While our fifteen companies made money and stated without equivocation that such was their goal, they framed the achievement of that goal absent fraud and illegality. However, as stated later, some of our fifteen firms strayed from their avowed ethical positions. Their histories reveal guidelines in reporting which other firms can use today. These fifteen companies recognized the economic implications of cheating, which include the loss of reputation and a resulting impact on long-term success.

A simple examination of the language in their annual reports reveals a bygone era of virtue in the remarkable candor offered to communicate effectively with shareholders. A 1959 *Forbes* article quotes an analyst as describing Pennwalt's annual report as "relaxed." The *Forbes* piece went on to note that in the annual report, "the analyst could sense the mood of a man who is happy with the road his company is traveling."[26] The report was done under the helm of William P. Drake, and it was a report that reflected low debt and an increase in earnings in a year in which other chemical companies saw their earnings decline.

The disclosures and elaborations in these annual reports are striking in their contrast to some of today's veiled disclosures. For its 1939 annual report, as it was just recovering from the Depression and concerned about the possibility of war, Scovill provided the following assurances about its cuts in maintenance and repair dollars, all while disclosing that they were operating at only one-third their capacity:

> Our maintenance and repair work has in no wise been neglected though its cost has been reduced by care, and by reason of lessened operations which in general have averaged one-third of normal.[27]

The painful financial figures in the following excerpt from the Ludlow 1932 annual report indicate that the financial footnote is a creation of our era. Ludlow's language here is an example of how these fifteen companies laid matters right on the line.

> During 1932 the jute industry showed further falling off as compared to 1931. Our sales for the year amounted to $6,757,000 as against $11,007,000 in 1931. We believe we have maintained our relative competitive position in the industry, but the result of the year's operations shows a loss of $400,632.31 after taxes, depreciation, inventory markdowns and allowances for doubtful accounts.

> Your attention is called to the Land, Buildings, Machinery and Equipment Account. During the last three years the processes of deflation have caused a considerable reduction in the replacement cost of the fixed properties owned by Ludlow Manufacturing Associates and its subsidiaries. Under these circumstances . . . General Plant Reserve Accounts [are set up] on the books . . . totaling $5,000,000. . . . In setting up this reserve, it should be recognized that the Associates' assets are not altered thereby. Nothing is added to or taken from the properties by changing their book value to more nearly represent what is believed to be a conservative and fair figure at the present time.[28]

This painfully true disclosure was made without Financial Accounting Standards Board guidelines and requirements or SEC mandates. Telling the truth came quite naturally and without regulation to those in charge at these companies. "Attention is called" is an antiquated phrase in a passive voice. Today, some companies try to bury negative information in the annual report. Enron, a company forced to restate its earnings in 2001 to reflect an amount that is $600 million less than reported, used the following language in its 10K filed on December 31, 1999:

> In June 1999, Enron entered into a series of transactions involving a third party and LJM Cayman, L.P. (LJM). LJM is a private investment company which engages in acquiring or investing in primarily energy-related investment. A senior officer of Enron is the managing member of LJM's general partner.[29]

Translation: Enron's CFO was making money from contracts with Enron through his ownership on a nonpublic company. This disclosure was made in note 16 to the financials.

Contrast this disclosure mode with Ludlow's. Despite maintaining its major customer contract, Ludlow made the following disclosure on the front page of the same annual report:

> In our last Annual Report reference was made to the agitation by cotton interests to require the substitution of cotton twine in place of jute twine by the United States Government. To date, these efforts have failed, and

throughout the year we were the successful bidder for the jute twine requirements of the United States Post Office Department.[30]

When was the last time you read an annual report that revealed, "We got the contract" and then went on to add, "But, we could still lose it"? This ethical parameter of honesty was an internal control for these companies. Their word was their bond to investors, and their disclosures to investors were candid and timely.

Ludlow's philosophy did not change over the next 20 years. Here are some excerpts in candor from its 1957 Annual Report, which was published on February 28, 1958:

It is a difficult thing, at this time, when business as a whole has been declining, to forecast, with any degree of accuracy, the progress of the Company for 1958. . . . The present demand for jute products generally is off from a year ago, and it would appear that, for the first six months of this year, this trend might continue. Carpet companies are forecasting better business for the last half of 1958; and it is also expected that the American cotton crop will be substantially better this year than it was in 1957, which should be reflected in our sales.

Although we cannot issue an optimistic forecast for the short-term future, we believe that, through our organizational efforts in the field of Research and Development, cost reduction, and Market Research and Sales program, the Company has a good long-term outlook.

On behalf of the Board of Directors and for the management, may we express our appreciation of the good efforts of the entire organization in doing a difficult job in 1957 that will pave the way for a brighter future.[31]

Here a CEO spells out the cold, hard facts that things do not look good short term, but that is not his focus. Today this kind of announcement would send the market reeling, for Ludlow did not meet earnings expectations. Instead, the report should be welcomed as a candid assessment of a company's potential given the economic cycle. Despite the rugged economic times, Ludlow paid dividends of 65 cents per share for the first three quarters of 1957, 50 cents per share in the last quarter and announced, with the annual report, a first quarter of 1958 dividend of 40 cents per share.

Johnson Controls' management discussion in its annual report included the following, "We have charged off certain accounts which one year ago were rated as assets, because the doubtfulness was not so great. While all of these are not worthless, I have thought best to put them in the lost column."[32] The same annual report put no spin on labor problems, "as to Chicago, one of our two major markets, owing to the labor troubles there of which all are cognizant, the outlook is not flattering."[33] Their annual reports read like a candid discussion at a board meeting where directors have been assured that the minutes will be generic only.

One final example from Diamond Match's 1902 annual report indicates not only the honesty of the disclosures, but, again, that link between social responsibility and profits that came to them so easily and with an admission that what they were doing was still making money for shareholders.

> In no year in the history of our Company have we met with such difficulty in the manufacture of matches, owing to the climatic conditions prevailing during the summer and spring, which compelled us to shut down our factories; but in this respect we have suffered no more than our competitors, and not as much as some of them who took the chances of manufacturing matches during the prevalence of these conditions; and as a result the markets have been flooded with snapping and dangerous matches, to the extent that the Board of Fire Commissioners of the City of New York, issued an edict prohibiting the sale of parlor matches in that city on and after the first day of January, 1903. Subsequently, on further investigation, they concluded that the restrictions were too general and they modified the same by a code of regulations which no doubt will very materially improve the standard of matches to be sold in the city of New York.

> In an article so cheap as matches, quality should not be sacrificed to cheapness, especially as in this case where life and property are endangered by the poorer article. It occurred to us some time since, that it would be useful and economical to the public if they could be induced to use the highest grade of matches. To that end, at the beginning of the year, we added to our corps of travelers, about twenty-five additional men, whose mission was educational among the jobbers and sellers of matches, that they might be induced to handle the better grades. This has been done at an aggregate expense of probably $75,000. The results of this mission have been rather gratifying, as we have sold a very much greater proportion of the highest quality of our goods.[34]

Amazingly, this turn-of-the-century report indicates that Diamond ceased production because of weather conditions and resulting danger of matches produced under such conditions snapping. Diamond bore the resulting loss of sales even though its competitors did not act as responsibly. Diamond acted voluntarily so as not to unleash an unsafe product on the market. Ultimately, New York had to place a ban on match use in parlors because of the snapping matches and lack of safety, and Diamond had to suffer through that regulation despite its own social responsibility. However, Diamond seized the moment to go after the market with its pitch of product safety and quality, based on its wise decision to voluntarily halt production. It gained great advertising credibility because of its responsible actions that other manufacturers felt would be too harmful to their sales. Diamond also expended funds to educate on the benefits of its matches and welcomed the resulting increases in sales from its reputation and emphasis on the quality match. The fiascos from the cheap matches that were manufactured during bad weather created a public hunger for safety assurances, and Diamond Match, with its image untarnished, seized the moment. Certainly, Diamond met a public need, but it turned around its sales in the process.

Even their introductions to annual reports were striking in their candor. For example, Ludlow began one annual report with the following, "During the year 1927 the demand for the products of our Ludlow plant was somewhat curtailed as compared with the last two years, and consequently the returns from our American business were less satisfactory."[35] *Fortune* magazine writers Julie Creswell and Amy Kover offered their analysis of what they refer to as "annual report sin":

> What Compaq said:
> *During the second half of the year we returned to profitability, reduced operating expenses, and began to focus on increasing growth and stockholder value.*
> What It Should Have Said:
> We had some major help in our return to profitability. Check out the one-time restructuring charge of $868 million we took and the $1.2 billion we got for selling off our stake in AltaVista.
> What Amazon.com said:
> *Amazon.com creatively applies technology to deliver personalized programs and services, as well as flexible merchandising. We employ a variety of media, business development, and promotional methods to achieve these goals.*
> What It Should Have Said:
> We continue to creatively spend gobs of money luring people to our Website. In 1999 marketing and sales costs increased 211%, to $413 million. We, too, wonder when we'll make a profit.[36]

Many annual reports of today and the prevailing annual report philosophy reveal a rather different perspective and set of values: What do we *have* to disclose and *when* must we disclose it? As opposed to the philosophy of these companies: be straightforward. Give them the details and let them decide.

One very telling and contrasting example is the following from the 2000 10K for Raytheon, Inc., a conglomerate with a heavy interest in defense contracts:

> Defense contractors are subject to many levels of audit and investigation. Agencies which oversee contract performance include: the Defense Contract Audit Agency, the Department of Defense Inspector General, the General Accounting Office, the Department of Justice and Congressional

Committees. The Department of Justice from time to time has convened grand juries to investigate possible irregularities by the Company in governmental contracting.[37]

A very relaxed report that gives the reader the impression that the Department of Justice simply convenes grand juries against this company, from time to time, as a routine sort of matter. One can rest assured that there is a different perspective from the Defense Contract Audit Agency on the regularity and routine nature of convening grand juries with regard to specific companies. Federal grand juries are neither good news nor routine news, yet the phraseology in the annual report makes it both.

HONESTY IN TRANSACTIONS

The painful honesty of these companies is not limited to their annual reports. That same honesty emerged in how they conducted their business relationships and, most particularly, their contract negotiations and commitments.

Just their reputations for quality in their products is an indication of their dedication to making money honestly. A former Procter & Gamble executive tells the story of how P&G tried to save costs by cutting back on the flavor drops in its Vicks Cough Drops. Slowly, the company decreased the amount of flavor droplets in the cough drops, thinking that they were reducing costs in a manner imperceptible to the customers. They were wrong. Customers complained about the weaker flavor, and P&G quickly returned to the higher cost, but higher quality and better selling Vicks.[38]

During World War I, the British government discovered that Scovill could provide additional materials it needed for the war effort. The British needed Scovill as a backup, for they were already taxing Bethlehem Steel Company for the development and production of the 21-second fuse, something used in the British "18-pounder" and artillery casings. Scovill offered to develop and provide 2,000 fuses and cases per day, and it sent Charles M. Schwab to England to negotiate the contract. When Schwab returned with a fully signed contract, many were ready to celebrate at the anticipated sales and revenues. However, John Goss looked at the quantities and times of delivery that Schwab had promised and realized that there would be a required increase in the company labor force. Goss felt that such an increase could not be so easily assimilated into the company and its culture, and the result would be that Scovill would not deliver as promised in the agreement. Furthermore, Goss realized that the United States would perhaps be drawn into the conflict and that Scovill needed to be available to serve its country. Goss turned down the contract with this candid explanation:

> The Scovill company [stated] that it could not accept the obligation to make delivery of all the cases and fuses called for in that short length of time, because of the danger of breaking down the existing good morals of its organization . . . ; that it was too great a risk to assume that such a large group could be assimilated without seriously threatening the stability of the organization . . . [and if that happened] Scovill Company's usefulness as a producer of these components and any others that might be offered to it could not be relied upon; that the officials of Scovill Company felt that sooner or later the United States might be involved directly on the World War and that, if so, the Company wished its organization to be available for production purposes and in a manner that could be relied upon.[39]

A savvy investor today knows that some annual reports are hardly the most accurate pictures of a company. For an accurate view, one must turn to the statutorily mandated documents that the company is required to file with the SEC in order to find an accurate and honest status report, and even in these government-mandated reports, there are no guarantees. However, as indicated by the Raytheon example, even these documents have been infiltrated with the attitude of "What must I disclose and how can I gloss over it?," not "What should I disclose to those who trust me?"

THESE WERE NOT SAINTS, THESE FIFTEEN, BUT THEY UNDERSTOOD PURPOSE WITH PARAMETERS

These companies remind us that it is possible to remain honest in business and still be successful. Occasionally, however, even those of character succumb to drive, hubris, or old-fashioned greed. In a recent Ponzi scheme based in Alaska, an investor lamented that he lost his retirement pension because greed got to him. Greed rarely got to the employees and officers in these fifteen firms because they had a set of clearly established values.

However, this being a discussion of ethics, social responsibility, and their relationship to earnings, we cannot tell lies. These companies were not angelic. PPG has its share of disgruntled observers for its handling of labor issues. The labor unrest was primarily in the 1880s, running parallel to the labor issues that were part of the country's fabric at that time.

While General Electric has been called the "original Boy Scout Company" for its wholesome business conduct, it pled guilty in 1961 to price fixing on electrical equipment and paid a $500,000 fine as well as $50 million in damages to utilities.[40] Three GE managers received prison sentences. GE also entered a guilty plea in a time card fraud scenario for overbilling the government on defense contracts, and it has been accused of price fixing in the industrial diamonds market.[41] The EPA announced in August 2001 that it would go forward in requiring GE to foot the bill for the dredging of the Hudson River in order to clean up PCB pollution allegedly caused by GE when it once dumped PCBs into the river. The estimated cost is one-half billion dollars, and tempers continue to run high over both the pollution and the proposed dredging. GE discloses on its website that it will spend up to $150 million per year for the next three years for environmental cleanups.[42]

General Mills agreed to offer $10 million in cereal coupons to settle a Food and Drug Administration (FDA) complaint on unauthorized pesticides in 50 million boxes of cereal.[43] The cereal was removed from store shelves, and the coupons gave customers credit. Johnson Controls entered a nolo contendere plea on charges of price collusion with Honeywell.[44] Coca-Cola has ongoing issues with respect to its distributors, and its recent handling of contaminated products in Europe has found it subject to intense scrutiny.[45] Corning's joint venture with Dow on silicon implants proved a litigation and public relations disaster and might have been avoided with earlier and more pervasive disclosure of possible risks of the breast implants, however minimal that risk might be.[46] P&G was required to divest itself of Clorox in 1967 following Federal Trade Commission (FTC) antitrust suits.[47] P&G has had its issues with phosphates and the environment and has reduced their use. Proctor & Gamble also settled its FTC antitrust case over its Folgers Coffee monopolization case with an agreement not to make coffee acquisitions for 10 years.[48]

These companies, comprised of humans, had their share of mistakes. But their missteps are rare, and their minimal levels of legal and ethical difficulty for over 100 years reflect climates in which employees at all levels earnestly strive to do what is right. In a LEXIS search of docketed litigation for these companies, these fifteen companies reflected low numbers of lawsuits with consumers, regulators, and shareholders.

These fifteen companies make an interesting case for the proposition of reexamining all of the issues involved in business ethics and social responsibility. Business ethics and social responsibility are complex questions for which these firms' commitments, activities, and performance provide insight. The history of these fifteen companies shows that the notion of contribution to community and others beyond shareholders is neither a new nor a novel concept. These companies just went about that responsiveness in a different and very quiet way. These companies addressed social responsibility because they understood its benefits to their bottom line.

Long-term success does have ethical parameters as well as social responsibility commitment. Cited by the fifteen companies as engrained values were honesty with customers, employees, suppliers, and shareholders, fairness in transactions, and accountability for everything from employee hours worked to dollars invested.

These companies were always able to articulate a clear connection between their social programs and their business. For example, General Mills launched a program in the 1920s to help farmers combat wheat rust. General Mills contributed funds for farmers' education on the disease and for research to help combat the disease. While General Mills looked like the benevolent soul, the contributions really were a way to keep costs down because less wheat rust meant more wheat and cheaper prices.

During the 1940s, General Mills launched a national campaign for improving public heath. Naturally, whole grains and cereals were part of a sound nutritional plan. Public education on the benefits of good nutrition meant more sales for General Mills.

A haphazard focus on social responsibility can actually result in destruction of stewardship. For example, many management and ethics books and writings point to Ben & Jerry's Homemade, Inc., a Vermont-based ice cream firm, as an example of a socially responsible company with a culture of ethics that produces results. However, when it was faced with the need for international expansion to effectively compete with Haagen-Dasz, Ben & Jerry's turned down a golden opportunity for a joint venture with a Japanese firm. Company officials explained their decision on the grounds that the Asian firm had not been active in social issues, and Ben & Jerry's felt such a firm not worthy of a joint venture. The profit goal and the shareholders were lost amid a narrowly-defined social responsibility role that ignored the first key of long-term success: Remember that you are in business to make money. Ben & Jerry's stewardship to their shareholders, many of whom are Vermont farmers and residents with meager resources, was critical; yet their interests were compromised for what seemed a generic goal of insufficient social responsibility of an international joint venture partner. Vermont, its economy, and its residents are helped by a successful ice cream company located in its state, not a failing ice cream company with passionate feelings on social issues.

The universal values of these centenarians such as honesty, fairness, and accountability are not universally practiced in corporations today. A recent survey by the Society for Human Resource Management found that 51 percent of employers confess to doing something illegal or unethical on the job during the past year.[49] Another survey by KMPG reveals that 76 percent of employees have seen a high level of illegal or unethical conduct during the past year at their places of employment, and 50 percent believe that if that conduct were revealed it would cause the public to lose trust in their organizations.[50]

The most common breach the employees cited was compromising product quality, and the second most common was falsifying reports. Perhaps the most revealing aspect of the survey is why employees engage in such behavior or fail to report it when they witness illegal or unethical behavior. A full 96 percent of the surveyed employees disclosed that it was their fear of being labeled "not a team player." Long-running compromises on product quality and report falsifications are not components of success. Such breaches of trust erode customer and shareholder confidence and place employees in a state of moral schizophrenia as they are forced by their company's lack of values to take actions they find personally reprehensible. A company cannot pursue long-term goals without dedication to a program of increasing quality and sustained integrity. For example, P&G lists as its core values: leadership, integrity, trust, people, passion for winning, and ownership.[51] Howard Morgen, once the CEO of P&G described his company's character: "It wasn't that complicated, once we had isolated the principles involved. There were really only two in this case. The first is that Procter & Gamble obeys the law. The second is that we sell products that are safe for use under normal conditions."[52] The values of trust and integrity are central to long-term success.

Throughout their long histories, all of the fifteen firms have had their missteps. Coca-Cola presently just settled one of the country's largest discrimination class-action suits with not only an agreement to pay damages, but also to be subjected to ongoing monitoring of its practices by an independent panel.[53] Procter & Gamble has sorted through its controversial and high-risk derivative investments with resulting litigation against Bankers Trust.[54] Johnson Controls was the defendant in a case taken to the U.S. Supreme Court with questions on its employment policies and their discriminatory impact.[55]

What distinguishes these companies in these missteps is their self-correction and the limited number of missteps given their century of performance. These companies recognize what recent management research has verified: that illegal activity or conduct in violation of regulation disrupts growth in shareholder wealth and adversely affects employees and employee morale because of their participation in stock ownership programs or simply because they are associated with activity they find to be at odds with their own value systems.[56] They also know that voluntary actions and disclosures serve the company best in the long run, and they have done both in exemplary fashion. Economy-based honesty came more naturally to them.

PURPOSE WITH FORTHRIGHTNESS

An outmoded word emerges from the histories of these companies: forthrightness. Employees in these companies felt comfortable halting shipments or reworking a process in order to prevent defects. Managers supported such actions and often participated in realignments. These behaviors provide a stark contrast with the emerging details in firms in which earnings reversals have been required. As the SEC investigates earnings reversals and accounting improprieties in Worldcom, Cendant, and Adelphia, tales of employee fears of raising issues, greed and cover-ups emerge. Their version of the what we will and won't do questions was: do whatever it takes to make the numbers. Would these firms trade their positions today for steady growth in a long-term culture? Many shareholders wish they had. There was no institutional value check to prevent what amounted to fabrication of earnings by these companies. Doing whatever it takes to earn a profit is wrong only when that pursuit is not encased in a set of values that dictate what you won't do. These firms' employees did whatever it took to earn a profit in the sense of hard work and dedication, not in a compromise of values. When the going got tough, they kept going, but never at the expense of principle.

A long-term culture recognizes the fleeting comfort of a compromise of quality or integrity. More importantly, in such a culture employees see virtue as the team for which they play. Deceit, cover-ups, and compromises are often the products of a business culture focused solely on the dimes without values. That same focus, encased in a simple set of universal ethical values, is key to a long-term culture in which employees share definitive goals achievable only within preestablished and uncompromising parameters.

NOTES

1. Dempsey, J. E., Speech at the Pugh Theological Seminary, Pittsburgh, November 28, 1995.

2. Advertisement in Pullman company archives.

3. Grossman, Louis, Interview, October 1980.

4. Rudolph, Barbara, and Thomas McCarroll, "Dropped Stitch," *Time*, March 11, 1986: 62–63.

5. Grossman Interview, October 1980.

6. Grossman Interview, October 1999.

7. History of Procter & Gamble, pp. 11–12.

8. Nicholson, H. B., *Host to Thirsty Main Street*, New York: Newcomen Society, 1953.

9. Ibid.

10. History of Procter & Gamble, p. 265.

11. Ibid.

12. Grossman Interview, October 1999.

13. Diamond Match Annual Report, 1900.

14. Diamond Match Annual Report, 1962.

15. Grossman Interview, October 1999.

16. Grossman Interview, October 1980.

17. Ibid.

18. Ibid.

19. Jennings, Marianne, *Business Ethics: Case Studies and Selected Readings* Cincinnati: West, 1999: 120–121.

20. Deogun, Nikhil, "Roberto Goizueta Led Coca-Cola Stock Surge, and Its Home Prospects," *Wall Street Journal*, October 20, 1997: A1, A13.

21. Ibid., at A13.

22. Ibid.

23. Hogan, Donna, "Day of Double Losses for FINOVA," *Tribune*, March 28, 2000: B1, B2.

24. Grossman Interview, October 1999.

25. Procter & Gamble Statement of Purpose.

26. "Salt and Savor," *Forbes*, April 1, 1959: 39.

27. Scovill Annual Report, 1939.

28. Ludlow Annual Report, 1932.

29. Weil, Jonathan, "What Enron's Financial Reports Did—and Didn't—Reveal," *Wall Street Journal*, November 5, 2001: C1, C14.

30. Ludlow Annual Report, 1932.

31. Ludlow Annual Report, 1958.

32. Johnson Controls Annual Report, 1958.

33. Johnson Controls Annual Report, 1958.

34. Diamond Match Annual Report, 1902.

35. Ludlow Annual Report, 1927.

36. Creswell, Julie, and Amy Kover. "Annual Report Sin," *Fortune,* May 1, 2000: 50.

37. Raytheon 10K, 2000, at *www.raytheon.com*.

38. P&G executive interview with Louis Grossman, 1999. The executive refused to be identified and denounce the quote despite clear notes verifying the anecdote.

39. Scovill Company Records.

40. *History of General Electric*.

41. Stricharchuk, Gregory, "Ex-Foreman May Win Millions for This Tale About Cheating at GE," *Wall Street Journal*, June 23, 1988: A1, A16; Kumarna, Amal, "GE's Drive to Purge Fraud is Hampered by Workers' Mistrust," *Wall Street Journal*, July 22, 1992: A1, A4; Peterson, Thane, and Amy Bonus, "Diamonds and Dirt," *Business Week*, August 10, 1992: 20–24.

42. For full information on the clean-up, go to *www.ge.com* (last visited April 1, 2002).

43. *History of General Mills*.

44. *Johnson Controls Company History*.

45. Farrell, Greg, and Marco della Cava, "Coca-Cola Boss: Company's Flat Days Are Over," *USA Today*, July 23, 1999: 1B.

46. Jennings, Marianne, *Business Ethics: Case Studies and Selected Readings* Cincinnati: West , 1999: 120–121.

47. *History of Procter & Gamble*, pp. 11–12.

48. Ibid.

49. *Ethics Today* 2(1), 1998:3.

50. KPMG 2000 Survey on Ethics in the Workplace at www.kpmg.com.

51. Schisgall, Oscar, *Eyes on Tomorrow: The Evolution of Procter & Gamble* New York: Doubleday, 1981: 259–272.

52. Ibid.

53. Hays, Constance L., "Black Executive's Departure to Complicate Coke's Diversity Drive," *New York Times*, November 9, 1999: C1.

54. Antilla, Susan, "P&G See Charge on Derivatives," *New York Times*, April 13, 1994: C1, C16.

55. *International Union v. Johnson Controls, Inc.*, 499 U.S. 187 (1991).

56. Baucus, Melissa S., and David A. Baucus, "Paying the Piper: An Empirical Examination of Longer-Term Financial Consequences of Illegal Corporate Behavior," *Academy of Management Journal*, 40(129), 1997.

7

Key #2:
Performance—What
Business Are We In?

Ours is the country where, in order to sell your product, you don't
so much point out its merits as you first work like hell to sell yourself.

Louis Kronenberger, *Company Manners*, 1954

Try novelties for salesman's bait
For novelty wins everyone.

Goethe,
"Martha's Garden,"
Faust: Part I

The second key to long-term success lies in answering the question,
"What business are we in (WBAWI)?" This is no easy question to
answer. But without asking the question and finding an answer, there
will be no long-term culture.

THE DANGERS OF THE STRATEGIC NOMAD
APPROACH

Sadly, some companies never get to the point of even asking the
question, and their strategic nomadic activities and lunges are evidence
of this void in their planning. Even the icon of fast foods, McDonald's,
has suffered from this problem over the past few years as its sales have
been slipping. One minute they are a burger-and-fries joint, and the next
minute they are selling McLeans and salads. They have a McRib sand-

wich, while adding frozen yogurt to the menu. Wendy's promoted the variety and health menu earlier and better. McDonald's business is fast, cheap food for kids, not adults. Their strength is in children and they keep trying to lure adults. If you lure the children, the parents will come. McDonald's missed the boat on some of the hottest kids' movies, and the children took their parents and headed over to Burger King. Burger King even recognized that there were children of different sizes who needed different-sized kids' meals and different types of toys. McDonald's is still offering Winnie the Pooh to 8-year-olds who left Pooh in preschool.

The McDonald's waffling is in direct contrast to Hy-Vee Foods, Inc., a midwestern grocery store chain that holds its own against the national firms that are merging and acquiring regionals in every other market in the country. Hy-Vee knows its customers and not just generally. They know the customer base for each store. This company, with a 50-year dividend record and hailing as one of the contenders for going the distance in the next generation of centenarians, has a deli/take-out section in a grocery store near an office complex that is so successful that its manager must put up temporary tables and chairs each lunch hour. Its secret? This was a yuppie office crowd, and Hy-Vee brought in a chef to lure them with highbrow deli dishes. For its stores in smaller towns, it knows that Iowa's own beef is the lure. For all of its stores, it has learned the dynamics of the modern family. At the butcher counter, you find stuffed potatoes ready to buy, take home, heat, and eat. At the checkout, you find stamps, ice, and a package place for mailing and shipping. There is a seasonal aisle for decorations and the types of unique bakery items that prove irresistible to shoppers ending a busy day at work. One customer commented, "When I walk into Hy-Vee, I feel like they asked me what I wanted, and it's here."

DATA GATHERING FOR WBAWI

Answering this critical question well and often was one of the keys of these fifteen companies' long-term cultures. They did what they started out doing extremely well, but they were not stagnant. Indeed, it was perpetual motion (more on that in the next chapter on their lack of satisfaction with most anything) that was key to WBAWI. These fifteen companies today do not produce nor market solely what they did when their businesses began. There was a fluid quality to these organizations. They followed, understood, and responded to evolving changes. Eyes were sharp, and ears were attuned at all levels so that no opportunity got away. They anticipated evolving answers to the question of what business they were in and found their answers through a successful business strategy that was not a result of a single decision but a web of interrelated strategies, substrategies, policies, and tactics.

Answering the WBAWI question meant conducting a complete global-view analysis of the company's operation along with anticipation of trends, needs, and demographic implications. These firms never knew what the answers were or where they might be found, so they looked everywhere. They looked behind them in their supply chains and forward in their distribution chains and to their customers. They looked sideways, always to keep an eye on the competition, but it seemed they were always one step ahead of the competition. To help them with the look-sees up and down their chains, they really had developed a checklist of sorts to use in evaluating what business they were in and whether their current answer needed some tweaking. The method in their chaotic searches is found in Figure 7.1—a roadmap with a series of questions focused on all aspects of business operations that can be applied to any business to gather data for answering the WBAWI question.

THE TWO-DIRECTION VISION OF WBAWI: VALUE CHAIN MANAGEMENT IN THE 1800s

The questions in the figure, developed from examining the fifteen firms' strategies, have one overriding theme: look both ways before answering the question. Look back, look forward, and perhaps look back again. Two-direction vision is a prerequisite for answering the WBAWI question. These companies looked at what, where, and why they were selling, but also looked at what, where, and why they were buying and what, where, and why they were not selling.

These companies also viewed their business operations as raw materials for consumer distributions, which meant that they found opportunities not just in their factories but in the way their products sold. They found their answers in viewing themselves as managers of an integrated process, from raw materials to closing a sale. The nature of this process is that it is never complete, and the risks of complacency are covered in Chapter 8. Never being satisfied with the status quo is a critical component of long-term success. Some of our companies suffered when they let complacency set in. However, this chapter focuses on the beginning and end of the two-direction visions. How do we redefine? What do we look at? How do we react?

The answer to WBAWI requires different responses. For some of these companies, the answer to WBAWI meant that they needed to go into an acquisition mode. This form of expansion through outside expertise was common among them. However, they were measured

Customer Examination
1. Why are they buying?
2. What are they buying?
3. What are they not buying? Why?
4. What needs do they have after the sale?
5. What needs do they have before the sale?
6. What would they like to have?
7. What would make their lives easier?
8. How do they see us?
9. What do they need?
10. Where are they headed? Trends?

Manufacturing Process Examination
11. What by-products are there in the process?
12. What cost-reduction benefits can we find?
13. What new systems/by-products are possible?
14. What can we do with our processing skills?
15. Are there supply commitments?
16. Are there alternative suppliers? Raw materials?
17. Do we need to manufacture everything we sell?
18. Should we manufacture at all?

Supplier Questions
19. Should we consider acquisition of suppliers?
20. Do we have the expertise for acquisition of suppliers?
21. What new suppliers could complement our processes?
22. What new products should we integrate?
23. Are there further refinements to be made in the chain of distribution?

Economy Questions
24. What is the competition? Is it a competitor or the nature of the product?
25. Can the product be redefined? Aligned with a different use or market?
26. How are we managing cycles? What countercyclical protections do we have?

Distribution Questions
27. Where are we in the chain? Can we go forward to the customer? Back to the supplier?
28. Can we parlay our expertise and name to other products for distribution?

Figure 7.1. WBAWI questions.

Community Questions
29. From a sociological perspective, what trends are moving product markets?
30. What needs are being unmet?
31. What does feedback through employees and customers tell us?
32. What are the characteristics of the community? Where is the best sales contact?
33. What is good for the community?
34. What do demographics show? Where are we headed?

Figure 7.1. (continued)

in their acquisition and diversification programs. They had to acquire and diversify within the parameters of their values, one of which was maintaining low debt. In some instances, this value dictated their strategic process in diversification (see Chapter 9 for a discussion of values, particularly the issue of maintaining low debt). These decisions on acquisition were no different from any other strategic choice—why are we doing this and what relation does it have to the business we are in?

For all the companies, the evolving answer to the WBAWI question meant diversification. All fifteen have diversified as a key to their long-term success. It was not diversification for the sake of diversification, however. It was diversification pursued after answering WBAWI. The stories of how each of the fifteen firms arrived at their methods and targets for diversification are unique. Each company's story is slightly different, but each story is illustrative of their vibrant sprints in a self-imposed, nonstop evolutionary process. Had they not diversified, they would not have survived. How they diversified provides fifteen tales of creative genius, but the common thread in the tale of creative genius is that they all arrived at their diversification decisions through the practice of two-direction vision.

Again, the biography theme emerges. What works for one company may well be a disaster for another. However, as the final portion of this chapter on mistakes in applying WBAWI demonstrates, there are fewer mistakes when this two-direction vision is applied with the discipline of understanding what you do well and using the creativity that springs from emerging trends, demographics, and feedback from all those who interact with the company.

Nearly 100 years ago, these firms had already envisioned today's pop management concept of value chains. With a two-direction vision (as depicted in Figure 7.2), these companies saw themselves operating in two markets, a supply market and a demand market, buying in one,

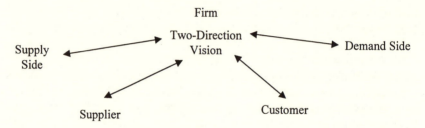

Figure 7.2. What business are we in?

transforming, and then selling into another market. Within this chain, these self-defined merchant-middlemen sought and found new opportunities as they continued to answer the WBAWI question.

These companies were looking back in their supply chain for opportunities and down their demand chain to determine opportunities. If their supply costs or deliveries seemed like potential bottlenecks, they explored acquisition and diversification there. If there were obstacles for customers' purchases, they explored removal of those obstacles by stepping in to meet their customers' needs. Not only were these companies minding their own stores, they were also constantly observing, soaking in problems, opportunities, demographics, and challenges, so that they could retain the entrepreneurial spirit that was at the heart of all of their beginnings.

Given the change from industrial to consumer markets during their 100 years of dividends, these firms' two-direction vision demonstrated remarkable foresight in helping them make this transition. These companies understood that this bird's-eye view of the input and output of their businesses was critical if they were going to survive business cycles. While their products were diverse, they all faced the potential impact of business cycles.

PENNSALT TO PENNWALT: FROM SALT OF THE EARTH TO THE SKY'S THE LIMIT

The old Pennsylvania Salt Manufacturing Company (whose history was covered in Chapter 2) reached a turning point when it signed that agreement in 1864 with the Kryolith Company in Denmark for the importation of cryolite, a rare combination of sodium, aluminum, and fluorine from Greenland. This decision to import this substance was a stroke of genius. Pennsalt dove into the uncommonly used waters of international markets in its quest for supplies. We do mean dove because its relationship with Denmark would provide this company with the unique position of having locked-up supply contracts for a commodity that would become increasingly important in an industrialized nation.

Pennsalt soon changed its name to Pennwalt because it had broadened its answer to the WBAWI question with its international supply chain from salt seller to chemical processor and importer. Pennwalt emerged not just a prime source in the United States for Kryolith, used as a processing agent in making aluminum, but also freed itself from the short-term sentence of being a staid salt company. With this international supply contract secured (a choice made by looking back in its supply chain), Pennwalt redefined itself more along the lines of a sodium chloride company or, in other words, a supplier of chemicals. A salt company is limited to sales of a product that graces supper tables and icy roads. A chemical company knows no limits in an expanding industrial world. With just one simple extension through a single contract reach back to a supplier relationship, Pennwalt created an integrated supplier/seller relationship that would continue for more than 100 years and provide an expanded answer to its question of WBAWI.

This simple redefinition and web outreach sparked creativity on the part of Pennwalt's seeming alchemists who then moved the company from chemical commodities and production to efficient marketer of differentiated chemicals and allied products. Once its employees understood that it was not just a salt company, they too began their contributions by responding creatively to the new answer to the company's WBAWI question.

Pennwalt's customers saw it differently as well. With this contract expansion and Pennwalt's international presence, Pennwalt had new credibility and was able to offer its commodities customers the bonus of its production experience. As part of this transformation from commodity seller to commodity processor, Pennwalt went back in the chain and secured rights to limited natural resources—oil, gas, salt, fluorspar, and sodium sulfate—on long-term arrangements so that its major requirements were assured. These rich supply contracts then permitted Pennwalt to embark on an acquisition program for firms with the technological know-how for processing the raw materials for which it had supply contracts. Pennwalt became a critical middleman for processing products. Pennwalt used its customers on one end, suppliers on the other end, and processing in between to answer its WBAWI question through a web structure of products that ran from raw materials to its customers.

With its processing skills and commodities access firmly in place, Pennwalt was poised for entry into fields unknown and unanticipated at the time of its value chain expansion, such as high-performance plastics, fluorine chemistry, aerosol propellants and refrigerants, and nitrogen products. Just a slight shift and expansion in business focus positioned the company for these new areas in what has turned out to be a broad and brilliant WBAWI. The new strategy of changing its image and product from "the salt company" also provided Pennwalt with credibility and a unique identity in the financial community. Pennwalt's original characterization by market analysts as a company with steady, flat growth sales changed with its new answer to WBAWI. Pennwalt was not a salt company; it was a savvy supplier. Figure 7.3 depicts Pennwalt's diversification and WBAWI evolution.

PPG: EXPANDING TO MEET ALL THE CUSTOMER'S NEEDS

PPG realized as early as 1900 that the business it was in, glass, was not completely dependable because construction and the resulting use of glass were tied directly to the cyclical nature of the economy. PPG was a one-product firm selling its product to contractor customers who were perhaps on the front lines when it comes to the impact of economic swings. If construction comes to an abrupt economic halt and you sell

Original WBAWI
We are in the business of selling salt

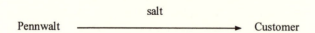

Pennwalt ————————salt————————→ Customer

Evolved WBAWI
We are Pennwalt—The International Processor

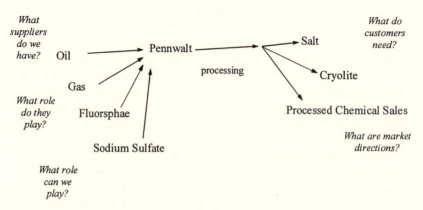

Figure 7.3. Pennwalt's evolving WBAWI.

only one product to those who are in the business of construction, you have landed on the formula for a short-term culture or at least an interruption in dividends.

To insulate itself, as it were, from economic swings, PPG looked at other products its customers used and then reached out to obtain those products. While PPG stuck close to home simply by acquiring other products used in construction, it was careful to make product acquisitions that were used even when construction was waning. For example, in an economic downturn, folks may not be building houses with new windows, but they may decide to paint their old ones. In 1900, PPG redefined its business from glass manufacturer to a much broader role, that of a supplier to builders. Now the business PPG was in was not glass, but construction materials. PPG had simply asked itself whether there were potential customers in the markets surrounding contractors and what it would take to tap into those customers.

Based on that strategic redefinition under WBAWI, PPG acquired Patton Paints of Milwaukee and began its diversification into the field of construction supply, which allowed it to smooth out business cycles with products that were sold to consumers for remodeling and other uses beyond construction. Furthermore, paint was not limited to use in home construction. Autos and other moveable objects required paint as well. Not only was PPG not tied to the glass market, but it was no longer tied to just the real estate market. By 1919, PPG had diversified into building supplies with product lines in paint, roofing materials, and sealants. PPG's WBAWI transformation is depicted in Figure 7.4.

PPG's answer to WBAWI did not stop with diversification into home improvement items such as paint—it kept listening to customers to refine its diversification. Once in the paint business, PPG began to learn the quality and use issues that were part of the paint business. Paint has its temperamental qualities. PPG discovered that customers struggling with paint's stubborn qualities want answers immediately. In the midst of their task, they want their paint problems solved. Because automakers were some of PPG's biggest customers and hence the biggest source of questions and issues, PPG decided to redefine its WBAWI just slightly. PPG was not just in the business of selling paint; it was in the business of selling paint and providing service to paint customers. So, PPG went right to its customers. For example, PPG built paint booths in automakers' plants to solve paint problems right on the product floor. Staffed with PPG employees, the automakers, in the midst of painting vehicles, could have their questions answered and problems addressed on a supplier's product right on the auto manufacturer's factory floor. The result of this customer complaint office in the field was that PPG's paint orders from auto manufacturers doubled and even tripled over the next few years. Their web simply expanded customer service to new

Original WBAWI

We Sell Glass

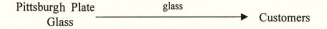

Evolved WBAWI

Pittsburgh Plate Glass

We Are a Full-Service Supplier of Construction and Repair Materials

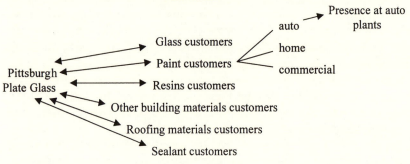

Figure 7.4. PPG's evolving WBAWI.

heights, at least new locations. Their WBAWI was not just a product; it was a product plus service.

This product line is still an integral part of PPG. In 1999, PPG made its largest acquisition ever with the $684 million purchase of Imperial Chemical Industries' automotive refinishing and industrial coatings businesses in North and South America. The acquisition was simply an international expansion of PPG's existing capabilities in this area of paint and a chance to bring its full-service approach to quality products already established in international markets.[1]

SINGER: A STITCH IN THE DISTRIBUTION CHAIN CAN NET A SEAM OF SALES

Singer Sewing Machine Company addressed the WBAWI question in a slightly different fashion from Pennwalt and PPG. At a critical point in its history, Singer came to the realization, based on feedback from its sales agents, that while the company had terrific sewing machines, no one could afford to buy them. Their customer information was that they had willing but unable customers. At that time, the average family income was $500 a year, and the purchase price of $125 for a Singer machine was a major obstacle for buyers. While Singer concluded that it was still in the business of manufacturing and selling sewing machines, it also recognized that its sales were hampered by consumer affordability. Any future success, despite the internationally acclaimed utility of the product, was tied to finding a way for consumers to buy sewing machines.

Singer made a decision, unique for its time, to offer the financing for its own product. Singer would carry its retail customers' debt. In 1856, Singer introduced the concept of consumer credit through installment selling. Singer's innovative "hire-purchase" marketing plan enabled thousands of customers to make the sewing machine purchase that was previously out of reach through a "buy plan," which required $5 down and $3 per month as a payment. Singer made a slight redefinition of its role with this change. It did not just manufacture and sell sewing machines—it helped consumers get sewing machines into their homes. Singer's WBAWI was no longer just "We sell sewing machines." It became "We help people buy the most useful product they will own, and we do it by showing them its utility and then helping them find a way to make the purchase once they are convinced."

Singer's next refinement of WBAWI came when it posed this artfully phrased question: "Do we just sell and finance sewing machines or do we become part of the customer's relationship with that sewing machine?" Through its commissioned sales agents, Singer had learned that many of their salespeople had only a small amount of technical knowledge about the sewing machines. This piece of information meant two things to Singer: (1) the salespeople probably could not demonstrate sewing machines properly and (2) the customer was being dropped like a hot potato once the sale was made with nowhere to turn for questions, repairs, and service. The first problem meant fewer sales. The second problem meant missed opportunities for revenues.

Singer had solved the problem of facilitating willing customers' purchases with financing, but how many potential customers were lost because there was no demonstration? Singer was tapping the sewer's market, but what about the nonsewer's market? Given its novelty, consumer fears about working these newfangled machines hampered many potential purchasers despite the ease of financing. Good sales-people did not always have the training and skills necessary for demonstrations of the company's product. Sales people trained as demonstrators would not only mean more sales, but it would also provide a way for customers to contact knowledgeable people who could answer customer questions and provide even simple instructions on using the machine.

Singer had a new WBAWI answer. Over one century ago, it introduced the concept of full customer service in the form of in-store experts. Before the term "marketing" appeared in a textbook, Singer developed the marketing concept of combining product with service to entice customers and develop enormous brand loyalty. Singer made multiple use of its remedy for closing the sales knowledge gap by using the trained sales experts in stores to handle repairs and provide service for customers' machines. These salespeople with sewing and mechanical savvy became a unique aspect of the Singer product. Singer was not just selling a sewing machine; it was selling a sewing machine and providing customers with the information and service that product needed. Such a slight redirection seems obvious given today's consumer market. But, at the time, most companies had salespeople who were manufacturer's representatives, working only on commission and moving from town to town. They were not interested in ongoing customer contact. They wanted a sale, not a relationship.

But Singer saw potential not only in cultivating sales, but also in maintaining the relationship. Singer parted ways from the traveling salesperson and opted to have permanent locations for sales, service, and repair. In an era when there was the general store and perhaps a Sears location in larger towns, the concept of a sewing center was a retail innovation. That retail innovation proved to be another source of revenue.

Singer perhaps created the original "help hotline" through these service agents. While the "hotline" could be done only by face-to-face contact in these pretelephone days, the concept was the same: give your customers help with your product and you provide a marketing tool, another source of revenue and brand loyalty because of the available service.

By 1859, Singer had opened fourteen sales branches, each with a female demonstrator, a mechanic for repair and service, a salesman or canvasser to sell the machines, and a manager who supervised the others and handled collections and credits. Singer's once cumbersome transitional regional distributor marketing had been replaced with these branch stores supervised by full-time salaried regional agents. Singer created the boutique concept. They answered questions from owners as well as potential buyers and also recommended and sold parts. With its financing, technical knowledge, and service available on site, Singer, in addition to being in the business of manufacturing sewing machines, became a full-service retailer and financing agent.

Singer expanded within its WBAWI web to reach its customers by filling those gaps created by the very presence of its product. Singer's WBAWI was not selling sewing machines; it was in the business of facilitating sales of sewing machines. A slight tweak and Singer was not only selling more machines, it had a product line in selling sewing machine parts and a virtual monopoly on service from loyal customers.

The answer to Singer's WBAWI would continue to change. The boutiques, designed as machine centers, soon expanded to become sewing centers. The boutiques proved to be a perfect contact point for women who sewed. Singer expanded its offerings at its store to sell patterns, materials, buttons, and all items necessary for the seamstress of that era. Singer centers became one-stop shopping for all sewing needs, from machines to fabrics to replacement parts.

Through this hands-on sales approach as opposed to regional distribution, Singer was able to refocus its efforts on the ultimate consumer. There was an additional benefit: its full-service retail outlets became a means of attracting and acquainting potential buyers with its products. Branch stores offered free demonstrations.

Despite its expanding boutique concept, Singer understood the geographic and economic limitations in boutique infiltration. It was not possible to have a boutique in every town, and Singer still had customers to reach in smaller towns and outlying areas. Singer continued its potential customer contacts within these communities by creating different and less costly marketing opportunities. Singer found a means for demonstrating its product even without the presence of its new retail outlets. Singer zeroed in on the hub of community activities at that time as a source for potential customers: churches. Through a sales program in which ministers' wives were offered new machines at half-price, Singer ensured that all women in any given town could not only see a Singer machine, but they could also see an influential citizen use one. If the minister's wife purchased a Singer, what nobler piece of equipment could you have in your home? By 1863, with these marketing innovations in place, sales of Singer sewing machines reached 20,000 per year. Singer's slight tweaking of its WBAWI answer took it from flat sales to exponential growth.

Singer expanded its business in the supplier direction when its purchasing agents reported to management that Singer was the largest purchaser of cabinets for sewing machines in the United States. Recognizing a potential refinement in its role and a slight strategic shift, Singer took over part of the supply chain of distribution and established its own cabinet factory in South Bend, Indiana, in 1867. The cabinets were then integrated into and sold through the Singer stores with the same financing plans. Singer's WBAWI is depicted in Figure 7.5.

Original WBAWI
We sell sewing machines.

Evolved WBAWI
We find ways to bring sewing machines to people

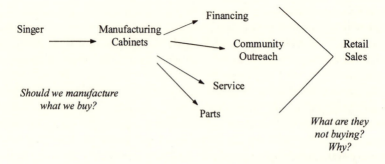

Figure 7.5. Singer's evolving WBAWI.

JOHNSON CONTROLS: SLIGHT EXPANSION, BIG MARKET

Johnson Controls was founded with the invention of the thermostat, but the company did not see itself as being in the business of selling thermostats. It was selling the comfort and uniformity thermostats brought to indoor environments. In fact, Professor Johnson insisted that Johnson Controls was a manufacturing, selling, installation, and service firm because "the business would fail if the sale of the thermostats, automatic controllers and similar devices were sold without installation and service by trained mechanics employed by Johnson Controls."[2]

Johnson Controls took its product from the mechanics of simple thermostats to the climate management of increasingly complex commercial buildings. Its first target in 1890 was public schools because of increasing numbers of students and facilities. From there the company moved to higher education and eventually into commercial buildings. Using evolving computer technology, Johnson Controls became the preferred central climate manager for companies with international facilities. The ultimate result was achieved: Johnson Controls assumed responsibility and earned the revenues for complete operation and maintenance of building heating and cooling so that the building manager could look to one firm to provide needed utility and maintenance.

Interestingly, General Electric has done the same thing today with its sale of jet engines to airlines. GE has the maintenance contracts on the engines, and the airlines and GE work as partners in keeping costs down while maximizing safety and fly-time goals. Arizona Public Service (APS), a public utility, has adopted a similar system for maximizing power sales. It developed a fast-recharging luggage cart to be used by the airlines. The airlines wanted to use electric carts for their clean and efficient operation but felt that the charging time and downtime for the carts were too much to fit their hectic and demanding flight schedules. APS set to work, and the result was a synergistic product as well as a full-service product for the airlines. APS manufactures, sells, and services the carts for the airlines while selling more of its core product—electricity—in the process. It is not just the juice provider; it is the company with innovative products that use electricity to save customers time and money.

This simple redefinition kept Johnson Controls in an expanding role through the 1970s. At that point, the company expanded into an area that seemed odd: automobile batteries. However, Warren Johnson's first business venture was not the thermostat but the development of a storage battery in 1883. That business fell by the wayside with development of the thermostat. It was only fitting that the company return to its roots. In 1978, Johnson Controls acquired Globe-Union, an automotive battery manufacturer, and became a major player in that market.

Johnson Controls' foray into automobile batteries gained it the expertise it needed to move more generally into automotive supplies. With its entry into the auto industry, the company gained information about auto suppliers and their burdensome system of component parts shipments, then used for assembly to automobile manufacturers. Ever the expert in systems management, Johnson Controls developed a better way to get batteries to auto manufacturers with a resulting increase in sales. Rather than buying cushions, frames, and tracks from various suppliers, automobile manufacturers could buy a complete interior system from Johnson Controls, including the seating and instrument panel. Figure 7.6 illustrates how Johnson Controls' WBAWI evolved.

Original WBAWI
We sell thermostats.

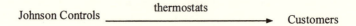

Johnson Controls ————————thermostats————————→ Customers

Johnson Controls
Revised WBAWI
We sell Building Comfort

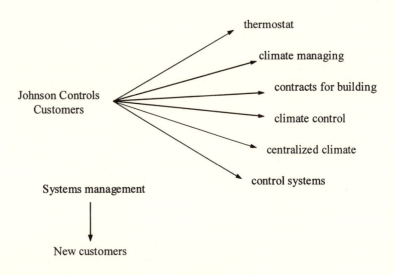

Figure 7.6. Johnson Controls' evolving WBAWI.

STANLEY: IF YOU SHOW THEM THEY NEED IT, THEY WILL BUY IT

When Stanley was founded in 1843, it was primarily a hardware and builder's goods company. Stanley was the tool company for commercial builders and professionals. But Stanley soon realized from its customers' end and the ease of use found in its tools that it could easily move from the commercial to the consumer level. By jumping to consumer sales, Stanley was now not simply a commercial supplier and seller; it was a seller of tools to all who used them, in whatever capacity.

Its first diversification occurred in 1920, when Stanley merged with the Stanley Rule & Level Company, a small manufacturer of hand tools and measuring devices. This diversification by acquisition added 1,200 workers to Stanley as well as a complementary line of products for consumers.

Stanley further refined its answer to WBAWI when it realized that tool purchasers had varying levels of sophistication and various needs. While Stanley's in-house strength was in manufacturing quality, standard tool items, it recognized that its name was associated with quality tools and that there were customers looking for more specialized tools. Stanley reached those customers through the acquisition of various companies involved in the manufacture and sale of specialized tools. Stanley acquired the manufacturing expertise on items it had traditionally not carried and then added the strength of its name to these specialty items. The result was that Stanley's customer base expanded to include those customers in search of specialty items.

Stanley's next diversification came by looking in the other direction—to the supply side of its chain. Stanley looked at what it was purchasing in order to manufacture its tools and diversified with the acquisition and operation of steel mills that produced the metal it needed in its manufacturing. This diversification into raw materials proved profitable for Stanley for a number of years. It not only had a better deal in terms of costs for its production, it was selling to others.

Stanley also made the transition into international markets with sales in foreign markets. However, it was able to add to its international customer base while reducing distribution charges by purchasing foreign tool manufacturers and simply implementing its quality-control processes at those factories.

Interestingly, that cheap foreign production was not just a benefit for Stanley. It was a benefit for foreign manufacturers not acquired by Stanley who saw the potential for sales of their low-priced products in the United States. In the early 1980s, low-priced tools from Asia (primarily hammers and screwdrivers) began flowing into the United States, with a resulting significant reduction in Stanley's market share. Robert Widham, a vice president of Stanley, noted, "Imports were killing us." By 1982, the question was, "Should we be in this business?"[3]

Pressed by the intensity of foreign competition, Stanley realized, late in the twentieth century, that marketing was part of its WBAWI answer. Stanley's president commented in 1980:

> This company was originally built and based on manufacturing. We still have hinge-making machines that were designed by us and that no one has improved on, anywhere. But we realize now that we don't necessarily have to manufacture what we distribute as long as the product meets our

quality standard. We have discovered our marketing strength. For example, we introduced weather-stripping, an energy-saving product. We subcontracted the production and eventually we will produce some of the product ourselves. Then we did the same thing with fasteners, hundreds of different screws, bolts, brackets, picture hooks, etc. We designed ingenious little packages that became drawers in a plastic storage box. We found out that there is an almost universal recognition of 'Stanley' as a quality product, a tremendous strength. Important as the name is in the industrial products markets we learned it is even more significant in the consumer products markets. This impelled us to refocus our resources on the do-it-yourself market. Now we posture ourselves as the leading company in the do-it-yourself industry.[4]

Stanley's obsession with quality manufacturing had paid off in terms of its consumers and its resulting reputation (see Chapter 8). However, Stanley had not maximized that competitive advantage of quality because it had answered WBAWI too simply: a manufacturer of tools. Stanley really was in a very different business and had the potential for being the ultimate quality seller for do-it-yourselfers—it was to the tool market for Yuppies what BMW was to the car market. Stanley, through its manufacturing obsession, had failed to see a way to pull the market through customers. In short, Stanley's lack of marketing resulted in a failure to focus on the customer end of its value chain. Stanley had been so focused on acquisitions and suppliers that it had ignored the evolutions in customer needs on the other end.

Finally, when Stanley did focus on the customer, it was able to pull demand for its quality tools by becoming a driving force behind the return-to-home improvement movement. Stanley fueled a "Do It Yourself" movement with effective advertisements touting examples of the wonders Stanley tools can work in a home. In fact, Stanley made it a point to feature women in their ads either actually using Stanley tools or observing their use. The presence of women in Stanley's earliest ads was an advertising innovation that brought Stanley into more homes because of an attributed "female factor." Stanley recognized the baby-boom generation as potential customers with their desire to return to simplicity, as well as their desire to experience the joy of self-repair in their aging homes. The same quality product but a redefined business role has seen Stanley through everything from foreign competition to lagging demand. Stanley's evolved WBAWI is shown in Figure 7.7.

SCOVILL: REDEFINING THROUGH PURCHASE AND BY END PRODUCT ACQUISITION

Scovill saw opportunities for product expansion, and it redefined itself initially from brass manufacturer to brass products producer. Why

Original WBAWI
We Make Quality Tools.

Stanley ——————→ Tools ——————→ Customers

New WBAWI
The Name You Trust for Your Do-It-Yourself Needs.

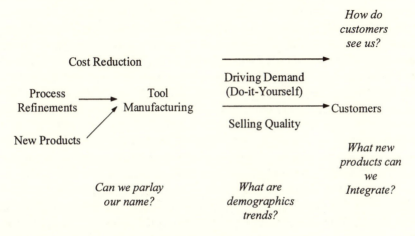

Figure 7.7. Stanley Works' evolving WBAWI.

just sell the brass when you can add a step in production and sell the brass fasteners? Scovill refined its manufacturing to include the additional step of turning the brass into fasteners. The result was that Scovill enjoyed a long-lived business relationship with the rubber boot manufacturers and garment industries as their near sole provider of their products' closings. Scovill seized the moment, expanded down the chain, and became the dominant market force in clothing closures. But, Scovill's dominant position was threatened in 1924 when Goodrich introduced its innovative "Zipper Boot," which incorporated a slide fastener as a means for closure. By 1926, Scovill had responded to the Zipper Boot, not just with a new product in the snap fastener, but also with machines it had developed that attached the closures to the clothing in an efficient manner.

The evolution of a mechanically attached fastener was Yankee inge-nuity at its best. However, garment manufacturers required a conve-nient workshop method of attaching the brass buttons and fasteners. Scovill developed presses that attached the tack buttons mechanically and by 1882 rented out machines to the clothing manufacturers/buyers of their brass buttons. This subtle addition of the machinery and pro-cesses for mechanical attachment of their products had Scovill redefin-ing itself not just as a clothing fasteners seller, but as a company serving an integral role in the chain of clothing manufacturing.

Once it had regained its market position with its attachment technology, Scovill further revolutionized the clothing and laundry industries with its "Gripper" fastener, a new product that underwent continual modifications until Scovill had slimmed down clothing fasteners to a thickness that eliminated the bulk of the original Goodrich product that had presented such an obstacle in laundering and dry cleaning. Furthermore, the sleeker look became a retail customer favorite. This new device with its consumer appeal brought Scovill executives to the realization that Scovill's role as a supplier could be maximized through the branding of its products, which even though integrated into other brand products, seemed oddly capable of taking on an identity of their own.

Scovill further refined its WBAWI by initiating component branding, which took it to the level of the premier clothing fastener company preferred by retail customers. Clothing manufacturers then featured their lines and advertisements with the winning tag "featuring Scovill fasteners." Scovill got the benefit of free advertising as well as an ongoing pull from retail clothing customers for Scovill's component good. The manufacturers saw it as a distinguishing feature for their clothing lines. In fact, starting in 1939, Scovill even went so far as to pull demand by launching a new and different kind of advertising campaign in which Scovill, a manufacturer of component parts, went directly to consumers and in the ads asked them to demand from retailers garments made with "Gripper" fasteners. Scovill "pulled" demand through distribution channels with a new direct marketing approach that prodded consumers to look for "Scovill" in their clothing.

Scovill was also nimble with a diversification strategy tied to the development and expansion of their customer base. The Scovill broth-ers often invested small sums in other enterprises, with the idea that these businesses could become useful customers for Scovill's mill prod-ucts. They invested back in their supply chains in companies they might be able to tap for the new materials they might need for expansion. For example, in 1858, Scovill purchased a thimble business with the idea of broadening the range of products offered to the garment industry, then a growing industry. For the same reason, Scovill purchased a cloth-covered button factory for more products to sell to its customers and all in the related clothing fastener business.

Scovill's diversification also focused on another common theme of acquiring "potential customers," but these acquisitions were made only after Scovill's management had reached a level of comfort with the target and its industry. A major customer of Scovill, Hamilton Beach, established an enviable reputation through its skill with "fractional horsepower motors," an essential component in soda fountain equipment, hair dryers, sewing machines, and other industrial and consumer products. Scovill not only supplied Hamilton Beach with brass as a basic material; it offered manufacturing advice to Hamilton Beach. This familiarity and confidence with Hamilton Beach production and products led Scovill to acquire the financially beleaguered firm in 1923. While the purchase seems beyond Scovill's WBAWI, it is important to understand that Hamilton Beach had been a Scovill brass customer for 56 years prior to the acquisition.

Another potential customer WBAWI strategy began in 1839, when Scovill used its expertise and knowledge in metals to expand into the evolving field of photography. With Louis Daguerre's development of a new process of "fixing an image" on a metallic surface, the importance of skill in the use of a sheet of copper plated with silver was critical. Scovill had long established an industrywide reputation as a master producer of rolled metal plate. Rolled metal plate now had a new use in a new and evolving technology. Scovill's management recognized this evolving technology as a source of potential customers. Scovill seized the opportunity, and by 1845, Scovill was nearly the sole supplier of these plates for use in photography in the American market. The volume of sales for the plates with the New York photographic trade increased so rapidly that Scovill opened its own store in that city in 1846. In addition to plates, this retail store sold cameras, photographic supplies, and an array of products from the Scovill mill. During a 25-year period (1850–1874), the photographic store generated almost as large a profit as its parent. Management reinvested more than 75 percent of these profits from photography sales in order to modernize the factory for the core brass business.

Future Scovill diversifications centered around the successful photography venture. A distributor, Edward Anthony, had competed with Scovill by importing Voigtlander camera and lens products. By 1855, due to changes in distribution, Anthony and Scovill began profitable joint ventures in production and distribution of photographic products. By 1902, the companies made their relationship permanent with a merger into the Anthony and Scovill Company or ANSCO. Figure 7.8 illustrates the Scovill WBAWI strategy.

Original WBAWI
A Brass Manufacturer.

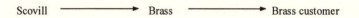

Scovill ⟶ Brass ⟶ Brass customer

Revised WBAWI
A Manufacturer of Everything That Involves Brass.

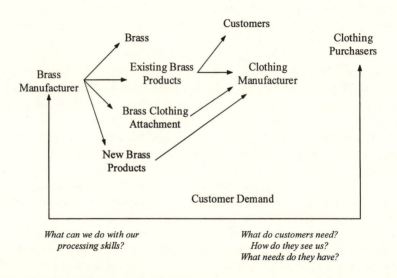

Figure 7.8. Scovill's evolving WBAWI.

LUDLOW: THE EVER-REACHING PRODUCT LINE

Ludlow began in 1868 as an importer of jute from India for the manufacture of twines, carpet yarns, furniture webbing, and cords. Ludlow was primarily an importer and seller of raw materials that had a variety of uses. Until 1910, all of Ludlow's raw material, generally from India, had been purchased through brokers, located either in the United States or in Europe. Ludlow realized its dependence upon others produced a vulnerability and lack of stability in supplies and suppliers. Furthermore, jute standards were fallible. Ludlow faced endless arbitrations for breaches in quality and difficulties and delays in shipping. Apart from the considerable dissatisfaction and frustration among management over these issues, there were resulting expensive interruptions in the conversion process.

In the face of these handicaps, Ludlow decided to obtain complete control over its purchased jute in order to secure a steady supply for high-grade production. Ludlow opened an office and plant in India for purposes of buying, selecting, and baling jute. This extension of functions backward in the supply chain allowed Ludlow to sustain its favorable position in both the supply and product markets. By 1920, Ludlow had stepped deep into its web to include the processing of jute in India as part of its business. By expanding its business role back into the chain, Ludlow was able to purchase the highest quality jute in India prior to processing. Unlike other sellers, Ludlow, by this expansion, obtained exclusive control over quality and even greater control over price.

But Ludlow was also a "know thy customer" and "watch those trends" WBAWI follower. Because of social changes in packaging, Ludlow realized in 1957 its limited WBAWI with its dependence on jute. At that point, Ludlow redefined itself from small jute manufacturer of package string to complete provider of paper and packaging materials. With this small tweaking of its business definition, Ludlow began a creeping form of product expansion. By 1967, Ludlow was no longer recognized as a jute company, but as a paper and packaging specialty company with products ranging from chart paper for scientists to gummed packaging paper. With the expertise Ludlow developed in making gummed packaging products, Ludlow expanded into rubber and vinyl products.

Slowly, Ludlow would travel far from its jute roots. With its expertise in rubber and vinyl, Ludlow then began making products for the automotive and shoe industries. Ludlow's fiber and processing expertise were combined for expansion into carpet manufacturing. Such a step was logical because its skill allowed it to make jute-backed carpet. With such high-quality raw materials, over which Ludlow had complete control, the company became an uptown name in carpeting. Ludlow then built upon its developed name in quality carpet manufacturing to expand into carpeting sales and home furnishings. With this foray into home furnishings, Ludlow again redefined itself as a producer of products for the home. Because Ludlow was now known inside homes, it was poised to move in to the sales of homes themselves. In 1974, Ludlow entered the business of selling mobile homes.

Ludlow answered the WBAWI question with slight refinements in an ever-expanding though interrelated web of products. The result was a shift in Ludlow's jute sales from 90 percent in 1956 to just 20 percent in

1966. By the 1970s, home furnishings sales constituted 50 percent of gross sales. Ludlow expanded backward into its chain in production and expanded horizontally at incremental paces with slight variations in product offerings at the consumer level, as consumers knew its name. Expansions into other fields were gradual. For example, Ludlow simply found different paper users, assessed their needs, and then altered production processes for expansion. Ludlow saw its expansion as different uses of the same product—not as an expansion into a new field. For example, Ludlow did expand into the medical field, but it was in the area of paper applications for medical use. Ludlow's dual WBAWI expansion strategy is shown in Figure 7.9.

Original WBAWI
Seller of Jute.

Jute ⟶ Ludlow ⟶ Customers

Ludlow
Revised WBAWI
Processor of Raw Materials for Consumer Products.

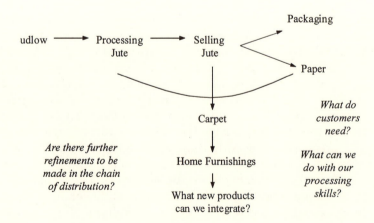

Figure 7.9 Ludlow's evolving WBAWI.

CORNING: INNOVATION THROUGH RESEARCH

When Corning began its glass business in 1851, it joined a field of stiff competition in a slow-growth market. The company entered a field in which everything about start-up was difficult, including plant location. But, within 25 years of its beginning, Corning saw something other glass companies missed. Corning did not define its business as that of selling glass, but rather as that of furnishing glass products that met the needs of their customers. As a result of this definition, Corning focused on consumer trends and sociological changes.

As technology changed in areas as simple as cooking devices, customers' needs and opportunities changed. A wood-burning stove has different utensils from gas-burning stoves. Different cooking equipment was needed. Corning's perception of itself not just as a glass seller but a glass product researcher or innovator positioned it to take advantage of these trends and changes. Beginning in 1877, Corning created one of the country's best R and D departments through its use of Cornell University professors for help in improving the quality of its glass lenses. At present, such partnering with academic institutions seems routine. At that time, however, Corning showed great foresight with this partnering. Corning's focus on research and improvement brought Thomas Edison to them, and the company made the bulbs for his newly patented light. By 1908, Corning had developed its own research laboratory, and in 1915, the scientists there developed Pyrex, a material Corning saw at first only as laboratory equipment, but which became a staple in every kitchen in America.

Research in the early 1950s provided the method for mass production of Pyrex, the material for Corning Ware, which was launched as a product line in 1957. Corning's triumph in cookingware only continued with the development of the microwave oven for consumer markets. Corning capitalized on its product suitability for microwaves by giving a free Pyrex/Corning dish with every microwave purchased. This promotion won microwave purchasers over to Corning's line. Corning was the near-exclusive choice for consumer microwave cooking despite its lack of both marketing research and direct ads. Corning's R and D-focused WBAWI is shown in Figure 7.10.

PULLMAN: AN ALL-INCLUSIVE WBAWI?

As a manufacturer of railroad cars, Pullman is the company in the group that began with the greatest obsolescence risk. The Pullman Company diversifications were tied to Pullman's knowledge of steel, steel production processes, construction, heavy equipment, the manufacturing process in general used in building railroad cars, and their use

Original WBAWI
Glass Producer.

Corning ————————→ Glass ————————→ Customers

Corning
Revised WBAWI
Finding Uses of Glass for End Products.

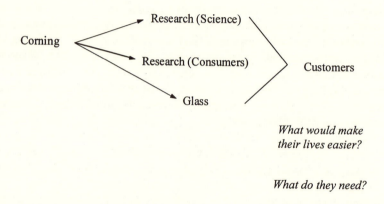

Corning

Research (Science)

Research (Consumers)

Glass

Customers

What would make their lives easier?

What do they need?

Figure 7.10. Corning's evolving WBAWI.

in transformation. Pullman's first logical expansion of its product line came through the creation of a subsidiary that leased railroad equipment. Antitrust litigation by competitors challenging Pullman's control of both the sale and lease markets for railroad cars forced Pullman, by a 1954 court order obtained by the FTC, to divest its railroad-leasing business. The resources from the sale of the leasing company were reallocated with the purchase of M. W. Kellogg Company, a leading engineering and construction business, which enabled Pullman to develop its global operations in manufacturing. This acquisition was a complementary union, joining engineering and construction capabilities. By 1976, revenues from services and materials related to engineering and construction, the revenues from diversification, exceeded those from Pullman's manufactured products.

As rail transportation decreased, so did Pullman's market. Pullman, although somewhat late in the risky game, redefined itself from rail car manufacturer to transportation specialist. That simple realignment of WBAWI put Pullman into both the truck manufacturing and aerospace industries. In its redefinition, Pullman was careful to define its customer and market as small trucking firms so that it was not in direct competition with companies focused on large trucking sales, but rather positioned as a seller to small companies who could count on Pullman service. With the purchase in 1951 of the Trailmobile Company, Pullman took its skills to the "open road." By 1980, Pullman had become the world's second-largest truck trailer builder. Pullman's WBAWI refinement is shown in Figure 7.11.

DIAMOND: UNMATCHED POTENTIAL

Diamond Match did not allow its original company name to self-limit its answer to WBAWI. Diamond defined its business not as matches but as a company serving consumer's ignition needs with the latest technology. That simple realignment of its business and product refinement made Diamond a market leader. Although it was not customary at the turn of the century to use census data for marketing and production decisions, O. C. Barber, president of the Diamond Match Company, wrote to stockholders in 1900:

> The increase in the Company's business during the past twenty years has exceeded the increase in the population of the country for the same period in the ratio of six to one . . .
> Should we be as successful in holding the trade in the future as in the past, the increase of the business will be following as great proportions as ever, and we shall have use of some of our surplus earnings to increase our output in order to keep with the demands made upon us. I think, therefore, that it will be the policy of the Company to make some extensions of its plants during this year.[5]

Diamond recognized demographic trends and then extrapolated to determine which would generate increased demand. Diamond went back in the chain and during the early 1900s acquired major tracts of timberland in New England and California to ensure ample supplies of wood for its match business at prices it could control. Internally, Diamond gained tremendous knowledge from its operations in forest products—growing, harvesting, and management in this venture led to entry into the secondary market of lumber sales, and expansion in this retail area continued during the next several decades. By the 1960s,

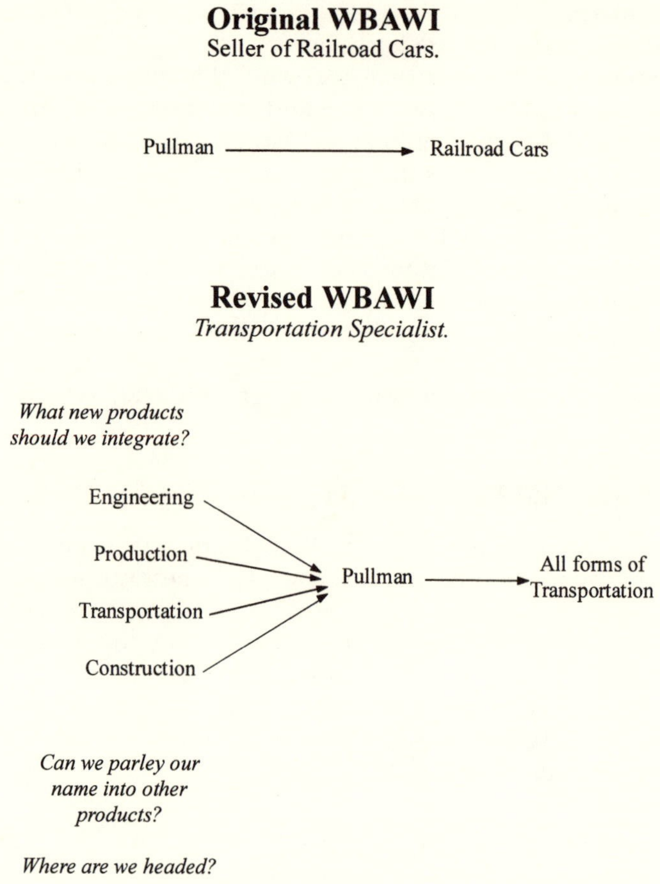

Original WBAWI
Seller of Railroad Cars.

Pullman ⸻⸻▶ Railroad Cars

Revised WBAWI
Transportation Specialist.

*What new products
should we integrate?*

Engineering

Production ⟶ Pullman ⟶ All forms of
                              Transportation
Transportation

Construction

*Can we parley our
name into other
products?*

Where are we headed?

Figure 7.11. Pullman's evolving WBAWI.

Diamond operated a chain of 165 very profitable lumber stores. It would later use its skills in the manufacture of small wood products to expand into other consumer products including ice cream sticks, applicators, toothpicks, and corn dog sticks.

Diamond's plant operations also expanded to include a print shop for use of by-products in the manufacture of matchboxes, toothpick boxes, and matchbook covers. Interestingly, the innovative book matches were initially returned to Diamond because consumers had difficulty using them. Diamond still made a go of this smaller convenient product by simply adding what would become universal matchbook instructions, "Close cover before striking." Diamond then helped Pabst Brewing Company launch book matches as a new advertising forum.

Over the years, Diamond also continued to perfect its original product with a focus on ignition and safety. Diamond's business began and thrived not because it invented the match, but rather because Diamond made them safe for consumer use, educated consumers on their use, and then utilized consumers for expansion ideas. For example, Diamond developed the first nonpoisonous strike-anywhere match and even turned over the patent to that new product so that other manufacturers could produce the same safe match. For the perceived good of the whole, Diamond sacrificed its first mover position. But Diamond was a master at understanding the value of goodwill in its continuing success. In fact, Diamond proved a master at parleying do-goodism into increased sales. For example, during World War II, when Diamond realized the U.S. government was a potential customer, it developed matches that could be used under water for up to eight hours and still light. This consumer, the U.S. Armed Forces, purchased 10 million matches per day for use by soldiers in combat. When environmentalism became a consumer concern, Diamond developed the Super Match, an ecologically friendly alternative for lighting fireplaces, barbecues, and campfires without the use of lighter fluid.

During the 1950s, then-president of Diamond Robert Fairburn realized that sales for some Diamond products were declining because of technological developments. Fairburn began expansion of Diamond's product line through the use of raw materials or waste by-products from its existing products and processing. For example, Diamond moved into production of molded paper products, paper-board, and carton packaging. In 1952, in order to expand its packaging expertise, Diamond merged with Gardner Board and Carton Company and acquired General Packaging in 1955 in order to obtain the equipment and plant facilities necessary for production. Both this merger and the acquisition enabled Diamond to become one of the leading producers of molded pulp products. In 1959, Diamond merged with U.S. Printing & Lithograph because its product line allowed expansion into the preprinted folding cartons, displays, posters, labels, and wrappers markets.

What started as a vertical extension in 1900 to bolster the primary business led the Diamond Match Company, by 1981, to a diversified manufacturing and marketing position. Diamond's diversification within its own manufacturing and marketing bases of knowledge was measured and undertaken only within its vertical chain of production of processes and, coincidentally, within its means.

The language of the 1899 "President's Report to the Stockholders of the Diamond Match Company" reveals an intense level of knowledge of both sides of the firm's markets.

It is much safer to be historian than prophet, yet I think it safe to predict that the future of the Company is as secure, and on a more lasting and permanent foundation than it has been for some years. This conclusion is formed from the firm hold we have on the trade by our exact knowledge that no competition in the world can successfully compete with us in the quality and cheapness of our product, of which fact we are more firmly convinced than ever, after finding out the cost of matches as produced by the several factories we have purchased.

Your Directors have, in a large measure, forecasted events and anticipated the wants of the Company for several years in advance of contracting for many of the articles entering into the manufacture of matches at prices prevailing two years ago. This must of necessity help augment our profits in the future.[6]

Figure 7.12 depicts Diamond's evolving answers to WBAWI.

Original WBAWI
Matchmaker

Diamond ⟶ Matches ⟶ Consumers

Diamond
Revised WBAWI
Ignition Specialist and By-Product Manufacturer.

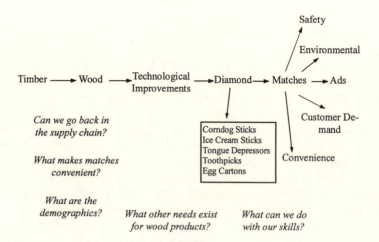

Figure 7.12.   Diamond's evolving WBAWI.

COLGATE-PALMOLIVE: CLEAN FOR CONSUMERS

Of all of the companies, Colgate-Palmolive was the most narrow in its focus in answering the WBAWI question, but despite its narrow response, it developed an enormous line of products. Colgate-Palmolive began as a starch, soap, and candle retail shop in New York but expanded its WBAWI to anything that cleans and primps consumers. The company's research focused on making new and better products.

Its first innovation was perfumed soap, introduced in 1866 based on customer feedback that lye and other soaps clean but certainly do not make one smell any better. From there, a good smell went into their toothpaste, and then their toothpaste went from the consumer-burdensome jar to the tube. Colgate developed these product innovations in its research and then fueled consumer demand.

With the acquisition of Robert Chesebrough's product known as Vaseline, Colgate expanded more into personal hygiene products that would eventually include Colgate's line of lotions, deodorants, and shaving gels. Other acquisitions over the years included Palmolive soap, Softsoap, Vipont Pharmaceuticals (the company responsible for developing antitartar toothpaste), several bleach manufacturers outside the United States (which have made Colgate-Palmolive the number-one bleach retailer outside the United States), Murphy's Oil Soap, and the Mennen Company.

Colgate's expansion through research, product innovation, and firm acquisition resulted, by its 100th anniversary, in product lines consisting of 160 different kinds of soap alone. Product innovations from its research have included the collapsible toothpaste tube, whitening toothpaste (Ultrabite), concentrated laundry detergent (Fresh Start), cold water laundry detergent, automatic dishwashing liquid, and the pump toothpaste container. Colgate's research center was established in 1896 for the development of new products and packaging, and today its center, affiliated with Rutgers University, is one of the largest academic/business affiliations in the world. Currently, the company spends 1.9 percent of total sales on research and 1 percent of sales profits on market research.

Colgate-Palmolive had some ventures that have deviated from its basic WBAWI, such as its acquisition of Hill's Pet Products and Princess House Crystal and Giftware. Both companies are wholly-owned subsidiaries and are also profitable. While on the surface these two companies are seemingly outside the WBAWI focus, they are both consumer products, and both are marketed with a focus on high quality. In fact, Colgate-Palmolive has followed the same research formula with Hill's Pet Products that it has used with its hygiene product. For example, in 1991, Hill's opened an $80 million high-tech manufacturing plant, which represented the single largest capital investment in Colgate-Palmolive's history.

Colgate-Palmolive very carefully defined its business as worldwide, not limited to the United States, and it has been a leader in international expansion. In 1924, having been in the international markets for over one century, Colgate-Palmolive once again demonstrated innovation by opening an actual plant in Paris for the manufacture of its products in Europe. Today, Colgate-Palmolive products are sold in 194 countries and territories.

Colgate-Palmolive introduced 55 percent of its products in the last five years, and its employees and officers describe it as a company seeking innovation and discovering what consumers want.

One of Colgate's CFOs described their WBAWI focus as, "We never accept the status quo; that is a dangerous place to be."[7] Colgate-Palmolive's WBAWI contrast appears in Figure 7.13.

GENERAL ELECTRIC: THE POWER WENT ON AND NEVER STOPPED

General Electric was founded as a light bulb company, but its simple refinement of its answer to WBAWI as the generation, transmission, control, and use of electric power has moved it from a consumer retail product to an international conglomerate, with 11 diverse areas. GE's expansion has come through constant exploration of the production, transport, and uses of electricity. For example, just 10 years after Edison founded the company, GE was developing electric streetcar systems. Less than 20 years after its formation, it was in the transmission business, which then led it to the manufacture of transmission equipment and then into the production of generation equipment, which included industrial motors as well as electric locomotives, markets in which it enjoyed a monopoly in the early twentieth century.

GE's research laboratory was in full operation by 1900 and results from that internal investment include everything from the X-ray tube (which gave GE the position it enjoys today in medical systems, including mammography equipment) to consumer appliances. Even GE's plastics division has developed products used by myriad manufacturers who need durable plastic for their products.

When its involvement in the electric utility industry (generation and transmission) presented antitrust problems for the government, GE refocused its WBAWI on engines for generation as well as on its considerable consumer products base for electric generation. The sheer cost of many of its large motors found GE in the financing business, which it

Original WBAWI
We Sell Soap.

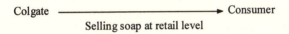

Colgate-Palmolive
Evolved WBAWI
We Develop, Manufacture, Package, and Sell Consumer Products.

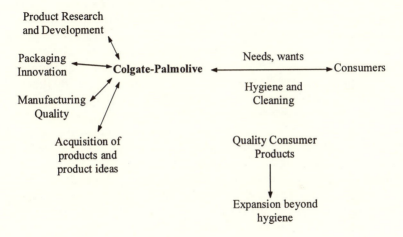

Figure 7.13. Colgate-Palmolive's evolving WBAWI.

has since expanded into GE Capital Services, now responsible for over 40 percent of its revenue with financial services in everything from the consumer market to real estate finance and bond insurance.

During World War II, with its shortages and supply interruptions, GE moved from a "make it" mentality to one of "buy it wherever possible and partner to bring down the cost." GE and its suppliers work together to share risk and cost benefits. GE went back in the supply chain with a program called "Partnering with Suppliers" because its rapid growth necessitated outsourcing to achieve efficiencies and expertise it could not build in-house.

GE began as a company with an innovative electrical product and expanded in both directions—backward for electrical generation and even further back for the production of machinery for the production of electricity. Still today it sells the equipment for electrical generation. But, GE also moved down into the web and made products that use electricity and then into even the financing purchases by consumers and industrial users. In that financing refinement of its WBAWI, GE found yet another of its strengths and has continued to expand its reach into the financial markets with success that has astounded the long-time players in that arena. Of all of the fifteen companies, GE has been the most nimble in adaptation and in seizing the moment based on customer needs, new technology, or when there is just a good old-fashioned market void.

Just recently, in a creative move into an area where GE saw a void, it has combined its abilities in engines with its honed skills in financing to further refine its WBAWI. GE now offers airlines fixed-price, off-wing maintenance of the GE engines it sells to them, including the cost of spare parts. The cost of selling and maintaining aircraft power, not just selling aircraft engines, is preset at a figure of dollars per flight hour. Referred to as "power by the hour," this arrangement shifts the risk of maintenance costs on engines back to GE. GE is seller, financier, and warrantor of airplane engines, and the demand is high. Furthermore, in development of a new long-range flight engine, GE will be the seller, providing guarantees on the engine's performance, but also holding a stake in the engine itself, for it has taken a share of airline revenues using the engines as part of its compensation for their development.[8] Innovation in its labs coupled with a culture of continual change and evolution makes GE a success in the past, a performer in the present, and a sure bet for longevity. GE's WBAWI is shown in Figure 7.14.

COCA-COLA: NEVER LOSE THE REAL THING

Coca-Cola's greatest struggle in WBAWI has been keeping its head level with an understanding of the unique nature of its products, particularly its flagship, Coca-Cola. Coca-Cola had to resist the tendency to expand its WBAWI because it has been blessed with a one-and-only type of product.

Coca-Cola's limited expansion products have evolved from consumer trends. These observations were responsible for Coca-Cola's entry into the diet soda market as well as its foray into the health-conscious market with its acquisition of Minute Maid, the world's largest orange juice company. Its main focus continues to be attracting and keeping consumers, and its international expansion, with the goal of more Coca-Cola drinkers, began as early as 1900.

Original WBAWI
We Sell Light Bulbs.

Light Bulb ⎯⎯⎯⎯⎯⎯⎯⎯→ Consumers

GE Evolved and Evolving WBAWI

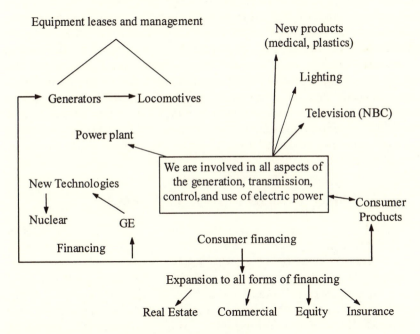

Figure 7.14. General Electric's evolving WBAWI.

Coca-Cola's decision to focus back into the supply chain centers around its dependence on the price of sugar. To avoid being at the mercy of sugar suppliers and tariffs, Coca-Cola made the decision early in the century to substitute high fructose corn syrup for sugar. The switch permitted a reduction in price for Coca-Cola's contracts with its bottlers and correspondingly lower and stable prices for consumers. Coca-Cola has also established an international supply network for sugar and corn syrup so that if one country overcharges on sugar, it can head to another country.

In its WBAWI, Coca-Cola has focused its energy on ever-expanding sales and has been a masterful marketer of a unique product. From its celebrity endorsements to movie placements to event sponsorships, Coca-Cola reaches consumers at their points of vulnerability. Its ads, "Things go better with Coke," "The real thing," "Coke is it," and "I'd like to buy the world a Coke," have become part of conversations nationally, and these familiar slogans were served to establish a loyalty among its customers. No more evident is this brand loyalty than in the company's product, TAB. TAB, Coke's original diet soft drink from 1963, continues to command a loyal following and is a profitmaker despite an advertising budget of zero. In fact, the placement of TAB in *Austin Powers* finds it experiencing new demand among a new generation, the same old strategy of movie placements to bring in brand-new customers and more sales.

Coca-Cola's WBAWI exercises are unique, for it has been required to understand its customer loyalty and not jeopardize that while at the same time expand the customer base. Furthermore, Coke maintains its quality through close relationships with its ten Anchor Bottlers and their assigned bottling companies. The relationships with these bottlers provide the stability for quality and long-term growth. Coke's unique WBAWI appears in Figure 7.15.

GENERAL MILLS: FOOD IN ALL ITS FORMS

General Mills began as a grain processor and evolved into a seller of food products in every form from whole grains to convenient snack foods to easy-to-make baked goods. General Mills honed its food preparation skills in order to expand into the food service business in school and on-site cafeterias. General Mills WBAWI was once a grain processor, but it is now food in all its forms and delivery mechanisms.

General Mills path from the narrow focus of grain miller to international food producer was steady but cautious. Its introduction of the Betty Crocker symbol in 1921 was its way of connecting with consumers beyond just selling grains. Betty Crocker was the human element that brought product distinction and identification. Betty Crocker has changed hairstyles and now wears a suit as opposed to a housedress, but she remains the icon of good things coming from the kitchen. Betty Crocker's face has long dominated home baking with all the benefits going to General Mills.

General Mills first foray into processed cereal was its 1924 introduction of Wheaties. The ready-to-eat cereal was unique but so also was General Mills marketing of it. While Betty Crocker brought in a strong

Original WBAWI
We Sell a Soft Drink.

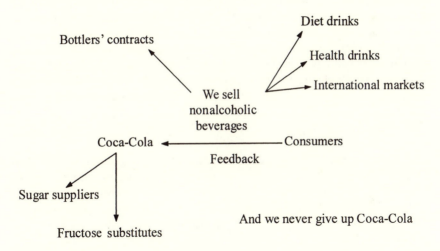

**Coca-Cola
Refined WBAWI**

Figure 7.15. Coca-Cola's evolving WBAWI.

homemaker market, sports figures drew children to the cereal products. This identification of its cereals with memorable fictitious and real characters made General Mills a leader then and has been responsible for its continued success in its ever-expanding line of cereals. General Mills created consumer desire through affiliation of its products with winners, icons, and pop culture.

While drawing consumer demand on one end with its cereal endorsements, General Mills was also meeting consumer needs through its R and D, which focused on making meal preparation easier. Its 1930 introduction of Bisquick was a landmark for the company as well as for the way Americans cooked. Bisquick was not just flour; it was a premixed base for baking breads, biscuits, pancakes, and cookies that shaved time and challenges from the chore of baking. General Mills is consistently the number-one or number-two seller in these baking product lines. This facilitation of baking would continue with even more products that eliminated even more steps in the process. General Mills product lines in this eliminate-the-chore-of-baking theme included cake mixes, muffin mixes, ready-made frostings, and desserts, packaged all in one box.

But General Mills' R and D was not limited to new product development. This company paid attention to the trends and lifestyles of homemakers. Even baking is beyond the time constraints of any family, so General Mills moved into packaging convenient meals, and its Hamburger Helper line is a staple for families with parents whose time is limited because of two or more jobs and incomes. The need for fast and quick but healthy snacks moved General Mills into that market. Its snack foods, well known for their quality as well as some redeeming nutritional value, include the top-selling Fruit Roll-ups, Chex Snack Mix, and Pop Secret popcorn. These products and others illustrate General Mills' strong brand presence. Since the time of its introduction of Betty Crocker, General Mills has maintained its growth through strong brand identification. Indeed, its most recent successes have been capitalizing on original brands such as Honey Nut Cheerios and Frosted Cheerios. Because this formula works, General Mills plans to continue its expansion with new flavors of old standbys with good name recognition.

Underlying these last few consumer product expansions was General Mills close attention to demographics. It is not accidental that its strongest sales have come with products offering increased convenience. Demographically, the country changed from home cooking to eating on the run. General Mills has been poised with products answering the call. Bisquick required the addition of milk and eggs. Now some General Mills mixes include a baking pan and require only water. Ultimate convenience in quality foods has become a refined WBAWI for them.

General Mills has a joint venture with PepsiCo in Europe, where the two now dominate the snack market. General Mills was also instrumental in forming a joint venture for cereal distribution in Europe and as a result has enjoyed high sales volume and growth there since 1990.

General Mills' WBAWI is shown in Figure 7.16.

PROCTER & GAMBLE: SELLING SOAP ON THE SOAPS

When Procter & Gamble began its operations, its goal was to build a loyal customer base through uncompromising quality. Its strategy

Original WBAWI
We sell milled grain.

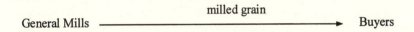

Revised WBAWI
We sell consumer food products

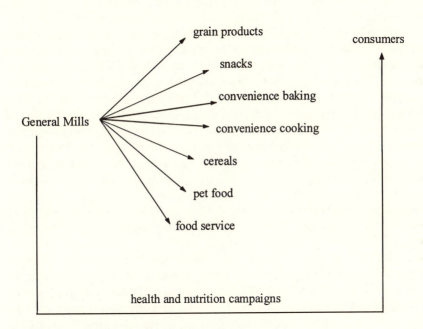

Figure 7.16. General Mills' evolving WBAWI.

worked well for its focus on manufacturing improvement, and the quality that resulted brought it, serendipitously, the product that would make P&G's mark internationally. Facing a rosin shortage during the Civil War, P&G experimented with new ingredients in making its soap (a new direction in R and D that it continues today). During this experimentation, born of a crisis, Ivory Soap emerged as the result of an accident of the laboratory workers mixing the soap base with too much air. This unique, soft, and light soap was then marketed aggressively and took this country, as well as many others, by storm.

Also as a result of its experience in handling oils and bases in soap manufacture, P&G diversified initially with Crisco, a shortening created from the oils and bases P&G was familiar with in its manufacturing process.

Its other consumer products were developed using its innovative technique called the Product Launch System, which included specific go and no-go criteria for managers to follow in taking a product forward. The go–no-go system was grounded entirely in consumer feedback—they controlled what a product needed and whether it would indeed fly. Products from the launch system include Pampers, Tampax, and Bounce. P&G was not adverse to acquisition, and Clorox was an example of its type of diversification still well within its cleaning product line.

P&G inspires zealous consumer demand, and it does so by heavy advertising. Its introduction of Tide was brilliantly tied to the afternoon television drama market. P&G is still inextricably intertwined with the "soaps." It not only advertises on these programs, it has become a joint venturer with them. P&G served as a party to a contract for the construction of three television studios for *Another World, As the World Turns,* and *The Guiding Light.* But it also responds to consumer needs and demands. Bounce is a product that was developed because no one had the time to add fabric softener at the correct time in the washer. Bounce has stolen the fabric softener market with new technology, providing an easier way to soften clothes. Like Colgate-Palmolive, Procter & Gamble has a narrowly defined WBAWI: Keeping consumers hygienic with innovation and then getting the word out on those innovations.

In what is a first, P&G is combining with another one of these 100-year companies. P&G is using the combination to better get out the word on its products and also use the distribution system to get its products out there. Coca-Cola and P&G have formed a joint venture that will market Frutopia (Coke's noncarbonated beverage) and P&G's Sunny Delight, fondly known by grade-school children everywhere as "Sunny D." Coke will also use its distribution system to market P&G's snack foods, beginning with Pringles, a potato chip in a can that lends itself well to widespread distribution, particularly for international markets. However, the companies have been squabbling since the time of the announced $4.2 billion joint venture. Coke has expressed a desire to scale back, convinced that it is sacrificing sales in its Minute Maid to sales of Sunny Delight, which were down 11 percent for 2000.

With this move to a unique joint venture, P&G had hoped to signal that it was a much more nimble company undergoing a WBAWI refocus. P&G almost seems offended that it is perceived as the grand marketer when it feels it is indeed an innovator, with over 1,500 PhDs on its payroll and patents totaling over 27,000. Being miffed on being given short shrift for its innovation, P&G has perhaps not so much changed its WBAWI as realized that it may not be capitalizing enough on its real strength and business focus.

As a result, P&G has entered a new joint venture stage. While its business focus has and perhaps always will be consumer products, P&G is looking to other companies to jointly exploit its ideas, innovations, and patents in consumer products. In what some have called a risky move, P&G is teaming with Whirlpool to create a cabinet-size clothes refresher known simply as "The Valet." The Valet represents the first new consumer appliance category in 30 years. The Valet is a cabinet-size machine that will take out wrinkles and deodorize clothes in 15 minutes. Alas, there is no stain removal. However, P & G sees that as the product's strength because it learned through marketing studies that dry cleaning expenses are formidable for many consumers and that they often send out for dry cleaning what simply needs refreshing. The Valet will save them the dry cleaning bills for when their clothes actually have stains.

While the product is fascinating and is enjoying good press as its launch approaches, P&G is adding an interesting twist to the way it does business. P&G will be creating demand with this product, showing consumers why they need it. This was not a product that consumers have demanded—it is a product consumers did not know could be made or what it could do for them.

P&G is also permitting the use of its brand names by other companies. P&G has always been a stickler for use of its brand names in combination with any other products or companies. However, this dual branding is new and increasing at P&G. For example, after asking for nearly 20 years, Dana Undies will now be permitted to develop and sell a line of Pampers Infant Wear. Marine Optical will develop and sell Cover Girl (P&G's makeup line) sunglasses. And P&G will join with Wrigley to produce Crest chewing gum—"tastes great, less fillings."[9] This joint venture is head-on competition with Colgate-Palmolive in order to oust Colgate from its longstanding number one slot in the toothpaste market.

These revolutionary changes at P&G are not so much a task of reworking WBAWI as one of reworking the culture of P&G. P&G's culture has always been highly secretive, and its employees perceived the company's success and advantage as stemming from its product development and the ability to keep that under company control. Now P&G is opening its doors to joint venturers as well as to the use of its once closely protected brand names. Managers are adjusting because the new mantra is that innovation that does not make it out to the customer does not make much return on investment. P&G even surrendered six of its patents to a university for further research and development there and had to cope with the company culture shock that resulted from both the revelation of the patents and their gift to scientists. Jeffrey Weedman, P&G vice president for external business development and corporate licensing, has noted, "You do not change a 160-year-old company in 18 months. But to see us do the venture with Coke and other initiatives, all of this should provide a very different look at Procter & Gamble."[10]

P&G has also put some food brands such as Jif and Crisco on the market, with no buyers as yet. With the Coke deal pending and these brands hanging in limbo, the authors would issue to P&G a reminder about the WBAWI exercise. Too much too quickly has proven a downfall for shorter-term companies, and P&G appears to be risking a hazy redefinition by not making firm commitments to what it knows it does well. Perhaps Coke needs P&G's R and D more than P&G needs its distribution system, and P&G should rethink its joint venture strategy.

Procter & Gamble's WBAWI is diagramed in Figure 7.17.

It is only fitting that this WBAWI chapter should end on a note of uncertainty about P&G and Coke's futures. That is the way WBAWI was meant to work. We leave with the unknown for two of the 100-year companies—which direction will they take? One of the observations about the Coca-Cola and Procter & Gamble joint venture is that there is always difficulty in combining two giants and trying to determine which has the greater strength and which benefits most from the venture. However, perhaps the better WBAWI question for both companies is, Do we lose the business we are in through this combination? Relentless review of WBAWI is part of these companies' long-term success, and both should ask, Will the long-term cultures mesh or clash? However, before determining the wisdom of a P&G and Coke combination, there is another part to WBAWI, which is determining when not to enter a product or company arena, when to scale back, and when to forge forward. The restlessness of WBAWI is covered in the next chapter, along with some cautions on avoiding mistakes.

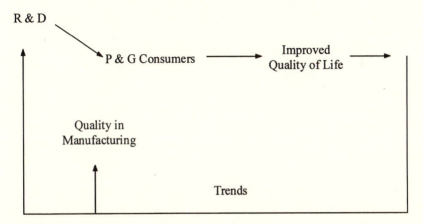

Figure 7.17.   Procter & Gamble's evolving WBAWI.

NOTES

1. "ICI Acquisition PPG's Largest Ever," *PPG Progress*, Fall 1999: 14.

2. Louis Grossman interviews.

3. Caloniuw, Erik, "Smarts Moves by Quality Champs," *Fortune: The New American Century*, 1991: 24.

4. Louis Grossman interviews.

5. Diamond Match Company, "Report to the Stockholders, 1901," obtained at the company headquarters, New York, September 1980.

6. Diamond Match Company, 1899 Annual Report (company archives).

7. Patrick interview, Colgate-Palmolive.

8. Banks, Howard, "Jack Welch, Engine Salesman," *Forbes*, August 9, 1999: 51.

9. Barnes, Julian E. I., "P&G Joins with Wrigley in Gum Deal," *New York Times*, August 7, 2001: C1, C8.

10. Barnes, Julian E. II., "Making Friends at Procter & Gamble," *New York Times*, March 16, 2001: C1, C4.

Key #3: Perfection—Will We Ever Be Satisfied? The Quest for Refining WBAWI

Keep thy shop, and thy shop will keep thee.

English Proverb

In democracies, nothing is more great or more brilliant than commerce; it attracts the attention of the public, and fills the imagination of the multitude; all energetic passions are directed towards it.

Alexis de Tocqueville, *Democracy in America*

These firms followed a simple rule. Savvy diversification works; do it. However, when heads are easily turned by cash temptations, the results can be costly. The firms in this group that diversified successfully used a measured approach with the benefit of background knowledge. There was some shoot-from-the-hip diversification. Such diversification and misreading of the two-direction vision proved costly.

This is the chapter where we acknowledge shortcomings and mistakes. We learn not just from those circumstances where these businesses did it right, but we learn from their mistakes. If there is a common theme among their mistakes and their quest for perfection, it would be, "Never shoot from the hip." This pithy phrase means do not diversify without knowing your product, your skills, and the nature of the new undertaking. It is the homework that makes WBAWI work. It is a matter of keeping the refinement going with the occasional spin-off necessary. An executive at Colgate-Palmolive described the ongoing refinement process, "We're in a jungle seeking sales. We see opportunities abroad as well as at home. Our motivation is primarily to provide a strong payout record for stockholders. And we see markets for what they are: turbulent and dynamic."[1]

This is also the chapter that reminds us that you cannot sit still. The mistakes are doing too much, not doing enough, and not cutting losses in time. To avoid any of these three scenarios resulting from being too satisfied, there must be an ongoing analysis of WBAWI.

CORNING: TOO MUCH WITH TOO LITTLE THOUGHT AND EXPERIENCE

We begin this adventure into missteps with the company that broke its dividend record in the summer of 2001. Corning has been paying dividends since Rutherford B. Hayes was president in 1881. Then came a $4.76 billion loss and July 2001 saw Corning's winning streak come to an end. The losses had begun in 2000 with the burst of the bubble because Corning was heavily invested in fiber optics and that demand slowed considerably. Its stock price dropped 88 percent between September 2000 and July 2001. Its break in its record was duly noted in the financial press.[2] Corning was writing off inventory it would not be able to sell in the troubled telecom industry and announcing layoffs of 6,000 employees in North America alone.

But the $4.76 billion loss is less than half of the $10 billion Corning had invested over the past few years in its attempt to buy up more companies in what it saw as a significant trend: telecommunications. The problems were several: (1) the estimates for growth were overstated; (2) Corning was buying companies for which it had little or no expertise in running; (3) the pattern of expansion was inconsistent with Corning's usual approach to diversification; and (4) Corning bought into the dot-com, live-for-the-moment philosophy that was defiant of the values and culture of its past as well as of the other fourteen firms that had achieved 100 years of dividends.

There was a certain sadness that hung in the air even as the young financial reporters on the cable networks reported on Corning's suspension of its dividends. As unlikely as it seems, these youngsters born and raised in an era of unprecedented economic growth seemed to appreciate the distinction between this company and this record and the breakneck fizzle of today's businesses. Now that we know they acknowledge the differences, it is worth examining what went wrong so that their seeming reverence for stability is not lost. This section of the manuscript and even its telling title was written in 1999—two years prior to Corning's end of its dividend record. At the time, the business press was touting Corning's aggressive venture into fiber optics.[3] One financial reporter wrote, "But Corning, best known for the cookware it stopped making in 1998, has shed its old-economy ties and bet the company on the new-economy world of high-tech innovation."[4] Corning sold off its cookware division to Borden in 1998, a decision CEO Roger Ackerman said, "Any fool would make," because cookware was not going to grow at "200 percent."

While the financial press refers to the sale as being to Borden, it was actually made to one of Borden's subsidiaries, World Kitchen International (WKI Holding, Inc.), which was the original joint venture partner for Corning in its expansion of its cookware line. Borden's World Kitchen had an entire line of kitchenware, including Chicago Cutlery and EKCO, and the fit seemed to be a good one. While WKI presently experiences the expected slowdown in sales because of the nature of the economic swing, its 10K indicates a $9 million decline in sales; it has not experienced the one-half billion dollar loss that Ackerman predicted. The unloading of the pots and pans part of the business is perhaps hauntingly regretful for Corning shareholders now.

Borden still survives with a profit, and Corning stock, once as high as $222, an increase of 734 percent from 1998, now hovers at $14. In 2000, those touting Corning's high-tech lunge noted that its stock had bottomed out in 1998 at $23. They were wrong. Indeed, Corning shareholders would welcome the earnings of Borden.

But, so also was Corning wrong about its fiber optic venture. Corning was not wrong about its foresight in the coming high-tech era or its investment in research to answer the needs of that era. Corning's venture into fiber optics was a natural turn for it. In fact, CEO Ackerman was hired at Corning Research Labs in 1962. Americans owe their color televisions to Corning laboratories' innovations with the television tube. Corning had developed the first viable optic fiber by 1970. It had really been experimenting with it since 1934 when Frank Hyde, a Corning researcher, experimented with making better telescope mirrors. His technology sat on the shelf for over 35 years until the 1970s when telephone companies were searching for better connections. Corning became a leader in sales to telecommunications companies and was perfectly poised for the Internet explosion.

If we look back at Corning's history, we could substitute "fiber optics" in several of Corning's WBAWI tales of woe and realize that history repeated itself with Corning's shortcomings in fiber optics. However, its zeal for the new economy and its resulting oversubscription (see Chapter 9 on the value of low debt) made this high-tech foray far more destructive than its previous faux pas in WBAWI. The following segment provides an eerie look at those mistakes. For these mistakes are eerie in the sense that the problems with fiber optics were déjà vu all over again.

Throughout its history, Corning realized that it was not just in the business of glass or specialty glass or even consumer cooking products. It was a product developer in the sense of developing new materials for old products that could make them perform better and even developing new products from the materials it developed in the laboratories. Corning was darn good at research and development diversification. However, Corning has been notoriously bad at joint venture diversification and acquisitions and has been able to, up until fiber optics, remove itself from the tar babies in the occasional briar patches of diversification into which it dove without the restraint of its values or even the underlying thoughtfulness of WBAWI. Its joint venture and acquisition strategies, begun to maximize distribution and returns on its lab products, were not measured and reflected shallow consideration of WBAWI.

Corning's experience with Signetics is an illustration of the flaws in Corning's approach that would eventually result in the fiber optics destruction of its longstanding dividend record. In 1962, Corning acquired Signetics, a maker of integrated circuits. Corning thereby entered an industry where technology obsolescence far outpaced the rate of change in the industries in which Corning had experience. Corning took years to develop cookware and was not prepared for the harsh reality of 12- to 18-month obsolescence. Corning's limited research, manufacturing, and marketing expertise in integrated circuits and ongoing lack of deftness in fast-changing markets forced it to abandon this venture and circuit manufacturing.

Corning's experiences in this era and realm, resulting from its lack of long-range planning and steady expansion, demonstrate the financial exposure of hasty acquisitions made without evaluation of expertise and careful answers to WBAWI. There was no logical connection or common experience between integrated circuits and cookware. It was the lure of high tech undertaken with the baggage of simple consumer products. Interestingly, this passage was written in 1998, long before Corning had any difficulties with its fiber optic investments.

Still, Corning did not take the lessons from this diversification flop to its next venture. During the 1960s and up until 1975, the Corning Glass Works was the dominant market force in the business of making the glass envelopes that house television picture tubes. Corning had pioneered the technology that made the glass envelopes possible. In 1966, half of Corning's sales and three-quarters of its profits were generated from this single product line. The glass envelope market declined in 1975 when the Japanese blitz of the American television market occurred. Orders for Corning's tubes dropped to almost zero, and Corning was unprepared for this market change. Corning scrambled to find alternative products and product lines and quickly obtained control of a French glass-related firm and a British glass producer. Both ventures, entered in haste without planning or expertise, produced either red ink or marginal profits. While both acquisitions involved glass, there were different products, international business issues, and import complexities. Corning entered into the marriages in haste and was forced to repent at leisure.

Yet another example from Corning's history demonstrates that while diversification may be a necessary condition for survival, it does not necessarily lead to success. Corning pioneered both the research and production of a smooth-top cooking surface made of glass. Because its costs were too high, Corning could not persuade any range manufacturer to incorporate its smooth-top surfaces unit into existing or future products. Corning decided to manufacture its own ranges. At first glance, this diversification seems parallel to Diamond's and Ludlow's. Yet, Corning did not know consumer appliances, and nothing in its marketing or manufacturing processes provided the depth of experience necessary for such a dramatic change in product line. Cookware is not the same as a stove with its complexity and evolving technology. The high-priced stoves achieved only a marginally profitable volume. Corning soon sold the range operation to the Amana division of Raytheon and relegated itself to the role of Amana's supplier for the cooking surfaces. Both firms fared better after the sale to Amana because Corning and Amana both returned to their WBAWI strengths.

Corning's diversification through joint ventures is legendary. Corning has one of the highest numbers of foreign joint ventures for U.S. firms, with nearly half of its profits in the 1980s generated by joint ventures. However, the same types of missteps Corning made in product diversification occurred with its joint ventures decisions. These joint ventures found Corning planted squarely in fields in which it had no knowledge of production, sales, or customers. The lure of profits and the merger/acquisition attitude of the 1980s found Corning a victim of bad WBAWI analysis.

Its latest and most costly lesson in terms of its dividend record is instructive in its oversights. Up until the time of the "high-tech economy," Corning had always referred to itself as a research company. If they didn't develop it, they didn't sell it. They had a strong pride of authorship. "We're still geeks, nerds, wonks, and researchers at heart," was Gerald J. Fine's description of Corning's culture when he served as vice president of Corning's photonics technology.[5] There apparently was something to that pride of authorship and intimate knowledge that brought Corning success. It was not until fiber optics that Corning reached out to others to acquire products. It was a first for a company that had always been the developer to whom others came to help with the marketing.

In less than a two-year period (between 1999 and 2001), Corning bought Oak Industries, a maker of laser gear, for $1.8 billion, followed by the $4 billion purchase of Pirelli S.P.A. for its optical components, the purchase of half of Siecor, one of Siemens' companies, and a joint venture with Samsung for production capacity. During the same period, Corning tried to purchase Nortel Networks in Canada and JDL. When John Loose took over Ackerman's slot as CEO, he said, "We caught one hell of a wave in telecommunications. I think we can keep growing the top and bottom lines by 20 to 30 percent a year."[6] Corning's theory in the acquisitions was that it would become the "one-stop shopping" company for the telecommunications infrastructure needed for the Internet.

Loose was wrong in his anticipation of growth, in ignoring the low-debt value of the company in making acquisitions, and in his pricing of those acquisitions. Corning paid $4 billion for Pirelli, a company that had only $25 million in sales and had not turned a profit. Worse, as it redefined its WBAWI, it became 70 percent invested entirely in high tech and dumped its tried and true product lines. Not only were Corning Ware, Pyrex, Corelle, and Revereware sold to Borden, but Corning also dumped all of its product line performers: housewares, medical testing equipment, and television and laboratory glass, the very products that had given Corning its original competitive niche in the cutthroat, as it were, glass industry.

Traditionally, when Corning ventured into unknown fields such as electronics with Signetics, there had been disastrous results. Signetics was sold for a pretax loss of $9.5 million. Its high-tech venture would prove no exception to the rule. Commentary on Corning's high point in the market includes colorful stories on scientists interacting with customers and Corning actually taking orders from these interactions. While Corning executives were proud and saw it as service marketing, these new roles for the scientists took away from Corning's strength—developing the products of the future in-house. It was as if the company had lost its self-esteem and could not envision itself a player in the new world of high tech. Hence, it acquired and then attempted to use marketing as a substitute for what had been its WBAWI—it was unsurpassed at R and D. It had learned early on with Corning Ware that it never had to market: if you build it right, they will come. During the high-tech boom, Corning was letting others do the building, and it was selling, with nearly everything invested in one high-tech basket. Corning committed a cardinal sin for a 100-year company—it rid itself of its diversification cushion and had everything riding on one high-tech bubble.

Corning's medical implantation devices joint venture with Dow on breast implants was a disaster that bankrupted the joint venture and resulted in still-pending litigation and liability exposure for both partners in the venture. Dow Corning, faced with international product liability class-action suits, settled those private suits for over $3 billion. The Dow Corning silicone implant diversification was a disaster because the joint venture lost sight of Corning's basic values in its quest to compete in the implant market. This diversification failed, not because of inattention to WBAWI but because of inattention to priorities and values (see Chapter 9).

PPG AND COLGATE: TOO DIVERSE

PPG's CEO noted that PPG fell victim to the acquisition frenzy of the 1980s and succumbed to temptation to reach beyond its mature and well-defined business mix. The financial market pressures caused PPG to pursue diversification in uncharted areas. PPG made several acquisitions during that time and one such acquisition found PPG operating a medical electronics business. However, medical electronics had no relationship to what PPG knew and could do well. In CEO John Dempsey's words, "the company lacked the specialized management skills necessary to manage it properly and achieve a critical mass."[7] Eventually, PPG sold off the medical electronics unit at some cost, leaving PPG with the difficult lesson that acquisition for the sake of acquisition can be costly. PPG's CEO expressed ethical and moral concerns about the leveraged buyout phenomenon based on the notion that aggressive investors could run a business more profitably than existing management. For PPG, acquisition post-1980s became a measured strategy rather than a response to a fad or market pressures that proved costly to the company. As noted earlier, its acquisitions remain in its core businesses but are pursued for their ability to provide sales growth, as in the acquisition of foreign manufacturers in order to obtain an existing product presence to which PPG adds its service mechanism and expertise.

One of the PPG officers reflected on PPG's WBAWI and described his company as "plain vanilla."[8] But he went on to add that the goal was profits, and they seemed most easily attained when PPG simply continued doing what it did well. Its focus in diversification was on global as well as insulation from economics swings. As a result, PPG remains perhaps the one company of the fifteen with the fewest WBAWI mistakes that required financial recovery. It also remains a continuing and steady earner.

Colgate-Palmolive experienced a similar problem to PPG, although its journey out on a limb was not near as far as that of PPG. Colgate had been saved from its first binge that was scheduled to close in 1929. Colgate would have formed a conglomerate with Kraft Foods and

Hershey. The deal was virtually done except for the formal signatures, with a ceremony scheduled. However, the day before the signing ceremony was to have occurred, the market crashed, and all bets were off. Those with the company still look back in wonder at how close they came to destruction through the ego and bravado of company executives who thought such a combination made sense. It would have been the destruction of all three companies.

It was over 20 years later before Colgate would try the acquisition mode again. During the 1950s through the 1970s, Colgate went on acquisition binges. One of the diverse companies it acquired was Helena Rubinstein, a cosmetics company. While the fit seemed logical, another consumer product line, what Colgate learned from the expensive acquisition is that the distribution system for cosmetics is very different from that of consumer products, the competition is different, and the advertising appeals are quite different. By 1980, Colgate had sold Helena Rubinstein and other purchases made during its binge modes. One executive noted that its ill-thought-out acquisitions mode, brought on by the pop theories of acquisition of the time meant "We almost committed suicide."[9] Colgate returned to the consumer products that it knew and emphasized growth in other ways (see the following discussion on global WBAWI).

Today, Colgate executives explain that they are always looking for diversification. "But, the targets are very narrow. It must be within the lines of business or only slightly expanding the lines of business that we do today. Except for the pet food business, that means exclusively cleaning products. Clean your hair, clean your skin, clean your clothes, clean your floors, and clean your teeth."[10] Colgate-Palmolive's WBAWI is simple: it is the "keep clean" company.

SINGER: HASTE IN DETERMINING WBAWI, REPENT AT GREAT EXPENSE

Singer offers lessons in hasty diversification that rival those presently experienced by Corning. In 1963, fearful of the continually declining sewing machine sales, Singer undertook a program of massive diversification. While the plan seemed to be an effective strategy at first as Singer reduced its sewing machine revenues from 90 percent to 35 percent, a closer examination and time proved that panic diversification is a disastrous strategic move. Singer's debt skyrocketed (see Chapter 7), and it was unable to manage effectively the various businesses involved in office equipment, calculators, gas meters, defense electronics, aerospace, home building, printing, telecommunications, and household appliances.

The 1975 write-off of many of these businesses totaled $411 million and reduced Singer's book value by 50 percent. This instability followed by a refocus on aerospace products resulted in Singer's spin-off due to virtually bottomless debt and a stock price that facilitated a takeover. That takeover, by Paul Bilzerian, was a disaster for shareholders and resulted in Bilzerian's conviction for fraud. Singer's fate is a story of near failure caused by panic diversification. Furthermore, Singer has been unable to shake the impact of Bilzerian. Its Chapter 11 fate in 1999 is indicative of the decades-long struggle it has faced in its diversification recovery.

PENNWALT: WBAWI MEANS A KNOWLEDGE-BASED WBAWI

While Pennwalt did an excellent job of defining its business not as a salt company but as a chemicals processor, it did not do as well with diversification outside of chemical processing. In the 1960s, Pennwalt began a program for new product expansion growth and acquired two health care concerns, Dental Manufacturing and Wallace and Tiernan. Pennwalt was in a PPG mode on this one. It is the kind of head scratcher we use in business schools to buoy the students' spirits when they seem overwhelmed by the demands of strategic analysis. Most can see the lack of analysis in the decision.

In this acquisition, Pennwalt was purchasing firms involved in chemical production and sales; so there was some logic. However, health care was an area in which Pennwalt had no experience. When the management teams of these newly acquired companies grew thin, Pennwalt lacked the depth and experience for running its newly acquired businesses. These acquisitions and the resulting debt also made Pennwalt an attractive takeover target, and Pennwalt's plunging stock price brought in the raiders.

This one misstep in WBAWI forever changed the company and saw it come to an end as it was absorbed during the 1980s (see Chapter 3 for more details on the complex acquisitions involved). A company that had been a leader in international expansion now saw itself acquired by an international conglomerate. Just a tad more adherence to its strength might have us seeing a different Pennwalt today.

GENERAL ELECTRIC'S WALL STREET WBAWI MOSEY

The most aggressive of the fifteen companies in terms of diversification was General Electric. When GE relied on the products it developed in its research laboratories, its diversification went from medical imaging to Lexan plastics. Sticking to its strength in the creation, transmission, and use of electricity, GE enjoyed success in its expansions into electrical generation, consumer products, and even in the financing of those diversifications.

When GE drifted from its WBAWI, it had near-catastrophic results. GE was a failure in computers, robotics, and semiconductors. Its foray into investment banking with Kidder Peabody resulted in international press coverage of a scandal and the resulting sale of the firm at a $600 million loss. The irony about the Kidder Peabody scandal is the embarrassing lack of management oversight with the investment firm. During GE's ownership, a young Harvard MBA, Joseph Jett, was able to find and abuse a glitch in Kidder's internal accounting system that permitted him to book as sales the simple act of bond and strip trades that are more akin to a bank giving change. Giving a customer four quarters for a dollar is not a revenue transaction, but Jett was able to book such bond and strips swaps as such under Kidder's system. The result was that Kidder's earnings skyrocketed. Joseph Jett was responsible for 20 percent of Kidder's bond section income and the bond section income rose from 7 percent of Kidder's income to 37 percent when Jett was made head of the bond department. Jett's bonus for one year was $9 million.

GE had invested over $1 billion in Kidder Peabody and had just begun to see a return on that investment when Jett was hired in 1991. In fact, GE was trying to find a buyer in 1992 when Jett appeared to be single-handedly turning the company around and providing GE with the returns it needed.

As a management and ethical debacle, the events at Kidder Peabody during Jett's time there are unsurpassed in their instructive quality. Other traders saw the problem. One who questioned Jett's earnings was fired. Another who questioned his results was told to work harder and was eventually fired.

When Jett's pseudo earnings were uncovered by outside auditors in 1994, GE had to take a $210 million write-down in one quarter. Subsequent reviews and investigations revealed that managers either turned a blind eye or did not understand the complexity of the system or the booking of the bond trades. Former SEC official Gary Lynch noted in his report that it was not enough to know that employees were making money, "You have to understand *how* people are making money."[11] Eventually, GE sold its Kidder Peabody investment to Paine Webber at a $917 million loss, taking another $500 million in one quarter to cover the loss. GE's income dropped 48 percent in one quarter as a result. Half of the Kidder Peabody employees were terminated following the acquisition.

In subsequent reports on the Jett era, many noted how complex the issues in the case were and how difficult it had been for auditors to get their arms around the issue. However, most of those providing commentary on the case noted that knowledgeable securities professionals with the right set of values could have halted the Jett bond activities within the first quarter of their occurrence. However, GE was relying on outsiders for management and did not have the internal depth for this type of acquisition. The investment in Kidder in an attempted diversification was a financial and public relations disaster for GE.

Since the time of these failures, GE has regrouped and put parameters around its diversification: If we cannot be number one or two in a new market, there is no competitive advantage to continuing the diversification. When Jack Welch took over GE, he bought 338 businesses and product lines for $11.1 billion and sold 232 of GE's businesses for $5.9 billion. Welch has played the role of buckling down the GE WBAWI to those things GE does better than the rest.

P&G: A GE MISTAKE

Procter & Gamble had its GE financial world embarrassment when it dabbled in the highly risky, highly leveraged derivatives market. P&G was out of its genre, and it incurred substantial losses ($157 million), which resulted in its suit against Bankers Trust and a P&G shareholder derivative action that challenged the wisdom of these ventures into such a risky proposition for a company lacking the internal controls for such risk management.[12] In fact, it was the P&G extensive losses that became the last straw for the American Institute of Certified Public Accountants and SEC, and resulted in new FASB rules on the reporting and disclosure of derivatives and other high-risk investments that are now a routine part of annual reports and 10Ks. Following the P&G derivatives adventure, the most common question at shareholder meetings in 1994 was, "What derivative exposure does this company have?"[13] There was a palpable loss of trust on the part of shareholders of P&G as well as other companies such as Gibson Greetings that were drawn into derivatives whether by attempts to maximize earnings or unwittingly by investment houses and rogue employees.

DIVERSIFICATION IS NOT A CURE-ALL: GENERAL MILLS

General Mills did have a period of odd and enormous diversification between 1950 and 1976. Cash rich, General Mills acquired 86 companies during this period, including Talbot's, Eddie Bauer, Gorton's, Kenner

Toys, Izod, Monet Jewelry, Red Lobster, Olive Garden, Good Earth Restaurants, and Wallpapers to Go. However, 73 percent of these acquisitions were divested within five years of being acquired. The companies brought results, but General Mills divested to avoid forthcoming slumps and other problems. Furthermore, the expansive range of companies often proved too diverse for General Mills WBAWI strengths.

Since 1976, General Mills has divested itself of nearly fifty businesses. The company spun off those divisions that did not focus on consumer food products such as the chemical business or were not in its area of expertise such as Wallpapers to Go. The toy companies (Kenner, Rainbow, and Parker Bros.) and restaurants (Red Lobster and Olive Garden) were spun off to the shareholders in the 1980s. The result was a company more focused on its strength of consumer foods and a company better postured to tailor its products to meet consumer needs and trends. General Mills has returned to what CEO Charles H. Bell, who took over in 1952, said was the strength of General Mills, "Any and all products that travel the avenue to the home."[14] General Mills was back to what it did best: consumer foods.

In 2000, General Mills announced what may be one of its best WBAWI moves in a century—the acquisition of Pillsbury. Pillsbury had its stodgy side with Progresso soups, but it also has that brand recognition for consumer foods in the form of the Pillsbury doughboy. General Mills knows brand recognition and how to make food products convenient and hip for today's consumer—the one who wants to multitask and use only one hand to eat. Pillsbury has always had quality but has had a tough time with keeping up with the consumer pulse. Once again, the combination goes right to the strengths of General Mills.

COCA-COLA: NOT RUINING A GOOD THING

Coca-Cola perhaps had the greatest faux pas of the fifteen companies when it attempted to change the formula for Coca-Cola and introduced New Coke in 1992. It was a failure for Coke because it did not understand the strength of its unique formula and the customer loyalty associated with it. It was almost as if customers resented the company for even trying the ill-fated experiment. Sheer hooting caused the product's withdrawal. On the ten-year anniversary of Coke's ill-fated messing around with "The real thing," then-CEO Roberto C. Goizueta noted, "Some people second guess everything the Coca-Cola Company does. History and hindsight require no vision. You only stumble when you're moving."[15] Coca-Cola uses the anniversary each year for self-deprecation, financial press, and motivation for employees to not take things so seriously. At the tenth anniversary of the demise of New Coke, employees were treated to a scene from *The Simpsons* in which four hobos discuss their downfalls. One of them is the inventor of New Coke. The cartoon was followed by a montage of video on New Coke's unveiling to the tune of R.E.M.'s *It's the End of the World As We Know It (And I Feel Fine)*. The session finished off with the lesson of this WBAWI mistake: Pleasing consumers is important, and Coca-Cola's market value has increased since that time as it realized that it had a customer-pleasing product.

Interestingly, Coca-Cola had planned Diet Coke with lemon, an idea that has come to them through customer habits. Marketing studies have shown consumers are fond of putting lemons into their Diet Cokes as a means of adding a little snap to the taste. Coca-Cola now proceeds with its second form of Diet Coke, although it is not a substitute.

THE MISSED OPPORTUNITIES—THE IGNORED REFINEMENT OPPORTUNITY

There were occasions in which the firms missed opportunities for diversification because the answers they had formulated to the WBAWI question were too narrow. Scovill referred to its pass on the opportunity to acquire George Eastman's business in 1890 and expand into photography as a "mistake."[16] Its struggle with the cyclical nature of brass motivated diversification, but the venture into photography required a level of capital that company executives labeled "too risky."[17] That delicate balance often produced a "road not taken" effect. Among these companies, error seemed to fall on the side of caution with a great respect for the company's self-imposed debt levels and limits (see Chapter 9).

WBAWI WORKS GLOBALLY

Colgate-Palmolive has perhaps been the best example of the fifteen companies of how WBAWI applies globally. In fact, Colgate believes that its early international expansion saw it through economic cycles in the United States. Colgate-Palmolive built its international presence with knowledge built literally from the ground up. For example, Colgate has a strong market in India. The reason is simple. When it entered that market 60 years ago, it did so with salespeople on the ground learning the territory, the culture, the people, and the stores. Colgate sent out salespeople with suitcases full of Colgate-Palmolive products and told them to have at it. They returned with empty suitcases but a head full of information on how to sell Colgate-Palmolive products in India. Their acquisitions, following the Helena Rubinstein debacle and others, followed the simple suitcase model—do we know how to sell this product and do we understand the territory where it is being sold?

Colgate has been in Mexico, Brazil, Thailand, Malaysia, and the United Kingdom for over half a century and watches in awe as the rest of the companies "go global." Colgate has been there and done that long before the term "global" became part of business studies and strategies. These companies always saw the world as their oyster, from Pennwalt's initial agreement with Denmark for importation to Singer's infiltration of the world with sewing machines, understood that people have needs to be met, and designed and delivered products to do just that, wherever the people may be.

In its 1901 annual report, Diamond Match reflected a similar global expansion as part of its WBAWI.

> Our progress in England has been very satisfactory. The trade of 1899 increased over that of 1898 by ten per cent and the trade of 1900 increased over that of 1899 by 40 per cent. It would seem possible for The Diamond Match Company, Limited, of England, to take the entire English trade in time. The English Company owns a majority of stock in two factories in South Africa.
>
> The factory in Peru, in South America, is in successful and profitable operation.
>
> The factory in Germany is just starting, and we hope for good results after it has passed the formative period, which all factories must undergo.[18]

UNIVERSAL WBAWI: BUILDING STRENGTH FROM WITHIN

While diversification was a key to long-term success, it was not undertaken at the expense of an internal focus on quality and manufacturing efficiency. All of these firms were in the business of manufacturing a quality product efficiently. Their focus was not just on the world around them and where things were headed, but on their internal worlds and what could be done to improve everything from production to distribution.

When The Stanley Works originally answered the WBAWI question, it perceived itself as a quality manufacturer: Build them well in production, and they will sell. As a result, Stanley developed a never-ending obsession with production, and maintaining consistent quality became a Stanley focus and trademark.

As a result of its definition of strength in manufacturing, The Stanley Works survived and grew in its earlier years because of "Yankee ingenuity," among other reasons, applied to manufacturing. Outstanding technicians constantly made innovations in both process and product. Innovative mastery of basic metal processes yielded better and new products. For example, in the 1870s, Stanley found better methods of cold rolling of wrought iron strip; in the 1880s, it developed a "softer" steel; in 1889, it patented a hinge with ball bearings; and in 1931, its production refinement yielded the first "Magic Eye"—activated operation of a door by a photoelectric cell.

Stanley's manufacturing focus resulted in the development of the skill of rapid response in improving the production process. For example, plagued by foreign competition, the president of The Stanley Works reasserted a company strength of refining and improving production.

> Japan was taking the entire hinge market away from us. They were shipping hinges to the West Coast at half the prices that we could produce them. We made an agonizing decision that we were going to stay in the hinge business, and we hired some very expensive engineers that were very creative, and we said that we want you to mechanize our hinge production and take all the labor out of it. You put coil steel in one end and get a package of hinges out of the other. That is what we did. We took virtually all of the labor out of it. We became the low-cost producer, and today Japan is out of the hinge business; we beat them at their own game. Now, in hand tools we were lucky. In Japan they use tools differently. They pull them toward—like chisels, planes, and saws—instead of pushing them away. So they design them differently, and Japan never really got in the world market with their hand tools. That is just luck.[19]

Stanley once again concluded that its business was tools, and it could compete on the basis of quality if its costs were reduced (see Chapter 6). Once again, Stanley refined its process and was able to cut costs and meet foreign import prices head-on—quality at the same price was their selling point. Stanley also capitalized on its reputation for quality by adding products, its first foray into consumer relations.

Scovill was a manufacturer at heart. Company records, brokerage reports, and other historical documents, especially those that focus on the 1802–1920 period, emphasize the firm's manufacturing orientation. Although J. M. L. Scovill, one of the founders, was himself a true "Yankee Peddler," he concentrated on manufacturing efficiencies and innovations, that is, the process, as the primary source for generating profits. In more modern parlance, Scovill, like the other centenarians, believed that manufacturing refinements and cost reductions were key links in a strategy for survival.

THE OPPOSITE DIRECTION: DIVESTITURE TO PRESERVE WAWIB AND WBAWI

Willingness to divest to preserve the goal of "making money" is also a critical element of WBAWI. Illusory manufacturing and marketing goals happen to the best of the best. But among these fifteen centenarians was the skill of knowing when to fold. Since its inception in 1802, the Scovill Company had been connected with the brass business. By 1975, however, it became apparent that even a preeminent position in that business could not provide sufficient margins for capital expansion in metals nor for necessary diversification. Even as a low-cost producer, Scovill's future in brass was not promising. Consequently, Scovill management persuaded the Board of Directors to assume what seemed to some a horrendous risk—divestiture of the brass business. Scovill sold the brass portion of its business, continued its diversification into home-related products, including safety and protection devices, and continued with consistent dividends.

Perhaps most telling about this divestiture was the board's reminder to Malcolm Baldridge about the stewardship owed the community where Scovill had its roots and where a large degree of economic dependency had developed. Baldridge struck a compromise with the board by (1) agreeing to find a local buyer for the business; (2) arranging for financing for the purchase; and (3) securing a promise from the buyer of continued use of local labor. The preservation of goodwill was critical for the board and a demonstration of stewardship toward both shareholder and community.

Tenacity is an Achilles heel when it comes to the WBAWI question. You cannot ignore business reality in the name of tradition. Interestingly, although these fifteen companies were steeped in tradition, they still seemed willing to examine their very cores when answering the WBAWI question. When they hung with tradition, they suffered. The Pullman Company refused to jettison a liability, the railroad passenger car part of its enterprise. Some directors, high-bound by traditions, would not yield to the president's pleas for deletion of this cash-draining division. The board tied the hands of the officers who wanted to move to cut it loose because the board focused only on present earnings and the bottom line and its fear of the reaction of the press and Wall Street. The failure to focus on WBAWI and not tradition meant a lost opportunity for carving away a loss source. The cashdrain of the railroad passenger car portion of the business should have been eliminated. But the board's refusal demonstrated a lack of timing that eventually caused stock market prices to fall so low that Pullman was taken over in 1980 by Wheelabrator-Frye, Inc., a much smaller firm. While the Pullman board had encouraged diversification into construction, the Trailmobile business, and several other industries complementary to Pullman's expertise, it failed to recognize the critical value of being in business to make money, not to preserve sentiment. It took an interruption in dividends before Pullman divested itself of its railroad car business.

Singer felt with its spin-offs of its furniture businesses and in 1986, the sewing machine company itself, that it was redefining WBAWI. But Singer had abandoned its market presence and strength with the divestitures. The result was that by 1995, Singer was reacquiring its furniture businesses as well as foreign sewing machine manufacturing companies such as Pfaff. Burdened by debt and takeover pressure, Singer, perhaps more so than any of the other companies, lost its bearings during the 1980s. It seemed to shift with the winds, and that strong presence has not yet been regained. A 1995 *New York Times* piece outlined the holes in Singer's financial picture, including one-time gains, lack of management vision, and too much debt (see Chapter 5).[20]

PPG has perfected the art of divestiture. With its eye on product successes, competition, and costs, PPG has divested effectively in all of its divisions in a timely and appropriate fashion. Its chemical division divested itself of the Columbia Cement Company and its related synthetic soda ash operations as no longer compatible with the strengths and market presence of PPG. While PPG had diversified in the 1800s from a glass company to a raw materials source, it continually reevaluated the various raw materials and their divisions, and was prepared to sell or end, on a timely basis, products and divisions not compatible with its vision of WBAWI.

Diversification as a raw materials supplier had brought PPG to fiberglass and fiberglass insulation. However, the weaving of fiber into fiberglass also brought further diversification into the weaving of tire cord and yarn. When sales of tire cord and yarn surpassed those of fiberglass, PPG sold off its insulation production and began innovations in the tire cord market.

The Stanley Works offers a unique perspective among the firms in that divestiture has not been necessary. While it has been active in diversification, Stanley has apparently enjoyed remarkable success in the fit and results of those acquisitions.

General Electric was the master of rapid divestiture among these fifteen firms. Never has GE been slow to divest, particularly when it diversified precipitously. Because GE strives for an atmosphere of entrepreneurship, it has had diverse product lines and acquisition, but it quickly spun off those areas in which it could not become a market leader, such as in computers. It was also known to divest when there was too much negative publicity, such as when it withdrew from nuclear power plan development and removed itself from the transmission market due to antitrust concerns. As noted earlier, Wall Street proved disastrous and GE spun off Kidder Peabody in the heat of the Joseph Jett scandal.

Coke-Cola had successfully invested in Columbia Pictures for an acquisition price of $2.2 billion, but it did not have the depth for management of a motion picture studio and was forced to sell Columbia for $3.4 billion, a $1.2 billion gain in just a few years. Coca-Cola divested just before the movie studios encountered substantial losses in the 1990s.

General Mills has a WBAWI divestiture that perhaps says it all when it comes to jettisons in order to get back to business strengths. In 1961, when Edwin Rawlings became CEO, he divested General Mills of all of its unprofitable business lines, which included electronics. This side road into appliances, begun in the 1940s, was the only outright business failure of General Mills. James S. Bell, who along with one of his heirs, Charles H. Bell, had begun a long period of diversification of General Mills, saying that the idea was to have General Mills "travel the avenue" to the home. As a result, General Mills entered into the locomotive, appliances, electronics, and chemical manufacturing businesses. None of them were ever profitable, and Rawlings unloaded them all to firms with far more experience than General Mills in these areas.

Still, there was a great deal of shareholder and employee consternation over the divestitures because the effect was that General Mills lost over $200 million in sales. However, the cash from the sale of these appliance businesses enabled General Mills to enter its era of refocus on consumers, convenience, and food. General Mills used some of the proceeds from the sales to acquire Tom's Snack Foods, Gorton's, Red Lobster, and Yoplait.

Procter & Gamble is presently shedding its noncore brands. For example, the abrasive and nonabrasive tub and tile cleaner market is shrinking dramatically. As a result, P&G has sold off Spic 'n Span. The sale of Comet, its century-old cleanser product, is pending. Other non-core brands that have been shed include Biz laundry detergent, Cinch baking products, and Oxydol cleaners.[21]

We offer the same thoughts in this WWEBS (will we ever be satisfied?) chapter as we did in the WBAWI chapter for P&G. As it makes these radical cuts, it needs to think more surgically and less about amputation. The cuts do not follow a pattern, and while spinning off to preserve WBAWI is good, spinning off WBAWI deprives the company of its strengths and defenses against cyclical storms. P&G is at risk for doing too much, too quickly, and without a discernible pattern of WBAWI. Bending to the whims of a demanding street often proves disastrous. Corning went too far into one field and the results were dismal. P&G seems to be at risk for not understanding which field, it will preserve.

Presently, P&G is struggling to emerge from a period of flat sales. Its since ousted CEO, Durk Jager, may have had the correct take on how it got into a defensive posture, "We've spent too much time playing not to lose. That breeds complexity and conservatism. We were penalizing losing more than we were rewarding winning."[22] Perhaps the better question and the real issue for Procter & Gamble is: Define winning.

Tell us what you want us to win at, and we can take it from there. The ill-defined WBAWI perplexes and confounds P&G executives, employees, and analysts. Still struggling, P&G sold Jif peanut butter to J. M. Smucker in October 2001, as well as its Crisco. However, in announcing the deal, P&G indicated that the sale is part of a new strategic refocus that will see it shed all of its food brands and focus exclusively on cleaning and hygiene products. Furthermore, P&G has indicated it wants only global brands, such as its Pampers, Tide, and Crest, and Crisco and Jif were simply North American brands.[23] Yet, almost simultaneously, P&G and Coca-Cola announced that they were no longer going through with their joint venture for international distribution of snacks and beverages.[24] The WBAWI question for P&G is not answered with clarity as yet, and the differing directions of decisions perhaps reflect that uncertainty.

In none of the firms was successful acquisition perceived as a magical wand, which when waved would guarantee success; rather, success resulted from intimate knowledge of both the supply and demand sides of a company's particular industry and markets. Success in one field does not ensure glory in another, that is, it was not diversification through acquisition, per se, that was the guarantee of security or the common thread among the nine firms. It was the nature of these acquisitions that provided the commonality among the firms.

These companies learned the lessons of diversification, acquisition, and divestiture that businesses today should heed. Begin with the fundamental WBAWI question with an eye on WAWIB and couple it with a realistic assessment of ability in both management and capital. The lessons amid processes for diversification through acquisition and divestiture are summarized in Figure 8.1, below.

THE WBAWI EXERCISE IS NOT A DEFENSIVE ONE

Panic in answering the WBAWI question can be costly. Because of measured reasoning at each juncture, these companies had very few dramatic swings in focus with resulting errors, costs, or abandonment of strengths. To the extent they were dramatic swings, they were quickly

1. **What business are we in?**
2. **How does this relate to our core business?**
3. **Do we have the management expertise?**
4. **What will this acquisition do to our capital structure?**
5. **When is it time to cut loose?**

Figure 8.1. The diversification/divestiture philosophy.

self-corrected. If, for example, Stanley had followed some current management mantras, one cannot help but wonder whether they would still be selling tools. These firms were not reckless, but they never sat still. They were not reactive, nor overreactive. They, their markets, and their products evolved continually but at a measured pace and because of predefined patterns of consumer demand, needs, and product development. Pennwalt's CEO summarized the WBAWI philosophy: "We have to accept what we all know to be elemental—that taking a defensive position can, at best, only limit losses. And we need gains."[25] The motto at General Mills headquarters, placed there during the 1930s: "Facts, not opinions." General Mills still follows this motto in everything from its marketing studies to feedback on sales and makes it decisions accordingly with an ongoing fact-gathering machine.

A PPG executive described its WBAWI exercise as one of constant review of where they are, in both directions.

> While PPG has always stuck to its knitting, it has also always evolved into new businesses, into new practices, i.e., no repotting. We have had backwards integration, have always looked for common interests within the company and with customers and suppliers.[26]

Johnson Controls executives described their ongoing innovation as resulting from their realization that while they were staying "with the curve," they were not "ahead of the curve." At that point, they began to encourage and reward engineers for the development of new products.

In answering the WBAWI question, long-term success requires innovation with an eye toward the world in all directions and an accompanying nimbleness in response. In their continual reevaluation of their answers to WBAWI, these companies defied current popular models of a firm's evolution. They were never far from the manufacturing process in reexamination of what could be made better. They were problem-solvers before other companies saw a problem. At once, they were refining markets, marketing, and production. In some cases, they pulled the market through consumers.

In response to competition and technological innovation, these fifteen companies shifted functional emphasis from manufacturing to marketing, to financial, and to research. They managed these functions as interdependent, not discrete, activities; they did not become "marketing oriented" at the expense of another activity; and they did not succumb to current business fads in management. A shift in strategy did not require downgrading or negligence of a function. They demonstrated that a firm could be both "marketing oriented" and "manufacturing oriented."

The lesson of longevity that emerges from WBAWI is that these companies thrived on change and reinvention. It was as if they were unimpressed with their own achievements. They had a Charles Schwab-like philosophy: We broke records yesterday, but what have we done today? Babe Ruth had a similar stewardship: "Yesterday's home runs don't count in today's ball game." A long-term culture of innovation is born of input and study of all the players in business, tangible and otherwise. For example, 55 percent of Colgate-Palmolive's products sold today were launched as new products in the last five years. Colgate spends 1.9 percent of sales on R and D and .5 to 1 percent of sales on market research. Sometimes the R and D is not sophisticated but is rather a response to market demand. Colgate's "Total" toothpaste is a highly successful product that Colgate developed in the lab after learning that consumers were frustrated with not being able to get all the new toothpaste features in one type of toothpaste. There were whitening toothpastes and tartar control toothpastes, but consumers wanted to use only one brand of toothpaste. A little tinkering in the laboratory and Colgate produced one toothpaste—Total—that had whitening and tartar control. The consumers expressed the desire, and R and D just made the product happen.

These fifteen companies underwent transformations in image as a result of the expansion of their product base. Their expansions were gradual through slight modifications in product lines, product resources, and product marketing. The result of their continual but gradual evolution was additional stability despite ongoing economic and social transformation. In fact, they follow transformation as a source for new products. For example, P&G, showing some of its fervor from its founding days, has dispatched 80 video crews with three-way cameras to homes around the world to tap into life's everyday and boring routines to see if P&G is meeting consumers' needs and what consumer life is really like. P&G has come to realize that consumer focus groups, interviews, and home visits are not the most reliable sources of information because, well, people lie. "They might say, for example, that they brush their teeth every morning or indulge in just a few potato chips when in fact, they often forget to brush and eat the whole bag."[27]

When watching one videotape of a woman in Thailand making breakfast, Procter & Gamble executives learned the following: (1) the woman does it all with one hand; (2) the baby is always rested on her hip; and (3) she watches television as she does both. From this videotape they learn what General Mills has learned about the lifestyle with one hand—the multitasking society. The reason they are watching homes in Thailand is because 98 percent of U.S. homes have P&G products, but only one-third of the world is acquainted with them. The global transformation is P&G's goal, and it expects to boost sales by 2.5 percent with this international expansion. P&G is amassing a full collection of videotapes so that anyone in the company can view the lifestyles of families anywhere in the world.

These companies also continue to revisit their relationships within their two-direction vision. P&G has long been heavily dependent on advertising agencies for the successful dissemination of product information. However, like other companies, P&G has been compensating ad agencies on a commission basis. The agency earns on the basis of ads placed. P&G canned that system in 1999 and tied advertising agency compensation to sales objectives set for the agency in advance. Not only was it a first for P&G in terms of modifying its ad agency relationships, but it was also a first in the industry.[28]

WBAWI AND RISK

There was a remarkable balance in these companies that never hesitated to take on risk, both in product and process. To be too conservative at various times would have been fatal to the company. On the other hand, to move too quickly into markets or products could have been disastrous. They were not risk averse, but they were not inclined to make leveraged bets. Furthermore, they understood that drastic steps sometimes alienate customers. Johnson Controls adopted a policy of introducing change gradually and incrementally. There was change coupled with customer acceptance. Johnson Controls nudged the customers along with each innovation and each new expansion of its role in climate management.

Their risk factor was tempered by their sensitivity to debt (see Chapter 9), and so their risk exercise was one that was necessarily financial. Colgate-Palmolive has described its risk posture as a function of sound financial management and capital budgeting. Patrick described the Colgate risk as follows:

> Yes, we take risks in the businesses we are in, but we won't take risks in the financial markets, and because of our heavy global requirements we will not take unrealistic financial risks in our hedging activities. Its like poker—you might be willing to lose your ante as long as you place your bets on informed judgments, but to extend your risks beyond that conservative stance is just plain reckless. You must operate so that there is a cushion between the cost of capital and what you can generate. Anything less is what constitutes risk. However, each market is different and the risk must reflect our judgment of what that market can develop.[29]

PPG eschewed the risky derivatives market many companies, including P&G, fell into. "We did not see where such investments truly created any value or value beyond the obvious risk."[30]

Stanley's Merriam also reflected on the financial aspects of risk.

> I think of it as risk-taking in the sense that it involves two things it seems to me: the imaginative approaches to a business development and the ability and willingness to commit capital to those projects. In today's business world one of the areas I think of as being entrepreneurial opportunities are in modern concepts of marketing. At the Stanley Works, for instance, the entrepreneurial contribution has been in just that area and in applying marketing ability on the part of The Stanley Works in the hardware and tool businesses. The conceptual idea of the do-it-yourself market and the exploitation of that market is an outstanding example of a type of entrepreneurial effort.
>
> I suppose another area in today's world, which is so important to many companies and I think of it as not as creative as we would like to have it, is the ability to seek out acquisitions and the entrepreneurial effort that goes into that. It requires perhaps another aspect and that is the careful and correct analysis of the profit opportunities that exist. Sometimes it is just a matter of employing capital, perhaps an older company that has established a pretty strong cash flow but can't use that capital in the development of its own markets maybe for reasons of obsolescence as far as their own products are concerned and they have to reemploy that capital in some other businesses.[31]

One Scovill executive described one risk that Scovill took in modified fashion.

> Oh, yes, they did make mistakes. I can remember myself—I have been here since 1948—meeting in the old offices there with the people from the Polaroid Company who wanted Scovill to be their sole supply for all their cameras, including the repair of the cameras. I was sitting there with our credit man at that time, his name was Homer Senior, and of course, Professor Land and the Polaroid Company just had absolutely no money, nothing, so Scovill would have to really bankroll the entire project. So Homer Senior talked to the president who at that time was Len Sperry. Mr. Sperry said Scovill would act as a subcontractor to somebody who wants to manufacture. But, the company would not undertake the risk of acting as banker or prime contractor.[32]

These were tempered risk-takers who made informed judgments and about remained cautious about the need for a budget cushion, a cushion that helped them not just meet the dividends, but also survive during economic cycles.

THE FINAL LOOK AT WBAWI

Figure 8.2 depicts generically the WBAWI question and the limitless possibilities of refocus when companies never stop asking and answer-

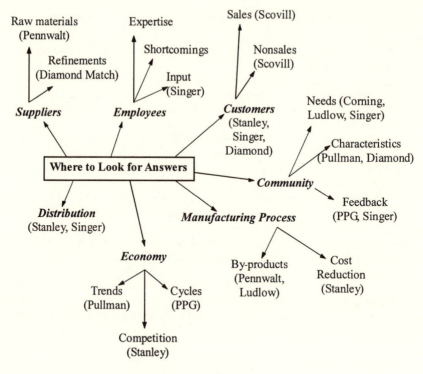

Figure 8.2. WBAWI and two-direction vision.

ing that question. Entrepreneurial growth continues throughout the company history when WBAWI reigns. After a review of the questions and individual schematics, a pattern emerges: look at the economy, look at distribution, revise manufacturing, check the supply side, rely on employees, and know thy customer and his world.

NOTES

1. Grossman, Colgate-Palmolive interviews, D. Davis interview.

2. Leonhardt, David, "Corning Reports $4.76 Billion Loss, Citing Write-Offs," *New York Times*, July 26, 2001: C5.

3. Norris, Floyd, "Disaster at Corning: At Least the Balance Sheet is Strong," *New York Times*, July 13, 2001: C1.

4. Jones, Del, "Old Company Learns New Tricks," *USA Today*, April 10, 2000: 1B.

5. Deutsch, Claudia H., "The Horse and Cart, In Order," *New York Times*, January 17, 2001: 3-1, 3-12.

6. Aeppel, Timothy, "Corning Buys Oak Industries, a Maker of Laser Gear, for $1.8 Billion in Stock," *Wall Street Journal*, November 15, 1999: A6.

7. John J. Dempsey interview, Pittsburgh, Pennsylvania, June 6, 1996.

8. Ibid.

9. Grossman interviews.

10. Ibid.

11. Nasar, Sylvia, "Kidder Scandal Tied to Failure of Supervision," *New York Times*, August 5, 1994: A1, C3.

12. *Drage v. Procter & Gamble*, 1997 WL 133381 (Oh. App. 1997).

13. Antilla, Susan, "P & G See Charge on Derivatives," *New York Times*, April 13, 1994: C1, C16.

14. Charles Bell interview.

15. "Coca-Cola Recalls, with a Laugh, New Coke," *Arizona Republic*, April 11, 1995: B1.

16. George Goss—Louis Grossman Interview.

17. Ibid.

18. Diamond Match Annual Report, 1901.

19. Davis interview—Louis Grossman.

20. Gorham, John, "The Wrecking of Singer," *Forbes*, November 15, 1999: 66–68.

21. "Procter & Gamble Is Considering Sale of Its Comet Brand." *Wall Street Journal*, July 3, 2001: A6.

22. Farrell, Greg, "Impatient P&G Ousts Jager," *USA Today*, June 9, 2000, B1, B2.

23. Nelson, Emily, and Devon Spurgeon, "It's A Natural: P&G Sells Jif to J.M. Smucker," *Wall Street Journal*, October 11, 2001: B1, B12.

24. McKay, Betsey, and Emily Nelson, "Coke and P&G End Plans to Form Venture for Their Juices and Snacks," *Wall Street Journal*, September 27, 2001: B4.

25. Leavitt, R. K., *Prologue to Tomorrow*, Philadelphia: The Pennsylvania Salt Manufacturing Company, 1950.

26. LeBeouf Interview—Louis Grossman.

27. Nelson, Emily, "P&G Checks Out Real Life," *Wall Street Journal*, May 17, 2001: B1, B4.

28. Elliot, Stuart, "P & G to Tie Agency Compensation to Sales," *New York Times*, September 15, 1999: C1, C6.

29. Grossman interviews.

30. Ibid.

31. Ibid.

32. Ibid.

9

Key #4: Priorities— What Will We Do and What Won't We Do for Results?

Better is a little with righteousness than great revenues without right.

Proverbs 16:8

Any worthwhile change in the conduct of a business must first and last have the element of lessening cost.

Cooper Procter

Just as these fifteen companies constantly visited what they needed to do to survive, they constantly engaged in self-examination to be certain their values were not compromised in the process. Within their cultures was the clear parameter of WWWD or What we will do and what we won't do to get there.

To avoid succumbing to greed and its powerful origins in the quick fix, these companies embraced five key values critical to long-term survival. Those values are low debt, low cost, high quality, a focus on the long term, and it is not our money: stewardship. One value often controlled another. For example, the reliance on employees for their input and efforts produced not only the input for WBAWI, but also the depth for management succession. These companies could grow managers from within because there was constant interaction among and between all levels of the companies.

Throughout their archives, executive speeches and company materials reflect continuing statements about values. While we remain possessed of a healthy skepticism about company archives, we are satisfied that our third-party sources offer independent verification of the values we found reflected in the companies' own materials.

When asked how Procter & Gamble determined the right posture to take on particular issues, Howard Morgen said, "It wasn't that complicated once we had isolated the principles involved. There were really only two. The first is that Procter & Gamble obeys the law. The second is that we sell products that are safe for use under normal usage conditions."[1] When Ed Harness became CEO of P&G in 1971, he addressed the management group straightaway with this thought, "We are built on sound principles and practices and are not dominated by a group of individuals. Though our greatest asset is our people, it is the consistency of principle and policy which give us direction."[2]

Harness called values for a company "the art of finding principle." He noted that, "Making the hard decision, consistent with principle, usually involves two things—hard thinking by a disciplined mind and short-term sacrifice on the part of the company."[3] Harness reminded managers regularly of their obligation to seek out new employees in the company and acquaint them with P&G's value system. One example P&G uses to illustrate its commitment involves a decision on whether to pay a "facilitation" or "grease" payment to see that its diapers were unloaded after a shipment to a country in Africa. The government agent demanded $5,000, or he would not permit the diapers to be unloaded. The diapers were a legal product and had prior government approval for importation. However, this was a local official who was exercising his authority, and he refused to allow the diapers to enter the country for distribution and sale. P&G refused to pay the $5,000. The result was that sales were delayed, and the shipment sat there as P&G tried to resolve the issue another way. Why not just pay the $5,000 and begin earning the margins on the diapers that could then be sold immediately? Because P&G executives knew that this time it would be $5,000, but the next time it would be $10,000, and P&G preferred not to do business that way. There was the short-term cost of not being able to earn the money on the sales of those diapers. However, structured thinking helped executives and managers to realize the implications of their decision. P&G went to the central government and discussed with officials the need for diapers, the importance of the P&G presence there, and the long-term possibility of a P&G factory there (something that has since happened), and P&G's diapers entered the country without any premium to local officials as the central government stepped in and dealt with the corruption.

Value-based decision-making is very different from the expedient choices some companies make today. These values provide the frame for the formula for doing business outlined in previous chapters. These values, in effect, make decisions for the companies. They do not bend with the winds but rather remain a stable force of reason in these companies' plans, expansions, and strategies.

These values create in these companies an overall culture of camaraderie: we know why we are here, we know where we're going, we are in this together, and we don't pull any stunts to get where we are going. There is no feeling as you visit these firms of hand-wringing managers overwhelmed by strategic planning. There is a feeling that together the employees of these companies made decisions and then all signed on for the ride together with complete understanding of the plan of action and appreciation for the steadiness of the course ahead.

MAKING IT CLEAR UP FRONT: THESE ARE NOT SAINTS

It is critical to state at the outset that these companies were not ready for sainthood. Because both authors together have been involved in business ethics research and instruction for over half a century, we can state without equivocation that, on occasion, these companies pulled some scary stunts, in the ethics sense.

In order to clear the air, we listed examples in Chapters 5 and 6 that demonstrate humans ran these companies and that they made their shares of mistakes over the years. In addition to those examples, P&G recently agreed to pay Unilever $10 million to settle a suit that alleges P&G took documents out of the trash cans outside Unilever offices in Chicago.[4]

We know of no perfect humans nor firms. The list could go on as long as human beings run companies, for there will be mistakes in judgment. However, these companies are unique in their ability to recognize errors, self-correct, and return to the value system that has served them well for over one century. For example, Coca-Cola not only agreed to the EEOC settlement, but it has, by all accounts, including those of the regulators, gone the extra mile in changing the culture of its company in terms of diversity. Furthermore, P&G brought the case of the trash bin spying to the attention of Unilever and fired the three P&G employees who took the materials from Unilever's trash bins. Their ethics in the breach are exemplary—if their values are violated even by rogue employees, they take the necessary steps for compensation and correction. It is on these values that we focus our discussion.

VALUE #1: LOW DEBT

Among these hallmark companies a strange anomaly, a seeming contradistinction persisted. Managers were admonished not to shrink from assuming risk while at the same time they were reminded about the parameters of debt and other exposures. These companies eschewed debt. Throughout their cultures was the attitude that debt was a last resort financing strategy. If debt became necessary, the firm strove to retire the obligation as quickly as possible.

From 1908 to 1927, the Scovill Company reported in its "Statement of Condition" a column headed "Admitted Assets." A 1928 market analysis pointed out that the Scovill Company is "not a borrower" and that it always kept itself in position to pay cash to obtain discounts for their purchases. In another annual report, the president commented openly in the early 1920s that the cash account should be discounted because he anticipated there would be some inflation during the next two to three years. Conservative in their reporting standards, these companies painted an open, honest, and anticipatory picture of themselves each year.

The 1899 PPG annual report to stockholders reflected assets of $15.5 million and a debt of $3 million. Language within the report noted, "During the year our bonded debt has been reduced by $219,000 and the mortgage on our Ford City Property has been satisfied."[5] In 1958, PPG's long-term debt was 9.1 percent of its total capitalization, although this was the high point to date because its rate had hovered at 2.6 percent. By 1968, its ratio was 25 percent, and it now keeps that ratio at 32 percent.

One of the reasons for this low-debt mantra was the companies' great familiarity with risk and the business cycle. One of P&G's executives shared a story of a certain light-heartedness when P&G was facing the results of the 1929 crash. Orders were being canceled, and the company was reeling from the ripple effects of the fall of the stock market. When one of its larger customers came by with the bad news, one of the P&G officers told him, "You'll have to wait your turn; there are several cancellations ahead of you."[6]

However, fiscal conservatism occasionally collided with development and acquisition. As noted in Chapter 8, in 1948, the Polaroid Company approached Scovill to be its sole supplier for all cameras. The president turned down Professor Land's request because the company did not feel comfortable in undertaking the risk of acting as a banker for Land or as a prime contractor for the joint venture. The diversification decision was made not for the sake of preserving the value but in order to avoid too much debt exposure in a risky expansion.

Despite their respect for their positions as fiduciaries of shareholder wealth and an aversion to excessive risk, these companies still accepted risk as a part of their responsibility of maximizing shareholder wealth and undertook expansion programs that were fraught with peril, so long as the programs served the best interests of the shareholders and were well thought-out under WAWIB and WBAWI. These companies understood when expenditures and risk were needed.

Ludlow's officers described their roles in business by using the term "stewards" and viewed themselves as trustees assigned to protect stockholder interests. In their annual report for 1920, the directors pointed out that "the aim of the managers was to place the business in a liquid condition and in a position to withstand the period of readjustment through which the business world is now passing."[7]

Ludlow was willing to expend funds to construct new hydraulic power plants but did so in order to reduce annual energy costs. Still, Ludlow's working capital at the end of 1920, following construction of the plants, consisted of $8.1 million in current assets and $121,687 in current liabilities. This conservatism on debt exposure was not misplaced. For example, Ludlow's 1921 annual report reflects depressed worldwide jute prices, continuing unrest in India (partially led by Gandhi), and declining profit margins. These uncontrollable and often insurmountable external conditions did not faze Ludlow because of its low debt exposure. A cash payment philosophy prepared these companies for the turbulence of politics and economics.

For these companies, discretion was the better part of valor when it came to debt and risk. By all definitions, Pennwalt was one of the more fiscally conservative long-lived American firms. A profitmaker since 1856, in 1938 its president said,

> You cannot keep anything by trying to safeguard it from change; that is false conservatism, for it is the surest way to lose what you have . . . the only way you can really safeguard any undertaking committed to your trust is to keep it moving ahead.[8]

Coca-Cola enjoys an enviable position of a capitalization ratio of 47 percent debt and 53 percent equity. While General Electric has tended to carry greater debt load than its S&P counterparts, its return on equity is 2 percent higher, and its gross margins have exceeded both industry and S&P 500 by nearly 10 percent.

VALUE #2: LOW COST

Peter Drucker once noted that "pricing does not stand as a monolith." Pricing depends upon costs, and the mass markets that all these firms found as their competitive playgrounds required low prices. These firms met their competition and still limited debt through near obsession with controlling costs while maintaining high quality. Attention to manufacturing costs was a constant emphasis. Throughout all of their chronicles and records are repeated references to the need for low costs, if not the lowest costs, in the industry.

Scovill was a true cost-minimizer and used the technique of consolidating all product lines into one facility early in its existence. Consolidation was an often repeated cost strategy. In 1969, when it acquired Old Dominion Electric, it folded operations of that company into the Hamilton Beach facilities and cut costs. By 1971, Scovill had purchased Westinghouse Portable Appliances, a company struggling with the problems of extremely high overheads due to multiple plant operations that Scovill solved instantly with its refined consolidation skills.

The Stanley Works devotion to improvement of production techniques through capital investment even in the most difficult financial times established its tandem relationship of manufacturing and quality with cost. Stanley did not scrimp on manufacturing improvements, but those improvements ultimately reduced production cost. When the tool market shriveled due to the hard hits to manufacturing and construction during the Depression, Stanley managed to survive, largely due to its low costs. Furthermore, Stanley was not burdened by the debt service that proved the downfall of many firms facing reduced or no sales during the Depression. For example, Stanley had negative net income in 1932, but still had sufficient cash for dividends. While 1933 was a positive income year, 1934 was again a deficit year, but Stanley still made its dividends in all those years because both its debt service and costs were so low.[9]

At Colgate-Palmolive, employees have goals for reducing costs. CFO Stephen Patrick described the cost-cutting culture as follows.

> We budget people and we set our goals and we challenge ourselves on how we can take the waste out of the system. Taxes, interest, every line is a line to manage.[10]

Patrick of Colgate described Colgate's cost-reduction mode as one of shortening "the time from cash to cash." When Colgate began this cash-to-cash program, it was 153 days from the time of their outlay for suppliers and the manufacture of product until they saw cash for the sale of that product. That time has now been reduced to 75 days with the resulting increased cash flow as well as the use of the money for two times the number of days as before.

It did not escape our notice that downsizings have infiltrated even the culture of these companies that had traditionally avoided such cost reductions, even when new technology replaced jobs. For example, in 1997, Stanley cut 350 salaried workers and 450 other positions that the company said "reflect the company's decision to exit small underperforming businesses such as shoe-repair equipment and a line of generic fastening equipment."[11]

However, downsizings were the exception and not the rule and really not considered a tool of their cost-cutting cultures despite technological and production advances that would certainly warrant such reductions in the workforce. We conclude that these companies were so well positioned strategically and had such a culture of keeping costs low that "fat" never entered the picture. Like entrepreneurs pinching pennies and pitching in, these huge conglomerates retained a philosophy of every penny counts. The result was security of employment.

At Colgate, there was a modified approach to the cost-cutting motto. Their mantra was not managing the bottom line; it was managing "all 64 lines above the bottom line." Patrick gave a detailed example of how he managed the various lines that lead to the bottom line.

> One line pertains to margin. There are many, many projects related to accomplishing this margin. We put names on those projects driving up the margin. We put names on those projects and assign objectives to those names [persons] responsible for those projects and we use results for purposes of [their] compensation. Take another line, say, drive down the overhead. We budge people and we set our goals and we challenge ourselves on how we can take the waste out of the system and improve ourselves on an ongoing basis. There are others, say, quality in advertising. We must make sure that the advertising reaches the consumer in a way that they are going to intend to buy the product. Taxes, interest, every line is a line to manage.[12]

Diamond Match offered some interesting insights into cost cutting. Despite increasing sales, Diamond cut its sales force by 15 percent during 1927 with the result being that its sales force in 1927 was 55 percent of what it was in 1925. Interesting that a firm cuts costs while it is doing well. During the same period, the result was that the cost of making sales per unit volume was down 20 percent. When coupled with manufacturing cost reductions of 6 percent, this company had reduced costs by over one-fourth, all during a time of record sales.

Their keen attention to production, its costs, and the relationship with quality continues today. For example, Procter & Gamble was experiencing line shutdowns in its paper towel production plants too frequently. Often the shutdown rates exceeded 100 times per day. The company lost paper towels, time, and money. P&G brought in an engineering team to take a look at the production process and the equipment. The engineers focused on the machinery and the reliability problem. Following their recommendations, the shutdown rate plummeted so much that P&G estimates that it has saved over $2 billion in production costs and lost product since these 1990 changes. In fact, the quality system has worked so well that P&G is pursuing a joint venture with a software company in order to produce and sell the programs P&G used to realize such savings.[13]

Only creativity limited the methods for these firms' cost cutting. For example, it was in the midst of the early 1920s recession that P&G discovered a money-saving distribution method that also pleased its customers. In 1922, P&G began shipping cans of Crisco at more precise times so that they could arrive just as they were needed. By fine-tuning order processing, P&G cut storage time and shaved expenses. It was just-in-time delivery before its time. The Crisco tactic was then transferred to all areas of the company. Upon the implementation of this new efficiency in distribution, the following message was sent to the company's salesmen:

> We have been through the mill of reorganizing and refining for the past year and a half. We feel that the organization is shaped up well; we are in fighting trim and ready to go. . . . The company as a whole has cleared its decks, relieved itself of expensive operations, and is operating today on a basis closely approaching bottom. This means that we are in a position to give, and are giving, real value.[14]

VALUE #3: LOW COST IS NOT LOW QUALITY

When Thomas bought Coca-Cola from Asa Chandler in 1899, he made a promise that would forever change the founding company's destiny: "To make the name Coca-Cola better every day."[15] Coca-Cola's mantra of quality was not unique among the fifteen firms.

General Electric lists as one of its values, "Live quality and drive cost and speed for competitive advantage."[16] GE's Six Sigma program for quality is legendary not just for its reduction in production defects but its boost in profits. Sigma refers to a mark on a bell curve that measures standard deviation. The standard deviation for most companies is 35,000–50,000 defects per million operation, or 3 sigma. Defects range from forgotten bolts to misbillings of customers. In 1995, Jack Welch learned that GE was at 35,000 defects or the very low end of the corporate scale. Nonetheless, Welch began a program to get to 6 sigma, which means that defects can be only 3.4 per million. As of 1998, GE was at 3.5 per million. Anecdotes of specific quality changes abound.[17] One example centers around the tubes in GE's CAT scanners, a medical device for bone scans and other internal scans. The tubes in the scanners were lasting for 50,000–100,000 Xrays. The time for replacement was four hours. Four hours is a lot of downtime, a lot of patients, and a lot of lost revenue. Because of so many customers' complaints, GE sent in what Welch refers to as the "Six Sigma Black Belts" to examine the problem. The Six Sigma Black Belts focus on everything in solving the problem from design to materials to manufacture. In this case, the Sigma Black Belts found that they could lop off nine months from the process for developing new tubes. With the R and D time slashed, GE engineers have created new tubes with five times the previous life span, with the additional benefit of sharper photographs and images in the CAT scans. The Six Sigma approach reduces cost because defect-free tubes mean extra product capacity. The sigma findings in one area can be transferred to another. The CAT scan tube discoveries were transferred over to mammograms.

VALUE #4: THE TIME WARP: LONG-TERM BUSINESS SUCCESS OVER SHORT-TERM TANTRUMS

Businesses operate in two time dimensions, short term and long term. They accept the reality of the time horizon dilemma, the tug-of-war between demands of the immediate and the wisdom of long-run patience. But these companies handled the time warp in an effective way. The tension they experienced between long-term success and short-term performance pressures is best summarized by the dictum of Donald Davis, Chairman and CEO at The Stanley Works.

> Change under constant view is almost imperceptible. An executive can be so involved that he does not perceive change: or, his own interest can blind him from change. The dilemma is how to manage change when there is tension and conflict between short-term goals such as monthly results or quarter-per-share performance—versus pride in maintaining programs that will benefit the company over the next 5 to 10 to 15 years.[18]

Coca-Cola's mission statement begins, "We exist to create value for our share owners in a long-term basis. . . ."[19] The companies avoided situations in which management panicked also because their boards did not panic at the external environmental events. Both managers and their boards understood the requirements of patience and resources for adjustment and realignment under WBAWI. They did not support makeshift, ad hoc tactical leaps, which would jeopardize the company and its long-term survival.

Procter & Gamble was launched in 1847, a time of bank closings and general financial panic in the United States. Some even felt at that time that the United States was bankrupt. But P&G commenced business with a calm steadiness, for its concern was not the wailing about the looming crisis, but how to compete with fourteen other soap and candlemakers in Cincinnati. It did not succumb to the financial panic but kept its eye on the ball by producing quality products.

To avoid hasty changes in direction or falling victim to short-term solutions, executives in these hallmark companies looked, listened, and learned. Their very interaction with all those involved with the company was a unique way of visibly demonstrating their commitment. For example, at The Stanley Works, top corporate executives spend a great deal of their time in the field with division personnel, calling on customers and suppliers, and in the division plants, where they monitor production in order to participate meaningfully in the development of capital programs. All the Procters who worked at the company began their work there as common laborers in overalls to acquire a grasp of details at a level available only through experience. They continued a daily practice of eating lunch with employees at noon each day, which created interaction in a natural and informal way.

This top management interaction with all levels of employees and all the companies' constituents has the effect of emphasizing the long term. The ease of access to senior managers translated into several phenomena in these companies. First, the employees, suppliers, and customers knew top managers well enough to be candid with them. Second, employees understood right from the horse's mouth and with great clarity the parameters of WWWD. It is one thing for a CEO to issue a statement of values or code of ethics. It is effective, however, when that CEO takes his views to the rank and file and they witness his commitment to them.

Finally, the visible presence of officers and top managers is a signal for employees and customers that they are in for the long haul and not the stock options. Jack Welch is legendary for his interaction (see Chapter 10 on people), and in most of these companies, executives knew the workers and their families. These personal relationships served to establish commitment from employees because the clear signal they received was that the company was committed to them. Donald Davis, the Chairman and Chief Executive of Stanley, explained as follows.

> How do we do this? We do it by having a bunch of people in management who understand what we are trying to do and who are flexible enough to do it both ways. Now this is a little hard to explain. To make this work, the corporate management is made up of five group officers, each of whom has 5–7 divisions, and at the headquarters level of the Executive V.P., Chief Operating Officer, and Chief Executive Officer. All of these corporate people do not have to be thoroughly knowledgeable of the 34 divisions, but between us we are thoroughly knowledgeable of the 34 divisions and at least two out of that group would be thoroughly knowledgeable of all the divisions. So we have what I call a nurturing style of management. What this means is that we *don't* just look at numbers and say this is good and this is unacceptable, or that we have to get a new manager or get rid of the division or something like that.

We keep closely coupled with what is going on to the point that when they have problems, we know what the problems are and we are trying to help solve them. *We are not just sitting there in judgment.* We can be losing money in the division, and we are relaxed about it as long as we have a strategic game plan, which we all know about, and we all endorse, and we are working toward it. So, we have lived with losing divisions for a long time. As long as we were comfortable in knowing where we were headed. And as a result of that, many businesses that I think the average corporations would have gotten impatient with and cut the cord on, we have stayed with them, and they have paid off handsomely.[20]

There was, oddly, a strong sense of stability amidst the chaos of these entrepreneurial firms. That stability was the result of the firms' willingness to consider longer-term value for the company such as that of a loyal and motivated workforce or customers whose problems are addressed. Because of the dedication to uncompromising quality, the long term was a clear value. Short-term gains at the expense of reputation were not tolerated. Minute-by-minute management was not needed for the long-term goals, and overriding themes of WBAWI and WAWIB controlled and comforted.

During the frenzy of Singer's restructuring, Chairman and CEO Joseph B. Flavin told analysts that Singer was not a "growth company." He added, "The idea is absurd for Singer. We're not an IBM, a Xerox, or an industry in its infancy." This rare candor is indicative of the comfort levels of the executives of these companies. They reflected a comfort in knowing what their companies were about and in the ability to provide a decent return to investors over the long term. They have a pride in that ability along with complete realism about what they are not in terms of market performance.

VALUE #5: IT ISN'T OUR MONEY

Stepping into the histories, facilities, and mindsets of these fifteen companies was like stepping into a world of untapped resources. Their unique culture is perhaps best summarized in a word that emerged during the exploration: stewardship. The use of this word by officers and employees in these firms was striking because it is old, rarely used, and full of religious connotations. However, these fifteen companies unabashedly created and sustained a climate of stewardship. A climate of stewardship is best explained by employers' and employees' use and repetition of a very simple theme: It is not our money. The managers and employees of these companies had a singular mindset that the work that they do is on behalf of investors who have entrusted funds to them. The word "stewardship" emerged in at least four interviews with different executives in these firms. Even today, Coca-Cola's mission statement provides that, "We exist to create value for our share owners and . . . perform as stewards.[21] Trust and stewardship governed decisions and conduct in everything from their own motivation to curbing expenses. Working for someone else, preserving their investment, and providing a return as payment for that investment were the assigned tasks.

This notion of stewardship produced an atmosphere of complete accountability. Anyone who dealt with the firm and its employees had to walk away with the sense that they were treated fairly. Failure occurred when someone walked away without a positive experience whether it was the high school bandleader in need of funds or a major customer in need of a refund. For example, in its statement of core values, P&G lists integrity and trust as two of the five.

In reaching a decision on removing phosphates from their soap products because of possible environmental damage, Howard Morgen, the CEO commended for P&G's voluntary removal, explained:

> It wasn't that complicated once we had isolated the principles involved. There were really only two in this case. The first is that Procter & Gamble obeys the law. The second is that we sell products that are safe for use under normal usage conditions.[22]

William Cooper Procter gave at least one speech each year on the role of character in business and emphasized the importance of truth in dealing with employees, suppliers, and customers. That focus on truth to those three key groups spanned generations.

These firms had a confidence that originates from clarity of purpose—that is, it is not our money. In one set of minutes from Johnson Controls' board is a statement of their purpose "to introduce and extend the business entrusted to them . . . by proper means." Earning money within a set of rules and standards is their goal. A certain core strength is required to withstand management fads and weather the stormy business cycles without abrupt changes. Business cycles and fads bring moments of insecurity to all managers, and there is pressure from the turbulent waters of business and economies to make abrupt changes or abandon strategy. The culture of stewardship brings a confidence that allows weathering of storms because managers are not looking for temporary accolades nor succumbing to the pressures of outperforming everyone else. This climate of stewardship provides shareholder value and is not swayed easily by the quick fix.

Stating that these companies had a climate of stewardship is insufficient information for replicating their success. The question that arises as a result of this peculiar climate is what creates such a thing? How do employees come to understand their role in serving shareholders?

There are common threads among the companies revealed in strong basic values. Their mantras of accountability stem from ingrained values common in all fifteen centenarian firms. Each company had stated and clear values. Ed Harness, who became Proctor & Gamble CEO in 1971, emphasized "the art of finding principle" to employees and encouraged managers to stress a sense of responsibility about Procter & Gamble's principles to young people coming into the company . He urged managers and those who report to them to make decisions with character, being mindful of the importance of good relationships with customers, shareholders, employees, and suppliers.[23] Not only were they engaged in two-direction visions, but these companies were also engaged in applying their values in 360-degree fashion. Everyone was to be treated in an honest manner, and business was to be conducted with character. These centenarians understood what they were about, where they were headed, and what they could and would not do to get there.

NOTES

1. Procter & Gamble history.
2. Procter & Gamble history.
3. Louis Grossman interview.
4. Barnes, Julian E., "P&G Said to Agree to Pay Unilever $10 Million in Spying Case," *New York Times*, September 7, 2001: C7.
5. PPG Annual Report, 1899.
6. Grossman interviews.
7. Ludlow Annual Report, 1920.
8. Leavitt, R. K., *Prologue to Tomorrow,* Philadelphia: The Pennsylvania Salt Manufacturing Company, 1950.
9. Stanley Annual Reports, 1933 and 1934, company archives.
10. Stephen Patrick interview—Louis Grossman.
11. "Stanley Works: Charges of $44 Million Set to Shut Down Seven Sites," *Wall Street Journal*, October 10, 1995: B4.
12. Grossman interviews.
13. Barnes, Julian E., "Making New Friends at P&G," *New York Times*, March 16, 2001: C1, C4.
14. Deupree, Richard D., *William Cooper Procter: Industrial Salesman,* New York Newmen Society, 1951.
15. *Coca-Cola Company History*, p. 20.
16. Covin, Geoffrey, "The Ultimate Manager," *Fortune*, November 22, 1999: 186–187.
17. Conlin, Michelle, "Revealed At Last: The Secret of Jack Welch's Success," *Fortune* (January 26, 1998): 58.
18. Donald Davis interview.
19. www.cocacola.com.
20. Donald Davis interview.
21. www.cocacola.com.
22. Procter & Gamble history.
23. Schisgall, Oscar, *Eyes on Tomorrow*, op cit., pp. 268–269.

10

Key #5: People—
Who Matters?
Employees Do

Scorn not the common man.

"The Condition Called Prosperity,"
Joseph Wood Krutch,
Human Nature and the Human Condition, 1959

It is a bleak landscape for those who glance cross-country or trans-nationally at the numbers on company downsizings and the resulting lack of employee loyalty. Even as companies resort to litigation to keep their employees from leaving to work for competitors and taking infor-mation with them, they are slashing their workforces, seemingly indif-ferent to the consequences in both morale and loyalty. Even as they slash, they then seek to rehire and seem flummoxed by their inability to attract employees back and attract new and strong talent.

Harvard Business Review is a contradiction in terms in one issue. A 2001 issue contains one piece urging companies to shun layoffs while an-other piece offers, "The Right Way To Be Fired." When asked by a *New York Times* business reporter about the contradiction in philosophies, editor-in-chief Suzy Wetlaufer said, "I don't see the conflict. Human beings have complex minds and they can grasp the idea that organiza-tions need to build trust, but the possibility of layoffs is always there."[1]

While the possibility of layoffs is always there, these fifteen compa-nies seemed to manage the issue exceptionally well. These centenarian companies had fewer layoffs in 100 years than Motorola has had in the past five, and they worked their way through the Depression and industrial revolution. While double-digit growth is exciting, it is not sustainable, and most downsizings today are not because of company survival but adjustments from double-digit numbers to single-digit growth with the bump in earnings coming from the immediate cost reduction of terminating employees.

The difference between today's companies that downsize as a means of boosting earnings and stock prices and the 100-year firms is appreciation for the role employees play in a firm's success. There was not a disposable asset in their philosophies; employees were listened to and treated with respect. Procter & Gamble's first two core values focus on employees: "We show respect for all individuals. The interests of the company and the individual are inseparable." In its 1927 annual report, the Diamond Match CEO at the time, W. A. Fairburn, included the following as his closing paragraph:

> Your Management desires to again avail itself of this opportunity to definitely express its appreciation of the continued whole-hearted co-operation and enthusiastic loyalty of your Company's workers in all of its manifold operations, departments and branches. The spirit of the employees throughout the entire organization has been and continues to be a most important factor contributing to your Company's success.[2]

These companies had five things that they did very differently from the companies of today in terms of how they utilized and treated employees. The five factors in the people key to 100 years are:

1. Get input. Criticism from employees is always good.
2. Everyone counts. Keep it lean and flat.
3. Caring and concern, not slashing.
4. Presidents and tenure. Train 'em well and keep 'em.
5. Boards. Alive and feisty.

Historical commentary of the late nineteenth century as an era in which management and owners of companies ignored needs of its workers aside, these fifteen companies protected their workers. By their actions, several of these firms demonstrated conduct consistent with their creeds concerning the importance of employees. Their actions reflected again not only what they considered the right actions, but also what was good for the company. Indeed, General Electric, Coca-Cola, and Procter & Gamble consistently rank among the top firms in the United States to work for.

GET INPUT: CRITICISM FROM EMPLOYEES IS ALWAYS GOOD

These firms valued their employees, relied on their input, and encouraged that input. The Hollywood characterization of sycophantic stereotypical corporate employee and autocractic manager did not exist in these firms. In fact, it was typical for employees to do boardroom presentations. Furthermore, the questioning of managers and officers by all employees was an expectation.

Singer's redefinition of itself as a marketer and financier of sewing machines came from employee feedback. Employees told managers of the high cost obstacle. Employees told managers of the need for training. Employees gave managers the idea of using ministers' wives as contact points for marketing.

The Pullman Company's culture of employee input was evident in George Pullman's schedule. While he would often turn away heads of state, he could regularly be found kneeling on the carpet in his office with employees and would-be inventors who had an idea they were pitching for changing a product or improving manufacturing.[3] Together these novices and a master of business worked through the proposal and mechanics of the idea.

Corning's employee culture is legendary. Employees must have a voice, dictatorial managers are terminated, and Corning workers live with the following philosophies:

"I am responsible for my own job security."

"There's personal satisfaction in putting a quality product in the box and beating the Japanese."

"We can't pass problems up to the line managers."

"Everybody that works here is competitive. We're willing to work long hours."

"We want to be multiskilled and learn how we can make the product better so we can be best in quality and service to the customer. And if we do that, this plant will be around for a long time."[4]

Business Week described the Corning culture as follows:

> Corning does not just value its employees, it trusts them. Its managers speak of challenging employees to do more and do it better. Corning employees spend 5% of all their working hours in the classroom which includes job training as well as remedial education. Chairman James R. Houghton acknowledges the enormous expense of the training but notes that ROE jumped at Corning from 9.3% to 15.9% in the five years employees have had training, "In my gut, I can tell you a large part of our profit increase has come about because of our embarking on this way of life.[5]

Perhaps as significant as Pennwalt's redefinition from salt company to chemical supplier was its source. Pennwalt's redefinition came from its front lines as employees recognized that salt was not just a commod-

ity and that Pennwalt had potential in its role with respect to differentiated products. An executive of The Stanley Works described how his
company monitored its markets.

> I check, for example, with our general managers and they are in tune
> with the external factors. I get around the country rather frequently, and I
> talk to lots of people (either our customers or our suppliers, or our own
> people) and I learn from them what is taking place on the West Coast
> versus the Southwest, South and the Northeast and what-have-you, and
> over a period of time you sense this kind of thing . . . . You have to know
> what the external factors are, and suppliers and Stanley used its employees
> as information gatherers, analysts and reporters. The Stanley Works board
> chairman brings frontline managers to board meetings to describe to the
> board the trends and issues in their respective divisions. The division
> manager is then expected to answer questions about both sides of his
> market—the supply as well as the demand side.[6]

For the research needed to gather ideas and information in answering
WBAWI, these companies were dependent upon employee input. All of
these ideas for diversification and the tweaking of the answer to
WBAWI came from the front lines. Employees are valued, criticism is
welcomed, and questions must be perceived and received as good
things. Employees cannot fear supervisors nor can a protection of the
status quo be the predominant management thrust. In today's hierar-
chal organizations, what employee would feel comfortable comment-
ing, "Well, you just can't be an old salt company anymore"? Candor as
a universal value in these companies meant candor in all directions and
to all sources. A culture of stewardship recognizes a higher authority in
accountability. As stewards for shareholders, the freedom and comfort
of suggestion and opposition should arise. Imagine if a Microsoft employee had said in 1995, "You can't defy the Justice Department like
this. You'll need to work on the decree *before* we bring out Windows
'98." Apparently no one said it, for Microsoft's battle continues.

It is also interesting to note that a number of the executives mentioned
self-criticism as part of this factor. In other words, they were not afraid
to use introspection to determine what they could have done better or
what could presently be changed to make things better.

EVERYONE COUNTS: KEEP IT LEAN AND FLAT

Long-term companies are lean and flat. As a result of this simple
structure, there is a peculiar mutual respect between and among all
employees. Because each employee is accountable as a steward to
shareholders, communication lines are open, and brutal honesty is

preferred. This openness, born of flat organizations, produces a free flow of ideas and innovations within the companies because the common goal of serving the shareholder was clear and pursued with vigor. This free flow of information and ideas means shareholders are given full information, customers have input, and managers listen to employees. There is a resulting trust that increases the employees' sense of responsibility and accountability.

The flat organization was typical among these firms in order to encourage input. A Colgate-Palmolive executive explained their philosophy in the following way.

> There's a sort of informality there which I think breeds effective communications at the company's top level. That really works for us. Within the company there is no lack of originality. I haven't seen an organizational chart of how we're structured with boxes and arrows.
>
> When new people come into the company they sometimes say, "Well, can we see the organization chart?" And we don't have one. The significance? It almost doesn't matter who's reporting to what box or what levels. There's a task to be done, an opportunity to be seized. The idea is to round up the guys who know about it and you work with everyday, take charge and go do it. It doesn't make any difference who reports to whom. There's a team spiritedness that I think serves us well.[7]

Colgate even builds its product launches around this type of flat approach. When a new product is being contemplated, the salespeople, the marketing people, the general management, and the production folks are brought together and asked whether they are willing to have their bonuses tied to the success of this new product. The result is that together they can calculate what they need to do to make the product a "go." In some cases, after they have worked together and figured out the numbers, their conclusion is, "Nope, at this price point we can't make money." This planning tool and joint buy-in was used to launch Total toothpaste.

Procter & Gamble also follows a similar ownership approach for employees. P&G used a brand management model that gives managers control of a brand as well as full responsibility for results. In a P&G recruiting brochure, the following description appears:

> Brand management is the mainspring and moving force behind all our consumer marketing. The brand management concept assures that each brand will have behind it the kind of single-minded drive it needs to succeed. . . . The brand group is expected to know more about its product and how to increase its consumer acceptance than anyone else in the organization. The brand manager leads the brand group [in] developing the annual marketing plan; developing and executing the advertising copy

strategy; planning and selecting media; planning sales promotions; coordinating package design; and analyzing and forecasting business results.[8]

Part of the reason for flat organizations in these centenarian firms was the nature and experience of their officer groups. For example, in the P&G history, Cooper Procter, grandson of the founders, began his work as a common laborer in overalls. He was the man who sat up all night nursing kettles of soap. Not only did he understand the work and role of employees, but he acquired the detailed knowledge of the production process. Understanding and coming from the belly of the company gave him good gut instincts when he was at the head of the company. But, he never lost touch with the belly. All too appropriately for this analogy, he ate lunch with employees daily. This simple interaction gave him, as the history of P&G notes, "a reciprocal understanding," which gave Procter an edge when the labor movement hit. While other companies experienced strikes and the fallout from the enemy management theory that overtook the country, P&G thrived.[9]

PPG's CEOs have a longstanding history of employee interaction. When they visit a local plant, they invite twenty employees to have lunch with them. The employees are chosen randomly from the payroll, and all have the chance for direct conversation with the CEO during lunch.

If an employee came to Procter with an issue, he had one simple question, "What are the facts?" After a review of working conditions generally in the company, in 1885, Procter began the practice of Saturday afternoon half-holiday for all workers with no reduction in pay! P&G's new release time would soon become the standard for all companies in America.[10] P&G found increased productivity because its workers were well rested.

At the heart of Coca-Cola success is the sales team referred to as the "Coca-Cola men," revered for their dedication and attention to customers, details, and ever-increasing sales. Coca-Cola has created an atmosphere of "fierce loyalty" among its employees. Stories abound of Coke employees who refuse to patronize businesses that serve Pepsi. As Nike endured the sweatshop backlash from the labor practices of its subcontractors in Vietnam, journalists continually compared Coca-Cola factories there and ran footage of the clean factories, the uniform-clad workers, and the on-site training and education classes for employees.

Coca-Cola and GE are both among *Fortune's* list of the Top 100 companies to work for, as well as part of *Fortune's* list of the ten most admired firms. GE has been profiled for what it calls its "workout" program that had as its goal the tearing down of the hierarchical nature of the company along with the facilitation of communication and exchange of information. The result has been an atmosphere of entrepreneurship where ideas come from anywhere and anyone in the company with managers responsible for everything from development of the idea to the resulting returns.

GE rewards its employees for producing results, particularly in its Six Sigma program. GE employees earn bonuses based on savings that come through employees' changes that reduce defects. Six Sigma Black Belts, the troubleshooters who implement changes to minimize debts, are given bonuses based on savings when they can show that the problems are fixed permanently. GE managers have 40 percent of their bonuses tied to Six Sigma goals.

GE also encourages employees to look outside the company for "best practices" and then bring those ideas into GE for continual improvement. GE instills a value to have the self-confidence to look outward for change and resolution. One executive described the culture of the company as one in which any employee could reflect on an idea, process, or change with a simple cut-to-the-chase "B.S.!" No offense is permitted, and the discussion proceeds to explore why the employee offered such sharp critique.

Despite the culture of "What's your point?" that dominates GE, managers and executives have tremendous regard for the work of all employees and acknowledge the work and contributions of many who have brought GE to its nearly unequaled status. GE is the only company from the original Dow Jones index still around today. On the 100th anniversary of the Dow Jones Index, Jack Welch rang the opening bell at the New York Stock Exchange. In GE's company history, there is a segment with Sir Isaac Newton's self-description of his accomplishments, "If I have seen further it is by standing on the shoulders of giants."[11]

CARING AND CONCERN, NOT SLASHING

Even in the face of changing and dismal economic circumstances, these firms recognized the value of their employees and took care of them in every sense. The Panic of 1873 affected every business and industry, with survival being the only goal. Frederick Stanley and William Hart met the challenge of economic hardship by keeping loyal, well-trained people on their payroll. Stanley underwrote employees' debts to banks, and Hart (then the chief assistant to Stanley) personally borrowed money to help local stores preserve their positions and keep their businesses going.

The challenging decision of how to manage the man–machine relationship, particularly when introduction of change in the latter is likely to affect the former, was ever present during their era of industrial revolution (as it is today). In the late 1800s, the founder of The Stanley

Works, Frederick T. Stanley, recognized these possibilities and challenged future management with the following guideline:

> Machines are no better than the skill, care, ingenuity, and spirit of the men who operate them. We can achieve *perfect harmony* when shortening of an operation provides mutual advantages to the workmen and the producers.[12]

Donald Davis, president of The Stanley Works from 1964 to 1989, commented on the founder's philosophy on the workforce.

> It is applicable today . . . as long as the employee can get as good a pay or better as he did under the old method without having to put forth greater effort, that is, if the machine makes the job easier he is more than willing to increase his output. The only time you have trouble is if you are trying to put in a new method and the old standard was fair but with the new method the employee has to work significantly harder and doesn't make any more or even less money, then obviously you have problems. So harmony comes when both parties benefit. That's obviously what we try to do.[13]

PPG has always reflected the value of its employees in its public documents. In its 1899 annual report, the following appeared: "Our company has made great progress in reducing the cost of manufacture and handling during the past year. We have been able to do this, not by reducing the wages of labor, but by our improved methods."[14] PPG's public documents and conduct reflect a sense of partnership with its employees. In a 1926 history of PPG, it was reported, "There are now nearly thirty-five hundred stockholders, many of the fourteen thousand employees holding stock in the company."[15]

PPG was one of the early pioneers of employee stock ownership and facilitated the process by discounting employees' purchase price. That ownership by employees declined in proportion during the period from 1940–1960, but in response to the 1980s threatening atmosphere, PPG revived and expanded employee ownership stake and was thereby able to thwart several takeovers. Today, the single largest block of stock in PPG is owned by PPG employees. Employees can purchase stock continuously through payroll deductions and with substantial discounts. In addition, the company has a contribution plan: for every $1.00 an employee invests, the company matches with $0.50. PPG has a culture in which employees discuss three things daily: time, temperature, and PPG's stock price.

Like the other companies, PPG faced times during its history when it possessed the technology to do more with less. These companies faced the dilemma of labor-reducing technology and employee loyalty along with a duty to the firm's owners to take advantage of cost-saving measures. Decisions in these dilemmas that would affect jobs and economies were not made easily and always involved the parties affected in their decision-making processes. For example, PPG pleaded with the union in the 1950s to work with the company so that the company could provide employees and their riverside town with some economic stability. It was only when PPG was met with a refusal from the union to work together to solve the new dilemma that PPG closed its plant there.

Executives in these companies did more than value their employees. They worked with them, and they knew the people in the shop and in the sales, engineering, and financial organizations because they spent time "in the field" on plans, budgets, and forecasts as these documents were developed.

GE's Jack Welch describes leadership in his company as follows:

> Have a passion for excellence and hate bureaucracy.
> Be open to ideas from anywhere.
> Have the self-confidence to involve everyone and behave in a boundary-less fashion.[16]

Procter & Gamble's leadership provided examples of work ethic unsurpassed by shift workers or salespeople. William Cooper Procter served as a voluntary member of the State Council of National Defense, an appointment made by Governor James M. Cox of Ohio, and his level of dedication to even public service is demonstrated in this excerpt of an article by Merle Crowell from *The American Magazine*.

> Governor James M. Cox of Ohio sent out a call for all members of the State Council of National Defense to meet in Columbus. Right on the heels of the governor's summons came one of the worst storms of the winter, a blizzard that drifted roads and tied up all railway traffic. When the hour for the conference came around there were only two members present from the whole state—the chairman who lived nearby and William Cooper Procter of Cincinnati, 100 miles away.
>
> "How did you make it?" the governor asked. Procter pointed to his open, topless automobile that had snow and ice caked in every crevice. "I drove up," he said. It was after midnight when they finished, and the temperature had dropped far below zero.
>
> "The last I saw of Mr. Procter," the governor said, "he was getting into his car for the 100-mile drive home."[17]

What is perhaps most fascinating is that Procter walked into his office the next day at 7:40 AM, ready to go to work with hands numb from the cold. He was determined at the time of war (1915) not to let production slip.

One executive described this officer-level hands-on involvement as follows, "Anyone can read the monthly financial reports; what we need to do is to interpret them so we can spot trends. We call on customers, on suppliers, we look at the bottom line of course, *but we know how that line reached the bottom*. We live with our divisions; we are involved with them. We think that is part of our success."[18]

One description by Colgate-Palmolive indicates the humility of officers in a flat organization. Colgate-Palmolive was experiencing a crisis in Brazil in terms of sales and the economy there. The officers in the United States immediately called employees in Brazil because "the controller in Brazil is smarter than Brian and I," the phrasing used to describe their reasons for calling and their attitude about input on the crisis. "We talk through these things" was the final observation on using employees in other countries to try and resolve issues and disputes with their experience in the culture there and their firsthand information about issues and product.

> Colgate also holds a global managers' meeting every two to three years.
> I know this sounds corny, but we try to create the reality of a family situation. Colgate people like each other. Dumb? Yes, but it's true. If you've been in the trenches fighting A and B, you'd like to talk to other folks about what went on and what we might do. Top management doesn't say "Here's what we're going to do, you guys." We have a genuine debate and where we're going to go [next] takes place. The sense of participation is very high.[19]

There was a challenging combination of respect and high expectations as a fundamental tenet of management in these companies. Numbers, figures, and data aided them in understanding events, but people, activities, and goals were equally important. Each party visualized the whole and his or her role in that system.

However, it is important to note that in some firms input from employees that proved to be wrong resulted in head-rolling. There was an ethical trust implicit in these flat organizations, and the attitude of "Gotcha, you're it, you're the fall guy," as one CEO described it, was not part of their flat cultures. The idea was to encourage creativity and entrepreneurship and both carry fairly high levels of failures prior to ultimate success. The companies were careful with retribution for mistakes in product launches and accountability. From the frontline to the washroom and back, every employee in these companies had input, and it paid off in the form of dynamics in strategy.

REPEAT—CARING AND CONCERN, NOT SLASHING

There was a sense of community derived from concerned work with employees and commitment to stability of employment. This type of culture produced a delicate balance between managers and employers. The atmosphere in the companies was not identical, but the input from employees was. At one point in its management history, an executive from General Electric was brought into Stanley at an officer-level position. A fellow officer described the executive's short tenure at Stanley as follows, "He came in and began to manage in the same way that you do at General Electric and this just did not go either. The people here were too sensitive and they couldn't take that kind of rough management. He was able, but that didn't work. . . . [t]his precipitated a real crisis in the company." Stanley followed a simple philosophy with employees, "It's having visions and setting goals and challenges and trying to stay out of it and let other people do it. Try to be patient." [20]

Stories abound of executive concern for employee well-being. During the tenure of Harry Ellis as CEO of Johnson Controls (1912–1937), Honeywell in Minneapolis suggested that Johnson Controls merge with them. Ellis would have benefited by millions in stock options had he agreed to the merger. However, Ellis declined because he knew some Johnson Controls employees would lose both their jobs and the sense of pride they had in building the company.

Johnson Controls employees own stock in their 401(k) plans, and employees in total own only about 5 percent of the company's stock. Johnson Controls began selling stock to employees in 1914 with a purchase payment plan of $10 down and $2.50 per month, a means of buying stock on time, with the company carrying the purchase price interestfree.

Johnson Controls was a defendant in a Supreme Court case in which its employees challenged the company's safety policy for workers on the battery lines.[21] Concern about lead exposure caused the company to prohibit women of childbearing age from working in that area. Because pay for line workers was high, many women wanted the jobs but could not hold them without proof of sterilization or medical impossibility. The women (and one male employee) challenged the safety policy as discriminatory. Johnson Controls maintained its safety concerns, even with signed consent, because of possible long-term damage to the fetus in pregnant women. While the case has been used to demonstrate subtle discrimination on the part of employers, it is more a case of Johnson Controls focus on safety while assuming the risk of the backlash and litigation that resulted.

The notion that companies really are nothing more than their employees gave these firms a sense of the utilitarian ethic, and they often acted, without desire for recognition, for the good of the whole. In 1911, Diamond Match Company earned the approbation of the general public when it "deeded its patent for the (nonpoisonous) sesquisulphide match to the public, giving anyone the right to use it free." The reason for patent transfer was employee safety. In addition to giving its secret formula to its competitors without charge, Diamond explained its valuable technical processes for making the new, nonpoisonous matches. Diamond even sent its own employees into other factories to show the most efficient way for producing the new, safer, sesquisulphide matches. This series of benevolent gestures "saved the employees of every other matchmaking company of the United States from phosphorus necrosis and caused the removal of a poison from every American home."[22]

Treating workers right in everything from pay to hours was nothing unusual for these companies. As noted, in 1885, Procter & Gamble was the first company in the United States to implement the Saturday afternoon half-holiday for all workers. At about the same time, Procter & Gamble employees were brought in on a profit-sharing plan (1887). The company remained remarkably free from labor disputes. Its policy of 12 percent semiannual dividend based on each employee's wages went a long way in pleasing workers. In 1844, P&G offered its employees a pension, illness, and death benefit plan known as "Ivorydale Pension and Disability Plan," which was supervised by employees of P&G by 1915.

When any changes were to be made in work conditions or pay, Procter used the Employees Conference Committee (responsible for handling the pension plan) and instructed, "I want you to call the workers together in each of your departments and get their views on wage schedules and other matters. Then go over their recommendations at a general meeting and bring in a report."[23]

The report came back as a vote of confidence for P&G and included the following:

> We want the eight-hour day . . . but it is our unanimous decision that we don't want to say what you shall pay us. You know as well as we do that the cost of living has gone up, and you will take that into account. You have always treated us right, and we know you are going to keep on doing it.[24]

Encouraged by the workers' report, Procter introduced sweeping changes and incorporated into those changes his idea that what workers want most is assurance of steady employment. To guarantee steady employment, Procter understood he needed to avoid seasonal variations. To do this, Procter established the Department of Economic Research, which would establish schedules and quotas based on forecasts so that production could be even throughout the year. The result was not just steady employment but reduced costs as the company ran a smooth production stream.

Such a change is typical of all fifteen firms, for they saw benefits to employees as benefits to the company in the sense of nearly no labor disputes, exceptional productivity, and enormous loyalty among employees. As other companies struggled through epidemic strikes, P&G and its fellow centenarians had already moved to the next level of employee relations. While other companies quibbled over wages, P&G gave employees profit sharing. While other companies held fast on the six-day workweek, P&G gave Saturdays off. While other companies laid off workers on a regular basis, P&G strived for steady employment.

Interestingly, the P&G plan for profit sharing was met with great opposition for perhaps the very reason it was instituted. An article in *Industrial Relations Magazine* included the following observation:

> It was to be expected that Mr. Procter's (William Cooper Procter) proposal for profit-sharing would meet with criticism before its adoption and with skepticism afterward. In the United States of America, employers had generally looked upon profit-sharing as a utopian idea, having little relation to reality. Many of them instinctively regarded it as a doubtful foreign importation.[25]

Johnson Controls reduced its workday for employees from 10 hours to 9 with no reduction in pay and did so in 1919, 16 years before any federal labor legislation was passed and almost 20 years prior to any legislation on hours and overtime pay. By 1930, it was providing health and dental insurance for its employees. By 1944, it had instituted a retirement plan for employees. In 1956, it began its program to provide employees with financial assistance for attending college or vocational training.

Scovill's attention to employees is perhaps best known because of the commitment to quality of one of its CEOs, Malcom Baldridge. Baldridge described the atmosphere at Scovill as one that causes employees to feel that they work for a fair company, that they are dealt with honestly and openly, that they work for a winning company, and that they are part of a team in which everyone contributes to the win. Scovill had training programs for employees that focused on leadership and teams in the 1920s. Those training programs continued through the 1950s when the Korean War produced employment shortages and the eventual demise of the training programs. However, Baldridge reinstituted this Scovill tradition in 1963.

In that training, employees are taught that Scovill is not antiunion, but rather, proemployee. Managers are taught to work directly with employees and to be responsive to their concerns and needs. The result of the culture begun in these training sessions was that Scovill officers were continually on the road visiting plants to review everything from personnel policies to employee concerns to relationships with local bankers. If productivity dropped, managers brought in consultants to help employees, but the consultants were required to work on the floor side by side with the employees to understand their jobs, their needs, and whatever problems were causing a drop in productivity. In other words, at Scovill, the consultants worked with the employees, not management. Yet, if the consultants got out of line, managers stepped in to help employees. Chan Goss was the legendary manager of the casting shop to whom employees turned for support when an outside "efficiency man" went too far.

> The gang knew him for a two-fisted, tough, square-shooting executive and they kept Scovill metal at the top of the list as to quality just because they liked "Chan." But one day an efficiency expert checking up on the casting shop at the East Mill discovered that the casting crews went across the way for beer after pouring a heat. Without consulting "Chan," the bright lad posted a notice forbidding any beer during working hours. A fireman smeared soot over that notice and the employees thought no more of it. The next move by the efficiency man was to have the main gate locked. After the casters went out for their beer, the gates were closed tight so they ran into "Chan's" office instead. Looking up from his mail, the brass master listened to the story, picked up his hat and went across the way with his men and ordered free beer for a week. The efficiency man vanished.[26]

There was a concern for employees among these companies, even during dire economic times. The following candid language was drawn from Ludlow's annual report for 1921:

> We have continued the system of foremen's conferences referred to in our last Annual Report and have extended the idea to include a much larger number of our operatives. Our managers at the Ludlow plant have been making it their aim to address meetings and to explain in conferences, to as many of our working forces as possible, just what actual conditions of the business are, and their efforts have met with very encouraging results. We feel that the better each one of our employees understands the conditions and problems connected with the business, the better we will be able to obtain his or her co-operation.[27]

Ludlow reflected its concerns for employees in the midst of the trauma of 1929 when its annual report explained the fallout for employees to shareholders.

> With the object of increasing the efficiency of our manufacturing operations, extensive changes and additions have been made in several of our

mills. As part of this program it has been found necessary to shut down the Andover plant and transfer its manufacturing operations to the Ludlow and Paterson mills. For such of the Andover employees as wished to move, positions have been found at Ludlow, and to a number of old employees pensions have been granted on the same terms as if their service had been with the Ludlow Manufacturing Associates.[28]

While not politically correct in description, the company was generous in providing for employees despite the century's greatest economic crisis.

The preceding excerpt shows an enlightenment about the importance of employee relations, which is striking. When Aaron Feuerstein's Malden Mills was destroyed by a fire in December 1995, he made the decision to rebuild the plant that manufactures the popular Polar-Tec fabric and also decided to continue paying his employees during the reconstruction period. He became a modern-day hero to many American workers. He commented after his experience that catapulted him to international fame that employees understand when there are terminations because of business issues. They do not, however, he added, understand downsizing for the sake of downsizing, and productivity, morale, and loyalty are affected when the business cycle is not at the heart of employee relations.

It is interesting to contrast just the levels of downsizing these companies undertook to today's standards. In 1997, General Mills chose to eliminate its oldest cereal facilities (Lodi, California; Chicago; and Etobicoke, Ontario, Canada). Despite high cereal sales (a 35 percent increase), General Mills was faced with obsolescence at these plants as well as ongoing changes in which particular cereal sells best. The total impact was a loss of 235 jobs with apologies from the company because its enhanced technology at other plants had given it excess capacity, and it could run those plants more cheaply than the old plants.[29]

Procter & Gamble has had its share of downsizings. Between 1991 and 1997, it slashed 13,000 jobs, and in 2001, it announced a reduction of 9,000 jobs, about 9 percent of its workforce. P&G attributed the downsizings to flat sales growth. In 1999, P&G began to seek volunteers for retirement, but the number who came forward was limited (only 7,200). P&G then had to undertake involuntary reductions, with a resulting loss of $1.4 billion. Interestingly, one employee of P&G had this reaction to the announced reductions: "I think it's the right thing for the company. While I hope I would not be one of the ones asked to leave, I hope I would be able to handle it with dignity and respect."[30] She also noted that P&G's effort to try voluntary reductions first was a "moral act." The president of the Cincinnati Chamber of Commerce said of P&G's announced downsizings, "We respect the leadership. Procter management will do the things that are necessary for the long term."

Colgate has a history of involving employees in its celebrations of company successes. For example, on its 100th anniversary of being in business, Colgate held a dinner for 1,000 at the Grand Central Palace. Every employee was invited, and every employee participated in the planning for the dinner. The factory and offices were closed early so that all could attend the celebration. Richard Colgate gave every employee $5 for every year of employment with Colgate.

For fifty years, the Pullman Free School of Manual Training offered those in the town the opportunity for a free quality education. George Pullman founded the school through a provision in his will probated after his death in 1897. Pullman left $1.2 million for founding the school with the following direction:

> That the children of those associated with him in the town of Pullman and its enterprises might be trained in the ideals of clean living, good citizenship and industrial efficiency, which were his own inspiration and through which alone the workman may hope to attain his true development.[31]

Johnson Controls begins its relationships with its employees before they are employees. Its officers recruit potential employees while they are in engineering schools. Interestingly, most of the engineering recruits go into sales, a means by which the company provides its customers with expertise in the field.

Bill Woodburn, a manager in GE's Plastics Division, once explained the caring nature of Jack Welch, who is known for his handwritten notes to direct reports as well as hourly workers. Woodburn turned down a transfer because he did not want to uproot his teenage daughter from her school. Welch sent the following note to Woodburn:

> Bill, we like you for a lot of reasons—one of them is that you are a special person. You proved it again this morning. Good for you and your lucky family. Keep your priorities straight.[32]

Interestingly, the companies were also at the forefront of providing benefits for employees, long before there were statutory requirements for doing so. For example, in 1894, Procter & Gamble adopted its Ivorydale Pension and Disability Plan because its studies showed that its workers needed protection against loss of income due to work accidents, illnesses, or retirement. With tremendous foresight, something that is now mandated was implemented at Procter & Gamble—a pension and disability plan. By 1915, Procter & Gamble had also put together an Employee Conference Committee to supervise the management of the fund.

Colgate-Palmolive sees its dividend record as a service to employees.

> We think it's important to our employees, for one. We've implemented stock ownership plans both here and elsewhere. For example, we have it in Mexico. I don't personally know of a single employee in the U.S. who does not own stock. We offer an incentive in both the savings and investment plans. Employees contribute into the savings plan and we contribute approximately one-half of their contribution in the form of shares. So, if you are an employee and decide to save $100 per month, we'll put in $50.00 or so in shares into your account.[33]

The attitude of these companies toward their employees is striking in contrast to the ease with which employees are dismissed today and without favorable results for the company. Employees who feel that they are treated unfairly by employers, particularly in the case of layoffs, engage in various forms of retaliation that are costly to their employers. With the computer age, many employees, upon learning of their terminations, sabotage their employers' security systems. For example, 70 percent of all companies experienced insider (that is, employee) attacks on their computer systems during the 2000–2001 period, including viruses and malicious codes.[34]

One company's manager of information systems who was downsized at age 56 sabotaged his employer's computer system before he left, at a cost of $20 million to the company. He wrote to the company president with candid disclosure about his deed.

> I have been loyal to the company in good and bad times for over 30 years. I was expecting a member of top management to come down from his ivory tower to face us with the layoff announcement, rather than sending the kitchen supervisor with the guards to escort us off the premises like criminals. You will pay for your senseless behavior.[35]

PRESIDENTS AND TENURE: TRAIN 'EM WELL AND KEEP 'EM

These companies also valued their officers and the constancy they provided. Their presidents provided stability during remarkably rapid change. Fortified by the obvious board support, confident that they would have time to initiate and sustain a strategy (and enough time to retreat, recreate, alter), and experienced in the marketplace, the executives of these firms had long terms and were able to achieve enviable records, as noted in Table 10.1.

In each company at least one of its presidents held office for a sustained period. Each company had at least one executive at the helm

TABLE 10.1. Presidential Tenure from Origin to 1982

Company	Founded	Consecutive Dividends Paid Since	# of Presidents	Average Tenure Years	President 10 years or more	Longest Tenure
Scovill	1802	1856	(Since 1850) 12	10	4	32
Pennwalt	1850	1863	(Since 1850) 15	8	5	23
Singer	1851	1863	9	14.3	5	44
Pullman	1858	1867	(Since 1858) 8	14.1	5	30
Ludlow	1868	1872	(Since 1868) 5	20	4	35
The Stanley Works	1843	1877	(Since 1843) 8	16.7	5	41
Corning Glass Works	185	1881	(Since 1919) 5	12.8	3	20
Diamond International	1881	1882	(Since 1881) 8	12.5	4	32
PPG	1883	1899	11	10.1	8	14
Johnson Controls	1883	1895	7	16.0	6	27
Colgate-Palmolive	1806	1895	10	19.4	6	51
Coca-Cola	1889	1892	5	26.6	5	60
GE	1878	1899	8	13	4	21
Procter & Gamble	1837	1891	9	18.0	4	53
General Mills	1866	1898	10	14.4	4	53

for almost one-quarter of a century. At least three executives in each company presided for ten years or more. The number of presidents has been surprisingly low, as few as five in the 100-year span. The range of CEO service extended from five (Coca-Cola) to 51 (Colgate-Palmolive) years. What is more telling is the average tenure of a president in these companies, 15.8 years.

The transfer of the Coca-Cola mantle has been described as an "orderly and matter-of-fact succession."[36] Coca-Cola and the other firms had an internal depth of management that made such succession, even in the face of the loss of a superstar, a nonissue (see Chapter 8). Goizueta's management style embraced Coca-Cola's simple goal of getting the whole world to have a Coke. However, Coca-Cola has had its share of succession issues since the time of Goizueta, as the company has departed from the traditional long-term CEO and the notion of growing those CEOs from within.

With only a few exceptions, the succeeding presidents in these 100-year firms were "homegrown," that is, they came up through the ranks of the company. Employees viewed these CEOs as "one of us" and offered the loyalty and effort that personal pride engenders. In order to promulgate values and to communicate personality and goals, both corporate and personal, a CEO must occupy the presidential office longer than "the short run," longer than a one-year trial. These firms offered their CEOs the opportunity and time to both sow and reap. An effective management succession program was present in each firm in order to continue their policies of homegrown leadership.

For example, Robert Woodruff became president of Coca-Cola in 1923 and retired when Roberto Goizueta succeeded him in 1981. Woodruff was a hands-on CEO who developed some of Coca-Cola's lasting slogans, such as "The Pause That Refreshes," and "It's the Real Thing." Goizueta, as Woodruff's protegee, was groomed by a rise through the ranks, riddled with every form of experience; Woodruff developed depth in Goizueta and his management team as he prepared for succession.

Procter & Gamble screens its employees carefully because they must be malleable in terms of Procter & Gamble values. The future executive team will come from those hires, "This is an up-through-the-ranks company with a vengeance."[37] However, P&G is having its difficulties with succession now, and its perceived upheaval (see Chapters 6 and 7) may be the result of its abandonment of its long-term policy of long-term CEOs. In 2000, Durk Jager, chairman and CEO of P&G, announced his retirement after only 18 months at the command. His attitude reflected the classic centenarian approach. In a discussion with analysts, he admonished them that "We can afford to take a couple of swings and misses. It won't wreck the company."[38] Jager's "retirement" seems to have been more of a departure. P&G's performance since then has not improved. It is important to note that GM gave Jack Smith a decade to turn around that company, and P&G requires similar types of cultural changes.

Some of the companies did experience a management succession crisis. There were periods during the 100-year histories when particular presidents held office too long. Striking a balance in tenure of the CEO was an ongoing focus of these firms. Often a long line of homegrown management reached a point of diminishing returns, or family-connected management lacked sufficient depth for innovation, given technological and marketplace changes. New expectations brought on by diversification or divestiture required new attitudes. Scovill reached such a crisis in the 1950s. The board consisted almost entirely of insiders, many of whom were connected inextricably to a management team which had guided the firm through some fifty years of successful expansion. However, in 1958, earnings were down to zero, and Scovill suspended quarterly dividend payments for the first time since 1885. Recognizing its own inadequacy and realizing the need for changes, the board agreed to appoint the first non-Goss, non-Sperry person to head the firm and also agreed, in effect, to change its own composition. Seldon Williams, a retired president of the Schrader subsidiary, was appointed president, and he expanded the board. After failing to pay dividends through the last three quarters of 1958 and the first two quarters of 1959, Scovill was able to pay twenty-five cents per share in September 1959 to tenuously maintain its 102-year annual dividend record.

THE BOARDS: ALIVE AND FEISTY

A board of directors is the ultimate arbiter of corporate direction, soundness, and personnel selection. Whistleblower on practices of dubious economic or moral worth, instigator of change in chief executive officers to save the firm or to conserve stockholder interests, provider of challenges and change to build strength through enunciation, and implementer of strategy are board characterizations found in the histories of these companies. Their boards of directors' actions or inactions have been pivotal in sustaining or in these firms, some cases causing decline.

Composition of the boards of these companies is revealing. Critical board members were welcomed. In one company, the president regarded the probing questioning by an outside professor member as crucial.

> The professor questioned the value and legitimacy of simply trying to get growth of earning through acquisitions. Picking up an old business or businesses without any real creative additions and trying to create your business that way does not necessarily lead to growth. He wanted to bring this out and the issue was clearly one of keeping management on its toes to the importance of new products and new strategies in order to retain the vitality and viability of the company's business products.[39]

In another company, a board member in the 1960s and 1970s inquired constantly whether the president was taking inflation into account in the total decision-making. He questioned whether the accounting methods enabled management to cope with problems of inflation, and keep up with the need for plant and equipment replacement. Underlying this interrogation was a concern that the firm might not continue its long-cherished control of costs, a great strength of the company. On the other hand, this same outside director rigorously monitored management's quality standards and resisted any effort to cut corners that might result in diminished product and service integrity. These firms had both leadership and openness on their boards. Management encouraged discussions and questions, and directors performed their responsibilities as stewards of shareholder interests.

The type of board member independence found at these companies is the very type of board member qualifications touted by investor groups today. While experts struggle to define "independent" with factors such as contracts with the company, these firms had a very simple definition for independent directors that they valued. Their definition was the ability and fortitude to disagree and offer constructive criticism.

Malcolm Baldridge described his ideal board member as follows:

> I think that in today's world the board should be largely a group of outside directors, who bring to the board and to the management a kind of professional understanding of the obligations and responsibilities to the stockholders and the publicly-held company. I think it is in this area largely that the board functions today. I never felt that the board could manage or shouldn't. But the board has to be experienced enough or self-assured enough to closely examine and question management with respect to its major policy decisions and directions. Also, the board has to recognize the responsibilities that the company has to its several constituencies: the stockholders, the customers, and the general public. It takes a person who has had considerable experience on the one hand and has an independence on the other, at the same time recognizing its role as an advisor to management.[40]

Implicit in the criterion of "feisty" for board members is that board members have achieved success in business. A look at the General Electric Board is a study in the confidence of Jack Welch who is willing to subject himself to what are surely lively board discussions. Five of Welch's board members are chairmen and CEOs of other firms, one is a former VP from Macy's, one is a Harvard Business School professor, one was the president of Cornell, and one is Sam Nunn. Apart from Welch, there are only two GE insiders on the Board. Credentials abound on these boards in an atmosphere in which no one fears a good challenging question. Colgate-Palmolive has only one insider on its board: the CEO.

The complacency of many boards today is the result of autocratic CEOs who lack the wisdom to understand that board members' criticism is healthy and not a coup d' état. The nature of these boards and their interaction with the CEOs of the fifteen companies is rough-and-tumble. But, these healthy exchanges at the top level served as a sounding board and often as checks and balances for times when the company was going astray.

George Pullman once described his company's philosophy with this statement, which sums up these companies' executive and board leadership:

> The principle upon which I have always acted is that the people are always willing to pay for the best, provided they get the worth of their money. I have always gone on striving to do something better, endeavoring to improve upon the best, in perfect confidence that the financial returns will look out for themselves.[41]

UPDATE ON CORNING

Following Corning's elimination of dividends, James R. Houghton, the company's longstanding CEO, came out of retirement to once again be CEO. John W. Loose, who had led the company, via fiber optics, into bankruptcy departed after a tenure of just 16 months. Houghton said, "I have a record of leadership and there's a feeling that Houghton is back, and everything will be okay." Corning's union head for its employees said, "Jamie's a very smart businessman, and getting him back is the best thing that can happen to us."[42]

NOTES

1. Uchitelle, Louis, "These Days Layoffs Compete With Loyalty," *New York Times*, August 19, 2001: BU4.

2. Diamond Match Annual Report, 1927.

3. *Pullman Company History*.

4. Hoerr, John, "Sharpening Minds for a Competitive Edge," *Business Week*, December 17, 1990: 74.

5. Ibid.

6. Davis interview—Louis Grossman.

7. Grossman interview.

8. History of Procter & Gamble, p. 113.

9. Ibid.

10. Ibid.

11. *General Electric History, www.ge.com*.

12. Davis, Donald, *Stanley Works: A 125 Year Beginning*, address to Newcomen Society in North America, August 16, 1968.

13. Donald Davis interview, New Britain, Connecticut, October 1980.

14. PPG Annual Report, 1899, PPG Archives, collected June 6, 1996.

15. Ibid.

16. "How Jack Welch Runs GE," *Business Week*, June 8, 1998: 5.

17. Cromwell, Merle, "War Makes Soldiers of Us All," *American Magazine*.

18. Grossman interviews.

19. Ibid.

20. Davis interview—Grossman.

21. *International Union v. Johnson Controls, Inc.*, 499 U.S. 187 (1991).

22. Diamond Match Company, Annual Report, 1899.

23. Deupree, "William Cooper Procter, Industrial Salesman," address at the Newcomen Society, December 6, 1951, New York, p. 18.

24. Ibid.

25. Deupree, "William Cooper Procter, Industrial Salesman," address at the Newcomen Society, December 6, 1951, New York, p. 18.

26. Scovill Company Records, archives at Scovill.

27. Ludlow Annual Report, 1921.

28. Ludlow Annual Report, 1929.

29. "General Mills Plans to Close Cereal Sites and Trim 235 Jobs," *Wall Street Journal*, September 30, 1997: B4.

30. Barnes, Julian E., "Procter to Cut 9,600 Jobs In Drive to Trim Its Overhead," *New York Times*, March 23, 2001: C1, C5.

31. Pullman, George, Will of September 1980.

32. "How Jack Welch Runs GE," *Business Week*, June 8, 1998: 5.

33. Grossman interviews.

34. Tahmincioglu, Eve, "Vigilance in the Face of Layoff Rage," *New York Times*, August 1, 2001: C1, C6.

35. Ibid. at C6.

36. Greising, David, "What Other CEOs Can Learn From Goizueta," *Business Week*, November 3, 1997: 38.

37. Collins, James C., and Jerry I. Porras, *Built to Last: Successful Habits of Successful Companies*. New York: Harper Collins, 1994.

38. Farrell, Greg, "Impatient P&G Ousts Jager," *USA Today*, June 9, 2000: 1B.

39. Davis interview—Grossman.

40. Grossman interviews.

41. *Pullman Company History*, p. 31.

42. Claudia Deutsch, "A Familiar Face Is Trying to Put Corning Back on the Right Track," *New York Times*, June 13, 2002: C1, C12.

How Do You Do It?

Getting to 100 Years: Creating a Climate for the Long Term

The last thing I would want to do is skip a dividend.
I wouldn't want to be tagged as the bad guy.
Fred Brengel, retired chairman, Johnson Controls

After studying everything from the quaint language of these companies' annual reports to stories of their employees' loyalty, a nagging feeling remains. Do all the research and the findings mean anything today? Is it still possible to create and operate a business that will survive? Is it still possible to create a company that will not announce next quarter that it is reversing the reported earnings from the last three years? Is it still possible to attract investors to a company that will deliver a return without interruption? Is it still possible to have a company that does not experience the dramatic swings of downsizings and "accounting irregularities"? Are we, perhaps, offering up quaint musings of the past?

Are these companies' stories just a collection of anecdotes? Did they not just benefit from sheer luck and simple random choices that worked? Is any of this information relevant today for those who are building and growing businesses? After all, these companies were formed and evolved in a different era when Wall Street was more forgiving, investor expectations were different, and consistent dividends were but one measure of value. They thrived in a time when there was a slower pace without the pressures of international markets. What about today's pressure for consistent, double-digit results? Do day traders not represent the level, interest, and commitment of shareholders today? These are great stories, but they have little meaning now. When the 1980s and their impact on several of these firms are factored in, some may want to conclude, "See, there are just as many casualties from following their leads as there are success stories!"

However, only four of these fifteen companies changed character and ownership in the 1980s, not because of their poor management but rather because of their wealth. Their low-debt, rich-cash positions and market shares were a temptation for those with good and bad intentions who were in the acquisition mode. Perhaps their eyes so focused on values and dividends made them blind to the realities of an aggressive market; they were easy prey in an era of greed.

Some may argue that these companies lack the sophistication to be a Microsoft or Intel. Yet, there is even a pattern in this type of dismissive thinking about the old-fashioned nature of these companies and their management philosophies. Technology companies are the current darlings of the market. Steel companies once occupied that pedestal of honor. Today steel companies have a very different position. The overarching lesson is that it is not the product of the company that determines its long-term success; it is how the company determines what that product will be, and it will change over time. Any company that sells the newly invented light bulb will be a winner as customers flock to it for the new product. The staying power is in the company that knows where those customers are going next, even sometimes when the customers do not realize it.

These companies and our research gnawed at us because it seemed that what we had found was the common sense of business. We conclude only that there are some eternal principles that make for eternal companies and that the practices of these fifteen companies establish both those principles and how to go about following them.

PATIENCE AS A VIRTUE: SURVIVING NEW ECONOMIES

The 1980s, with their barbarians at the gate, were challenging for these companies, but most of them also had to endure the humiliation of the high-tech and new-economy 1990s. There was a demand for investment returns at time-warp speeds. Exponential growth was the expectation. The tension was palpable as the market scoffed at the old-timers. In April 2000, Morgan Stanley's chief high-tech analyst, Mary Meeker, said, "There's going to be a story about traditional companies that miss the Internet revolution. Watch over the next year. Count the CEOs who fall."[1]

Meeker was correct. Durk Jager was ousted at Procter & Gamble. Doug Ivester was hurled from Coca-Cola. But, on May 14, 2001, Mary Meeker appeared on the cover of *Fortune* magazine with this question, "Can we ever trust Wall Street again?" The following points were featured in the story:

- Where Mary Meeker went wrong
- Inside the IPO racket
- Hyping Winstar to death
- Plus—you're right—blame the media too.[2]

The story inside is not a pretty one. Those who scoffed at these old-fashioned companies are now gone or struggling because they ignored the lessons of these long-term survivors. The fall of the dot-coms is really nothing new and different. This type of business cleansing has happened before, and it will happen again to too many. But our work leads us to ask: Is there any way to avoid these periodic cleansings that are so devastating personally and economically? It would seem that the application of these principles could at least smooth the business cycles a bit.

There are remarkable similarities in market crashes—from the 1929 crash to the California Gold Rush to the great Holland Tulip Scandal, when tulip bulb futures were being sold for $10,000. There was huge speculation, double-digit growth, and high leverage. In the end when the market finally collapses, there are survivors. They are like the companies we studied—slow, but certain. Steady and sure. Levi Strauss sold pants to the California Gold Rush miners, and while their claims, their gold, and their investors are long gone, Levi Strauss is still selling Levis. Long-term survivors, like Tolstoy's happy families, are all alike.

The managers of these fifteen firms behaved as stewards. Regardless of the economic forecasts, the predictions, and even perhaps their equivalent of day traders, these managers kept their eyes on the ball. They played for keeps and let the trendy deviations from quality and accountability take temporary hold and then fade. Within these companies is a certain confidence—an air of surety that "this too shall pass." But, that confidence emerged from their commitment to purpose, performance, priorities, and people. They were stewards functioning within the parameters of those values.

Johnson Controls executives explained that 1974 was a bad year for earnings for them—they made only $0.90 per share, and they paid dividends of $0.80 per share. When asked by analysts and employees what the management team planned to do, they responded simply, "We'll turn it around"[3] and then added a marvelous reflection of respect and insight into their self-described stewardship and said, "The shareholders deserve it."[4]

STEWARDSHIP AND TONY BENNETT

Stewards know their roles, their responsibilities, and their goals. They do not deviate from those responsibilities, for to do so would be a violation of fiduciary responsibilities. To do so would mean losing what has made them successful. Departing from or not fulfilling the assigned responsibility is intolerable failure. So we come full circle to the Tony Bennett factor. The man was given a talent he maximized as a balladeer. He has never lost sight of his calling.

Tony Bennett and our companies have in common the trait of long-term success spanning generations—no shifting paradigms, no buzzwords and quality without compromise. Bennett's changes came in recognizing new songs to perform in his style, not changing his style to the pop music of the times.

Bennett recognized his strength as a balladeer and stuck with it, through everything from the Beatles to Hootie and the Blowfish. Although each of our companies recognized the importance of diversification, they all held fast to a WBAWI—or "what business are we in?"—philosophy. They knew their strengths, developed strong market presences based on those strengths, and never forgot their roots. Singer suffered when it left its sewing machines. Stanley has its tools. Diamond held on to its matches. Coca-Cola nearly lost its customers when it tried to deviate from its magic. Colgate-Palmolive knows how to get things and people clean. General Electric understood it was not a player in computers, but it still knows electrical generation and equipment. Bennett never performed without singing "I Wanna Be Around."

The firms diversified only when their strengths allowed. Scovill began as a brass button manufacturer and backed into brass manufacturing because it knew brass. Scovill bought Hamilton Beach because Hamilton Beach was a major brass purchaser. Scovill understood this customer's business. GE built generators, then it financed its customers' purchase of generators, and when it had learned financing, it took off in that line of business. Coca-Cola stuck with beverages but expanded into consumer desires for diet drinks and healthy alternatives in the form of juices.

Other companies have forgotten the WBAWI lesson and paid the price. Sears abandoned its catalog, insurance, and real estate businesses and now struggles to find a retail presence. IBM suffered for not understanding its business was the workplace, not mainframe computers. But, you cannot rest on laurels. Phil Knight and Nike, a seemingly unstoppable force early in the 1990s, missed major trends such as skateboards, in-line skating, and snowboarding. George Fisher no longer heads Kodak because he did not see the digital camera competition coming. Avon has struggled to recover from losing both its Avon ladies and the resulting sales. The transition of women to the workplace was a trend with a direct impact on Avon, and it continued its sale model despite the declining availability of sales representatives and a market.

All Tony Bennett needs are a microphone and a pianist to make music. All fifteen companies were cost-conscious. Scovill executive vice presidents with worldwide responsibilities shared a secretary. Spartan company headquarters were the rule for these firms. By contrast, IBM's Louis Gestner hired an executive chef at $120,000 per year during his tenure. "Chainsaw" Al Dunlap commands a salary even after he departs the damaged company.

Bennett has used the same musical arranger for nearly thirty years. Our companies' management team histories are in direct contrast to the executive recruiting practices in vogue today. Scovill, founded during the Jefferson Administration in 1803, had only twelve CEOs during its 100-year dividend run. Three of the companies (Singer, Stanley, and Diamond) had CEOs who served for more than forty years; indeed Colgate-Palmolive leads the pack with a CEO for fifty-one years of nothing but growth. Seven of the companies never had a CEO serve for fewer than ten years. They were not afraid of homegrown management. Their officers and CEOs came up through the ranks. Management succession is handled quite nimbly, for depth abounds in the companies.

These companies were acutely aware of the pressures for immediate returns and results. The executives appreciated the tension between short-term results and long-term performance, but the short term did not control decision-making. Donald Davis, chairman and CEO of The Stanley Works, put it this way: "The tension is always there. One of the top management's toughest jobs really is to mediate between the two viewpoints—short term, profit results now versus investment for future development."

Tony Bennett did and does spend time on the road in concert, in direct contact with audiences—no megatours, just constant gigs. A full century before we heard of customer service, these firms sent their sales forces and vice presidents alike out on the road to talk directly with customers. They had an interesting approach to marketing studies: one-on-one feedback. Sales calls, follow-ups, replacements, and refunds allowed them to remain in the customers' minds and good graces. The "Coca-Cola men" are legendary for their sales acumen built on direct customer contact and familiarity.

Bennett has a reputation for quality in his recordings and performance. These firms had strong commitments to integrity. Their mantra was: "If there's integrity, there will be quality and profits." Their integrity manifested itself in more than just quality. Frederick T. Stanley, founder of The Stanley Works, spoke of the intricate balance between automation and employees: "Machines are no better than the skill, care, ingenuity and spirit of the men who operate them. We can achieve perfect harmony when shortening of an operation provides mutual advantages to the workman and the producers." This was ethics before its time, reengineering done correctly in the 1800s, and nothing at the expense of the customer or the employee.

Our firms were no less remarkable than Tony Bennett and his success with Generation X—his third generational conquest. The sad part of their stories is what happened to some following the takeover battles of the 1980s. Still, the majority survived, strong, dividends intact, and true to their values. It is reassuring to realize that cost-consciousness, focus, customer service, homegrown management, and integrity are keys to longevity. Today's management fads seem as shallow as Ice T and Madonna. There is a simple Tony Bennett factor in the success of these fifteen companies that makes today's management fads much easier to debunk and infinitely easier to question.

NOTE ON STANLEY

As this manuscript is completed, Stanley is facing challenges from shareholders regarding its proposal and subsequent proxy solicitation for moving company headquarters to Bermuda in order to reduce taxes for the company. The attorney general for Connecticut filed suit against Stanley to halt the company's move to Bermuda alleging that there were misrepresentations in the proxy materials sent to shareholders. State officials have also asked the SEC to investigate.[5]

NOTES

1. "Big, Hairy, Audacious Goals Don't Work—Just Ask P&G," *Fortune*, April 3, 2000: 39.

2. "Can We Ever Trust Again?," *Fortune*, May 14, 2001: 65.

3. Interviews with Louis Grossman, 1999.

4. Ibid.

5. David Cay Johnston, "Stanley Works Faulted Again By 2 Officials Of Connecticut," *New York Times*, July 4, 2002: C1, C5.

12

The Steps to the Long Term

The tendency upon reading about these remarkable firms is to immediately attempt duplication of their efforts. However, any business owner or executive aiming for the long term must follow a step-by-step process. The simple declaration of commitment to the long term is a far cry from actual longevity. What follows is an integration of the common threads of these long-term survivors into six steps. These steps integrate the principles of longevity and provide a guide for growing and sustaining a business.

STEP #1: CHECK YOUR EGO AT THE DOOR AND KEEP YOUR ORGANIZATION FLAT

As noted in Chapter 10, long-term companies are dependent upon candid feedback from employees and boards. It is very easy to put "employee feedback" as a step in the path to longevity, but the difficult part is creating a climate in which employees perceive that their feedback is welcome. In these centenarian firms, a factory line worker could talk candidly to the CEO about production issues because the CEO made himself available to the worker. A manager could speak freely to an officer about everything from lack of sales to travel expenses.

This feedback step is not an easy one because it requires officers, managers, and boards to communicate to employees that you are willing to listen to information you would rather not hear. If feedback is to work, employees have to understand that you want both the bad and the good. When employees bring the bad news, reacting to the news and not the employee is critical for not only taking action, but also for sending the signal to all employees that you listen and act. A dependence upon anonymous polls for the kind of information you want will not create a climate of feedback and the flat organization you need. Any form of retaliation against candid employees is a death knell for meaningful feedback. That retaliation can be as obvious as termination or demotion, but it may also be as subtle as changes in schedule, offices, or responsibilities.

The collective wisdom of employees in long-term companies exceeds the collective wisdom of management. That is, not only do employees know the vulnerabilities and issues, but they also know management's attitudes and sincerity. A sincerity about feedback is not something managers can fake! To the extent employees offer insights, views, and suggestions different from those of managers, the managers should think of Samuel Goldwyn's advice, "How am I going to know I'm right if you don't disagree with me?"

These 100-year businesses evolved based on employee and customer feedback, not management theory. "No sycophants allowed" is the type of sign these firms would welcome. Procter & Gamble faced an interesting dilemma in 1937 when the U.S. Supreme Court upheld the National Labor Relations Act and, in effect, separated management and labor through unionization regulations. To comply with the law, P&G had to abolish its Employees' Conference Plan, a means by which P&G addressed employee concerns and suggestions, because it was seen as a barrier to employee organization efforts. However, by the time the law required its abolition, P&G employees were so accustomed to direct communication with management that they continued their practice of letting management know of problems without the formality of the Employees' Conference Plan. Management continued to disseminate information to employees as quickly and as thoroughly as it could without the formal committee.

Restructuring for Flat Organizations

Apart from communication of an open mind on feedback, a business may need to have some restructuring in order to facilitate communication from frontline employees to the executive suite. A flatter organization is one like Colgate-Palmolive's, wherein everyone involved with a product, from its development to its shipping, has input before the company sells the product. Such universal input may come from teams. Thomson International, the world's largest publishing firm, has a team for every textbook it publishes. That team includes a representative from sales, a technology expert, a design coordinator, a production representative, a developmental editor, and a senior editor. That team works with the author from start to finish with the sales representative providing feedback on planned features and the design coordiantor calling attention to those features. The entire team has contact with the author, and the author's interaction is with employees through the organization. Apart from the full coordination of efforts is the feeling throughout the company that a sales rep can raise an issue with an author and an author can raise an issue of quality with production. A sales rep can tell a senior editor or an author that a particular feature or chapter will be meaningless in terms of sales or may actually detract from sales. The design member of the team can help the author develop an idea into a continuing feature for the book. By the time a book is published, there are at least six people in all areas of the company who know the book cover to cover.

But Thomson does more. It has its authors come to the sales meetings and actually meet all of the representatives who will be selling the book. It is not unusual for a sales rep to tell an author at these meetings that an instructor's manual needs improvement if the book is going to sell because that is the feedback the sales rep has from customers. To keep the feedback going, Thomson sets up an "Ask the Author" website. There, any student, instructor, or even sales rep can raise a question about the book, its content, or its coverage. Everyone on the team receives a copy of any questions that come in for their authors along with the author's response. There is a message of both accountability and counting. Everyone takes responsibility for a textbook project, but everyone also knows that their input counts.

Spending Time at the Front

One way of sending the message that input is welcome and that your organization is flat or getting there is to spend some time being visible. Time on the front lines is a certain means for getting that spontaneous feedback. Every manager should ask these questions: What is the time and distance between me and the sales force? The factory floor? The cash registers? When was the last time I visited the production lines? When did I last talk directly with a sales representative?

Jack Welch was legendary among General Electric employees for his direct contact with employees. There were stories in newspapers and archives alike about these fifteen companies that reflected a climate of comfort that employees enjoyed in terms of their input. They understood that when a manager or officer visited, it was not a visit for show but a part of their job of learning from those who knew best what issues and concerns needed to be addressed.

Whiting Brothers, a company that many thought of as a retail gas company, was actually a travel company. That is, its facilities, including gas stations, restaurants, and motels, were strategically positioned to take advantage of road trippers. They were in the business of providing the services drivers need when they travel by car. Their facilities were spread throughout the western United States. Whiting Brothers CEO and other managers took road trips themselves to experience the company facilities firsthand. Their CEO was known for eventually identifying himself to those running the gas stations and motels. If the employee the CEO encountered happened to have a copy of the company's code of ethics, which every employee received as a laminated, wallet-size card, that employee was given $25 on the spot as a reward. Whiting Brothers employees not only knew an officer could appear at their location at any time, but they also knew they might be rewarded for the interaction.

This discussion on checked egos and the flat organization can be summarized into some practical tips on creating the component of a culture of longevity that encourages employee zeal, feedback, and loyalty. The goal is a flat and feisty organization in which communication flows and employees feel comfortable in both their roles and feedback (see Figure 12.1).

Profit sharing—Give all employees a piece of the action.

Incentive plans—Give them bonuses for improvements, cost reductions, and meeting goals. Think of General Electric and Welch's Six Sigma quality dedication and reward employees who get your defects down.

Input—Let the employees decide what they want as benefits.

Personal care—In addition, give employees attention. Know their issues and concerns. Drop them a note.

Have an independent board and monthly board meetings. If there are no disagreements at board meetings, something is terribly wrong with your board.

Build depth in your company by immersing managers in all aspects of company operations. Remember William Procter often wore overalls to work, and he was CEO during an era when casual Fridays did not exist.

Get your managers on the factory floor, on the front lines with the sales folks in the area, and out and about with the purchasers.

Figure 12.1. The Steps to a Flat and Feisty Organization.

STEP #2: WRITE DOWN YOUR VALUES: TALK THEM, WALK THEM

These 100-year firms all had a short statement of values for all employees with one overriding value: No achievement counts if you cheated to get there. The job of getting out the message on your values is a tall order. It is, in effect, an internal marketing plan designed to get out the word that your company has inviolate values and everyone follows them in reaching company goals. By repetition, by clever pamphlet, and by example, the rules will eventually take hold to create a climate of values. Figure 12.2, below, summarizes the values of the fifteen long-term companies.

STEP #3: INTERACT WITH CUSTOMERS

Both Coca-Cola and Pepsi have recently launched versions of their cola products with a new lemon twist. The idea came from observation: Pepsi found that nearly 70 percent of the time when customers order cola in a restaurant that they put lemon in to add a new flavor to the

Without employees, we are going nowhere. Every supervisor considers the contributions and well-being of employees. Respect, dignity, fairness, and honesty for everyone in the company, regardless of position.

Keep the debt low. Leverage means less ability to survive economic cycles, materials shortages, and other unforeseen changes and issues. The larger the balance sheet debt, the less nimble the company is in responding to opportunities.

Keep your costs down and your quality high. Remember thy customer and continuing customer but remember thy shareholder and innovate so that costs decline but product quality does not suffer.

It isn't your money. Behave as a fiduciary. Remember your accountability to the shareholders. Be honest in everything from financial reports to prospects.

Obey the law. Shortcuts catch up with us and cost more in the long term.

Remember, we are in it for the long term. Do not stretch the rules to meet numbers. Value-based decisions sometimes cost us in the short term but ensure that we will be around for the long term.

Figure 12.2. The Written Values You Must Talk and Walk.

cola. Knowing their customers' habits has given both companies a new product.

These fifteen companies knew the people who bought their product because they observed them, talked with them, and then took their ideas. They also went further and found out why others did not need their product. Modifications, even just in advertising, as when The Stanley Works targeted home improvements, can bring in new customers. All customers in the form of demographic studies provided feedback on what future needs would be. Lye in powdered form, a foundation for Pennwalt's success, was an idea born by simple observation of their potential consumers' lives and the struggle with making soap.

General Mills has been in the process of reformulating "Dough Boy"—it is an icon. The Dough Boy has come to mean two things to consumers: "easy" and "quality." General Mills has followed its consumers and learned that the demand for quick and convenient foods has only increased. Steve Sanger, General Mills CEO, would like to take the Dough Boy to the next level, and so when someone proposes a new product, he instructs that everyone ask this question, "Can we make it one-handed?" Sanger notes that people now want one hand free to type or drive while they eat: "That's the way consumers are eating today. You have to make everything convenient."[1]

Figure 12.3, below, provides a checklist for getting to know customers' needs now, what their future needs will be, and how to keep them coming back.

STEP #4: KEEP YOUR DEBT LOW

Low debt was the margin for error among all fifteen of these companies. During economic swings, they survived and paid dividends because they were not leveraged to the point that any economic rumbling meant their destruction. Their low debt was a cushion for both their shareholders and survival. Furthermore, by maintaining

Visit when you are not selling.

Find what your customer needs.

Find what your customer needs but does not yet know he needs.

Where will your customer be 5, 10, or 15 years from now?

Follow up on all sales for satisfaction.

Make sure senior management makes calls on customers.

Make sure sales people report their anecdotes.

Figure 12.3. Know Thy Customer.

low debt, they were able to seize the moment when a WBAWI opportunity came along.

Southwest Airlines provides some additional insight on the importance of low debt. Following the World Trade Center and Pentagon attacks in September 2001, Southwest Airlines net debt to capital ratio was 33.3, the lowest in the industry. For purposes of comparison, the ratios for the other airlines, from highest to lowest were: Northwest, 96.4; US Airways, 91.6; Continental, 87.6; America West, 73.9; United Airlines, 68.5; Alaska Airlines, 61.9; Delta, 59.3; and American, 59.2. The announcements of route eliminations and employee layoffs proceeded in the same order as the debt ratios, with Southwest declining to lay off employees. In fact, Southwest is poised to begin grabbing routes as the other airlines struggle.

What is perhaps most interesting about the Southwest position is the attitude of the company executives about that position. Their own language reflects a clear understanding of long-term survival and a refined culture of the long term. When asked why it was not laying off any of its 30,000 employees, Southwest's chief financial officer Gary Kelly said, "We have short-term challenges. I don't see that we have a long-term challenge here, where fundamentally our business has been changed."[2] Not only is the statement a reflection of the luxurious position of low debt, but it also reflects keen attention to the question of what business they are in and how that question and answer have not changed despite some temporary changes in their surrounding world.

As the economy and market struggled post-September 11, the firms with the highest numbers of layoffs and distress were those strapped for cash because of high debt levels. These are the firms with no margin for error, even those kinds of errors that are not their own but rather the making of terrorists. With credit crunches and debt service, there is nowhere for debt-laden firms to turn. The cash burn rate for high debt firms pushes them toward bankruptcy.[3] Presently, General Electric with its high leverage (88.9%) in its capital finance business is at risk. A dry 2002 commercial paper market leaves it vulnerable as it has violated one of its longstanding tools of success: low debt.[4]

STEP #5: DIVERSIFY

Diversification—in production process, in product, in market, or some combination of these strategic elements, is a critical part of long-term survival. The evidence garnered from the study of these fifteen firms indicates that while they had the ability to act quickly, they did not do so without strategic thinking. Those times when their diversifications were not successful were those when they had not focused carefully on WBAWI. PPG was clearly out of its business and league when it ventured into medical care. Corning forgot the importance of diversification as a cushion when it went whole hog into fiber optics. Just as debt was a cushion for difficult economic times, so also was diversification. When one cycle was down, these companies were protected because their other areas of business had an up cycle. If home construction is down, remodeling is up, and PPG had a down position in one market, but an upswing in the other. If both are down, there was their entrance into automobile paint that offered further cushion for real estate market swings.

Successful diversification is not achieved because management, qua management, possesses a golden wand; rather, success results from intimate knowledge of both the supply and demand sides of a firm's particular industry and markets. Success in one field does not ensure glory in another; for example, diversification, per se, is not a guarantee of security.

Diversification provided an opportunity for early entry into international business as both buyers and sellers. Though conservative (as most of these firms were), they were willing to assume risk abroad to sustain security. Opportunities in international markets still abound, and some of the fifteen companies are seizing the moment as they expand their food product distribution systems into growing economies where those products are now within the reach of prospering consumers.

Diversification requires sensitivity to both the supply and demand sides of markets. These companies generated a web of strategies that encompassed manufacturing, marketing, finance, and personnel, all interactive. No opportunity or idea was ignored as the company decided who it was, what business it was in, and where it was to go.

Strategy is a rubric, an umbrella term, a web of interrelated substrategies, policies, and tactics. The evidence concerning manufacturing–marketing activities, man–machine relationships, values–priorities, risk–conservatism, and diversification challenges any executive to analyze how strongly constructed, how logical, and how clearly communicated is the organization's strategy. It is when the strategy is ill-defined, inconsistent, waffling in priorities, and insensitive to people that the firm falters, then fails.

History can be a diagnostic tool. Uncovering what happened (and why) can aid a firm toward—or away from—a "reorder" of the past. These companies focused on patterns in their company histories for possible application in current and future operations. These companies understood their longitudinal progression and patterns and all of the circumstances underlying both. This knowledge base was a means for their managers to sharpen their visions for the present and future. They were not dwelling on the past; they were learning from the cycles, the missteps, and the strengths of their pasts. These companies and their managers found the threads in their histories from which a pattern of experience could be drawn. History was a key for these companies and their strategies for the future.

STEP #6: ASK YOURSELF THREE QUESTIONS EACH DAY

Even six steps can seem overwhelming for managers. But perhaps the six steps could be reduced to three simple questions that these fifteen companies seemed to ask over and over again: Why are we in business? What business are we in? What will we do and what won't we do to get there?

These fifteen companies either provided the answers to these questions or the framework for answering them. The answer to the the first question is clear: You are in business to make money.

The answer to the second question is more complex, but in finding the WBAWI answer, there are fifteen patterns for success. These companies had fifteen different stories of diversification, both wise and imprudent, that offer a framework for strategic choices on where the company goes next. Those strategic choices involve a global view of the entire supply, production, and distribution chain of a company. An expansion through acquisition of the supply mode is as likely as an expansion of retail outlets. But it is that broad focus that spurs creativity in the means for diversification that is a requirement for survival.

Constant reevaluation of those strategic choices is necessary and comes from input from all levels. Review census data, resource data, and other external information in order to keep track of trends. Those trends are critical for determining the most effective path to long-term success.

It is only fitting that the last question should be on values. This third question reflects these companies' clear position on matters of ethics. For over one century they paid dividends, but from their inception they had clear statements of values. They knew what they needed to do to be successful, but they also knew what they would not sacrifice to get there.

Sometimes a shortcut on quality is tempting because of the short-term impact of the costs of quality. Stanley was tempted to lower the quality of its products when its market was infiltrated by cheap imports. Instead, remembering its value of quality products, Stanley focused on increasing demands and preserved its longstanding value and reputation. A sacrifice of quality is a sacrifice of long-term success.

When thinking about doing whatever it takes to be successful, focus on the work, the strategy, the quality, and the customers. But, it is that value system to which a commitment is made with resolve that will not allow compromise in conduct.

Stewards understand their accountability. That notion of accountability keeps stewards within certain guidelines on their decisions and actions. Acting with that accountability in mind preserves both assets and the steward's reputation. Stewards in business are no different. They understand that the next quarter is not more important than the next ten years or perhaps, the next 100. In fact, they understand that without the goal of 100 years, the next quarter perhaps will not go as well as it could. It is the desire to be around for 100 years that offers the vision, perspective, and insight a business needs for staying power and growth. With the goal of longevity so clear, the details fall into place, and the plans can take hold even during bad times.

The most wondrous part of studying fifteen companies with the unique achievement of 100 years of dividends is not that they achieved such during challenging times. The most wondrous part of these companies is that they did so with such common sense, which has remained untapped for so long.

AN AFTERTHOUGHT

As we close this book we realize that our final touches come on the same day that President George W. Bush has gone to Wall Street to ask business leaders to restore trust in business. During the production of this book we have seen the earnings restatements of Xerox (twice), WorldCom, Enron, and even our own GE. The president, with increased sentences for financial fraud, is asking for a restoration of long-term values among businesses and business leaders. Their fixation on the quarterly return has led to a loss of confidence that has created skittish investors despite signs of a healthy economy. Hesitant to trust, investors turn to bonds and CDs because they can see some immediate and tangible returns on those investments.

Perhaps we have an easier solution than regulatory reform as well as a means for businesses to raise the capital they need: Be companies of long-term values, focused on honesty and fairness in treatment of customers, investors, suppliers and employees. Be in business to make money, but make money the old-fashioned way, using and producing the cash that allows your investors the luxury of continuous dividends. All in all, it wasn't a bad plan for these 15 companies. All in all, it's not a bad plan for a market worthy of trust.

NOTES

1. Fig, Jonathan, "General Mills Intends to Reshape Doughboy in Its Own Image," *Wall Street Journal*, July 18, 2000: A1, A8.

2. Trottman, Melanie, "Southwest Airlines' Formula for Success To Be Tested in a More Cautious Market," *Wall Street Journal* ,September 24, 2001: A6.

3. Krantz, Matt, "Debt Weighs More As Firms Gobble Cash," *USA Today*, October 10, 2001: 1B.

4. Timmons, Heather and Diane Brady, "How Does GE Grow?," *Business Week Online*, April 8, 2002.

Appendixes—A Look at Financial Performance

HOW THEY DID: A LOOK AT THE FINANCIALS

This project has had its share of naysayers, particularly during the now-but-a-memory "new economy" when we were told that dividends no longer matter. Dividend payments seem to be a proxy for cash, and cash is king, or cash is at least indicative of a company teetering in solvency, as opposed to the phenomenal dot-coms who just needed an economic reality check from investors who finally realized the burn rate meant there was no cash in the company. With no other assets, the investors in the new economy had to wonder exactly what they had invested in—the air in the bubble?

The naysayers found no nouveau charm in this project. But, a quick look at these firms' performances in market context is a picture worth 1,000 refutes for the naysayers. The following pages are dividends graphs for these companies in comparison to the usual indexes. Exemplary dividends records are sufficient reason for further examination of the long-term culture. Appendix A is a graphic depiction of those payments. Appendix B is the dividend payout percentage.

Appendix A

Graphic Depiction of Dividends Paid

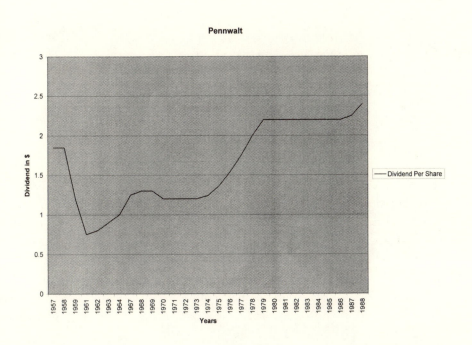

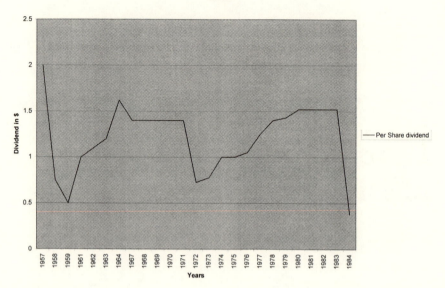

Scovill

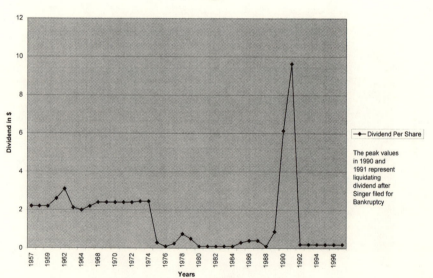

Singer

242

Pullman

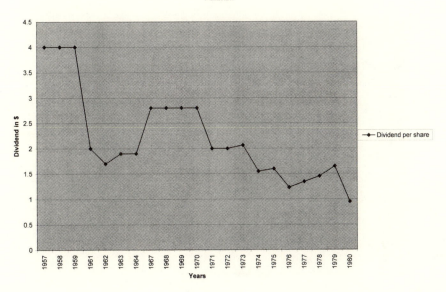

Ludlow

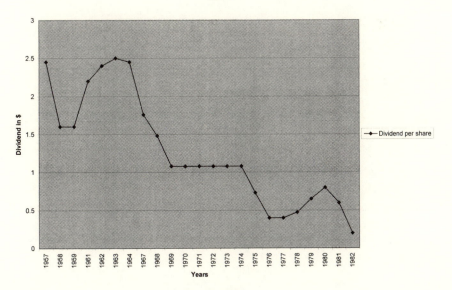

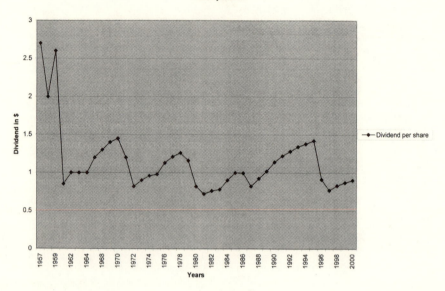

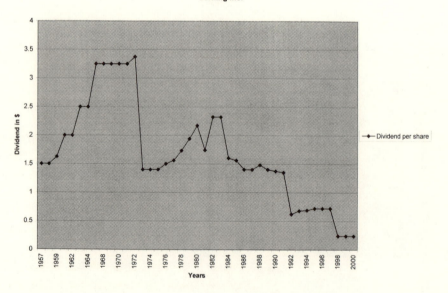

Diamond International

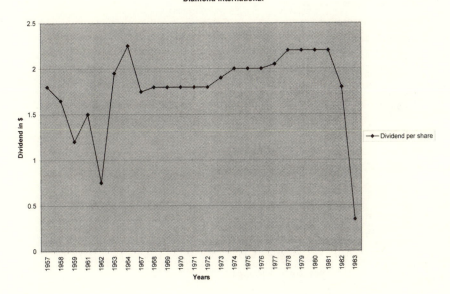

General Electric

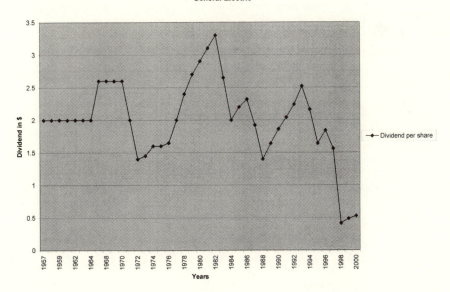

General Mills

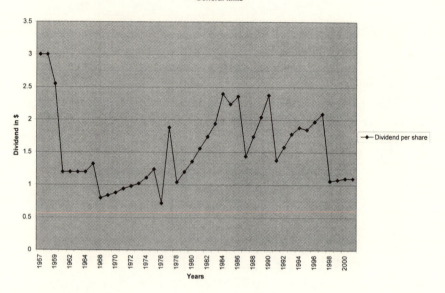

Coca Cola

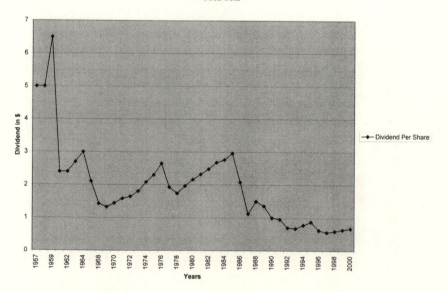

246

PPG Industries

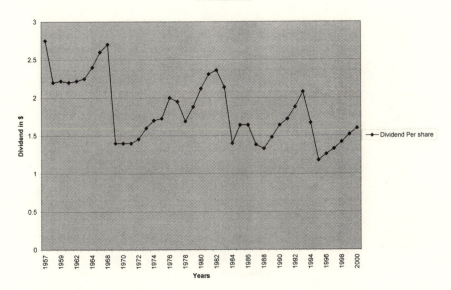

Colgate_Palmolive

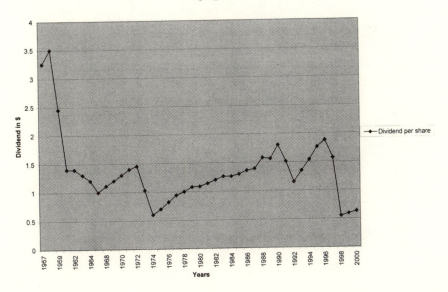

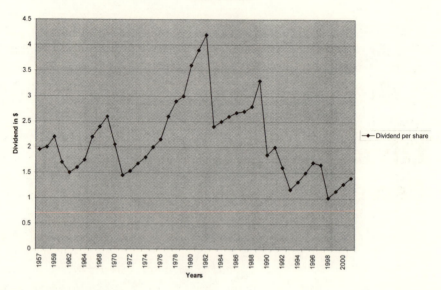

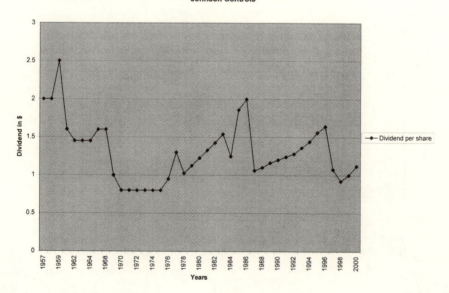

248

Appendix B

Dividend Payout Percentage

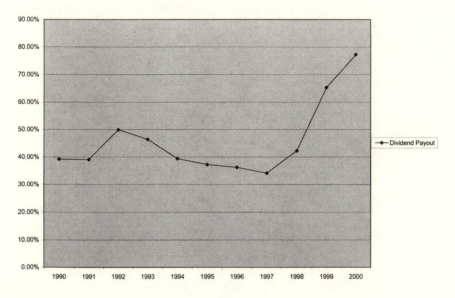

Coca Cola

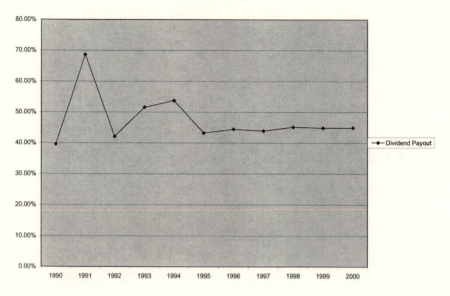

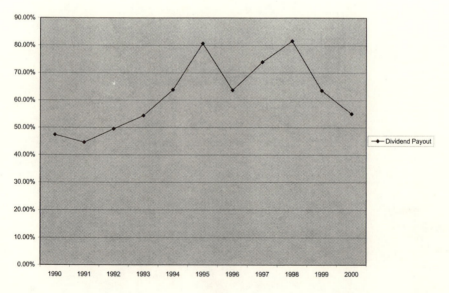

Procter & Gamble

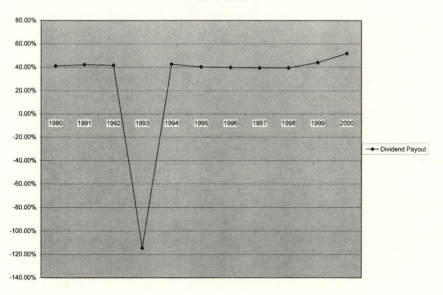

Colgate Palmolive

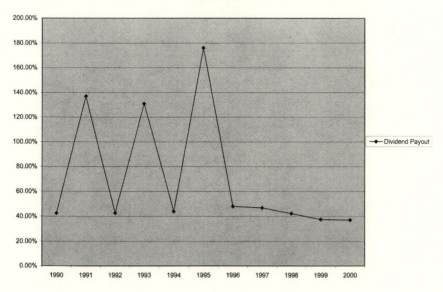

251

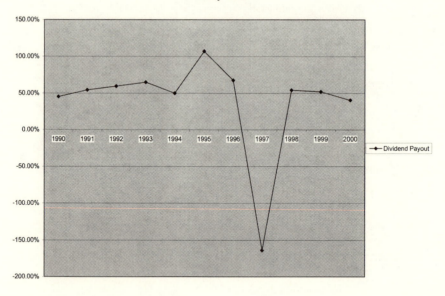

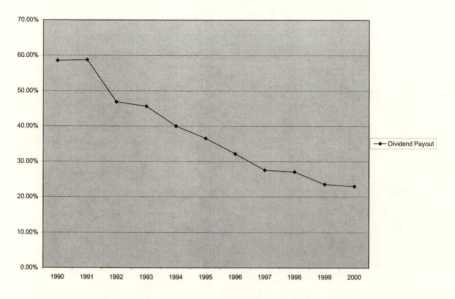

Corning Inc.

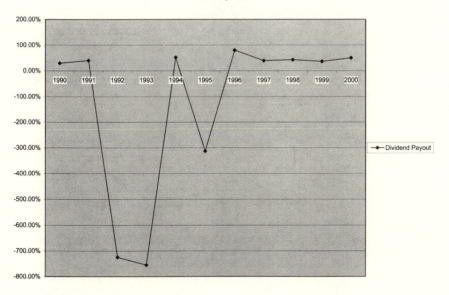

PPG Industries

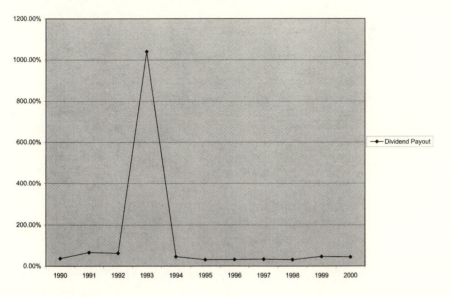

Index

ABOUT THE AUTHORS

LOUIS GROSSMAN is Professor Emeritus at Arizona State University.

MARIANNE M. JENNINGS is Professor of Legal and Ethical Studies, College of Business, Arizona State University. Author of award winning textbooks, monographs, and journal articles, her weekly columns are syndicated nationwide, and her other writings have appeared in the *Wall Street Journal, The Chicago Tribune, The New York Times,* and *Reader's Digest.* Jennings has conducted more than 200 workshops and seminars in business, human resource managment, government, law, and academic and professional ethics.